WHAT ABOUT ME?

By the same author

Anything School Can Do, You Can Do Better
(Arlen House/Fontana, 1983/1985)

Esperanto For Hope
(Poolbeg, 1988)

Early Reading
(Poolbeg, 1990)

WHAT ABOUT ME?

**A woman for whom
'one damn cause'
led to another**

Máire Mullarney

TOWN HOUSE

Published in 1992 by
Town House and Country House
42 Morehampton Road
Donnybrook
Dublin 4

British Library Cataloguing in Publication Data
Mullarney, Maire
What About Me?: Woman for Whom One Damn Cause Led to Another
I. Title
941.7082092

ISBN 0-948524-52-9

Acknowledgements
The author and publishers would like to acknowledge the following copyright
holders: Souvenir Press Ltd for *The Descent of Woman* (1972) and *The Scars of
Evolution* (1990) by Elaine Morgan; Methuen and Co. Ltd for *Love and Hate*
(1971) by I. Eibl-Eibesfeldt; William Collins and Sons Ltd for *Children's Minds*
(1978) by Margaret Donaldson; Constable and Co. Ltd for *Medieval Latin Lyrics*
by Helen Waddell; Faber and Faber Ltd for *Farming and Gardening for Health
and Disease* by Sir Albert Howard (1945); Professor Barbara Tizard for *Young
Children Learning, Talking and Thinking, at Home and at School*, by Barbara
Tizard and Martin Hughes (1984); Sheed & Ward Ltd for *Birth Regulation and
Catholic Belief* by L. Egner. Scripture quotations in this publication are from the
Revised Standard Version of the Bible, © 1971 and 1952 by the Division of
Christian Education of the National Council of the Churches of Christ in the USA.

Typeset by Printset & Design Ltd, Dublin
Printed in Ireland by Colour Books Ltd

CHAPTER 1

'Three, four, open the door.'
'I can do it myself.'

As far back as I can remember the 'me' that is somehow still me is standing on tiptoe, reaching up to turn the brass doorhandle above my head. My hand is not big enough to hold the handle; I have to edge it round by repeated nudges, until something clicks. The door begins to open. I don't bother to go through. It is only the door from the kitchen to a spare bedroom, nothing there. It's being able to open it that fills me with satisfaction and sends me running to my mother at the kitchen range, pulling her over to admire my success. Recently I watched a grandson opening a door in just the same way; he was nineteen months old.

Sometime later I'm inside a white dress with a pattern of flowers. It has several sleeves and no hole for my head. It's like a small white cave in which I struggle to find an exit. I am on my mother's bed, which is bouncy and unhelpful. At last my head and my two arms find their appropriate outlets and I slide down and go proudly to my mother, in the sittingroom next door, to accept her congratulations and let her button up the back.

The third remembered triumph glows with the deepest satisfaction. I'm kneeling on the mossy grass in the field beyond the paddock. There are tall trees around and from them little cones have fallen; larch cones, I suppose. With these and some mud I have built a wall. It is not very long, it is not very high, but I have made it myself and it delights me.

This time I must have sensed that my building would have to remain a private achievement. Probably I tried to tell my mother about it when I went back to the house, but if I had persuaded her to come up the steps, through the garden and on through the paddock, I can hardly suppose that even her sympathy would have recognised a work of architecture.

It interests me now to find that no memory remains of trying to open doors and failing, of having dresses put on, of aimlessly picking up larch cones. There must have been many experiences of failure, many more of having things done for me, but they did not register.

My adult deduction is that young children, female and male, are equally anxious to be able to do things, to make something happen. 'Mastery' is the word used by my favourite psychologist. But my reflection on that is that if I was then a small walking sundial, recording only the sunny hours, and if now, much larger, I am fortunate enough to have held onto that tendency, my mother's reactions must have contributed.

****

That small child who built with larch cones and mud lived in Ballydonagh, just above the Glen o' the Downs in County Wicklow, directly facing the main peak of the Sugarloaf. Sometime she was much impressed by the information that it had once been a volcano. When she heard about mountains falling on us at the end of the world she knew which mountain and she thought it would be just as well not to survive until then, but, on the other hand, she was sure that the best way to die would be all together.

We lived alone, my mother, Teddy and myself. The four-room cottage was attached to the farmhouse of our landlady but territories were distinct. We had house, cobbled yard, a sunny vegetable garden at a higher level, reached by steps. There seems to have been a lean-to shed under the garden, in the yard; I have two early memories of my father and in one of them I am sitting on the edge of the shed roof and he is below me squirting me with water from a large round glass thing — now seen to be a syringe — and getting plenty of fun out of the game. I think I am, too.

When you came out at the top of the steps you met red stalks of rhubarb on one side, the summerhouse, with walls of small sweet-smelling leaves — now I know they were sweetbriar — on the other.

Past the rhubarb, to the right, a path to a gate into the paddock, which was part of the farm but where I was free to wander. Did anyone warn me to keep out when the pony was there? I don't think so. There is no memory of danger anywhere. My mother told me how alarmed she was when she heard me call from the yard, 'Mammy! Mammy! The cock's eating my fingers!' I had been having my breakfast out in the sun. The fingers were 'fingers' of bread and butter, dipped in boiled egg; the cock had strayed in from the farmyard beside us.

Beyond the rhubarb and the summerhouse the garden stretched upwards to infinity, interspersed with apple trees. I have no picture of the upper boundary; what I remember is sitting on my heels on the brown earth, sometimes playing with worms, while my mother dug vegetables. She was careful that I should not be unkind to worms. Her spade might slice one in half, and the two halves wriggle interestingly and independently in different directions, but that could only be an accident; she would not put on a demonstration.

She often told me how her father used to be out in his garden at five in the morning, digging and planting to feed his family of ten. One of her favourite stories was of an afternoon when she was stealing gooseberries. Father came out unexpectedly, settled down to dig close by; she couldn't crawl out without being caught. The afternoon went on and on; the little robber under the gooseberry bushes got very stiff. At last Father said calmly, 'Time for tea. You had better come in now.'

Such a different world from mine, which was all women — apart from Teddy, who was referred to as 'he'. At weekends we seem quite often to have had company, my mother's former fellow-workers from the office, her closest sister, Gertie, whom I called Geg. They were next in age in their family and I used to hear how, when they were children together, Geg would coax Addie to tell her stories and draw pictures about them on her school slate.

Stories were demanded again when they were in bed, but it amused Addie to remember that the next youngest sister, Jo, had wanted the stories only to put her to sleep, and she'd be furious if they finished while she was still awake.

This practice in storytelling was of great benefit to me. Every evening before bed I would sit on my mother's knee and she would tell me about Teddy's adventures. Later on she told me that she had wondered how much I would consider sufficient; she told me seven stories, one after the other, and when she had finished I simply asked, 'And what happened next?'

Another evening she felt she was neglecting her responsibilities and she told me a confidence-inspiring story about my guardian angel. My question, 'But what did Teddy do?'

Not that there was any danger she would really neglect the task of bringing up a Catholic child. I don't know how she managed to get to Mass on Sundays when I was really small. I dare say we lived about two miles from the church in Kilmacanogue and as soon as I could walk we would set out in good time to walk there.

How welcome would be the sound of metal rims and a pony's hoofs clopping along the road behind us. We would never look around; there might not be room in the approaching trap. Usually there was; perhaps it was always the same trap, Mrs Smith's from the bottom of the hill, but we were always agreeably surprised and delighted at the offer of a lift back after Mass. Teddy, of course, always came too. I can see my smaller self kneeling at the elevation and holding him up to look when the bell rang. When I was six and living in Kenmare, I remember one particular walk, when I asked my mother whether Teddy would go to heaven. She very properly said yes. I would say the same myself now, in similar circumstances, thinking, Teddy — or equivalent.

> Vera Ierusalem
>   est illa civitas
> cujus pax jugis est
>   summa jucunditas;
> ubi non praevenit
>   rem desiderium,
> nec desiderio
>   minus est premium.

> Jerusalem is the city
>   Of everlasting peace,
> A peace that is surpassing
>   And utter blessedness;
> Where finds the dreamer waking
>   Truth beyond dreaming far,
> Nor is the heart's possessing
>   Less than the heart's desire.

(Helen Waddell's translation of Peter Abelard, in *Mediaeval Latin Lyrics*)

The strains of translation have introduced a dreamer who is not found in the original. A more informal way of making the point would be to say that whatever is loved here will be there — only more so.

My mother was similarly conscientious about Santa Claus. She made sure that he went about his annual business with imagination —

I am sitting up in bed in the dark — could there have been a candle?
— taking out of my sock a wooden tea-set with cups acorn-size, all red
with white spots like the (dangerous) fairy mushrooms we had found
when wandering among furze bushes up the hill. I imagine I must
have been three or four. Probably five, even six, and becoming rational,
when incontrovertible evidence of Santa Claus arrived — a doll's pram
in front of the sittingroom fireplace. Too large to have been hidden in
our small house, and nobody had called all day on Christmas Eve.
Because of this I believed for years longer than more sophisticated
children.

When I had a family of my own I asked Granny Ad how she had
managed; the sympathetic postman had left it outside the gate. And
how had she reconciled Truth and Santa Claus? No difficulty; Saint
Nicholas was as real as anyone else.

I like to think she had her reward. She made sure to give me a
happy Christmas, in spite of solid opposition when my father was
around. Once we had our own children she was part of their
Christmas. When they were small, present-opening had to be delayed
until Granny arrived and had been given a chair near the fire.

When she was about eighty she came to live with us. By this time
our eldest daughter, Barbara, was old enough to make quite elaborate
embroidered socks for Mama, Dada and Granny which would turn up
on our respective pillows when we got back from Midnight Mass. Not
quite midnight, in practice, but late enough for another family
tradition — a glass of wine, preferably Muscatel or Madeira, with a
slice of Christmas cake, sitting around the kitchen table. Meanwhile
three or possibly four Santa Clauses, of two different generations,
would be vanishing at intervals, trying not to meet on the stairs. Even
though Seán and I resigned completely a few years ago — our
youngest is now twenty-five — the children have not; we found golden
tangerines and delicious chocolates waiting for us last Christmas.

Christmas does somewhat stand out in my own childhood but the
rest of the calendar was studded with celebration or information.
There was Easter, with weeks of Lent before it. My mother found it
very long because she used to give up reading at meals. She used to tell
me about her family Lent; black tea and dry bread morning and
evening; how her father continued the fast even when he was old
enough to be excused, and then died the next year. Addie and Geg
would remember that date, his birthday in heaven, as well as their
parents' earthly birthdays.

Oddly enough, in later years I could never get a clear answer from either of the sisters to the question, just what age was I when Geg took over. At last, when both had departed I found a postcard from Tenerife dated in the year when I was four, written by my mother on her way to Nigeria. My father, born in the Argentine, working in the British Post Office, had been based in Dublin but transferred to the Colonial Service and took up a post in Lagos. For every twelve-month 'tour' he had six months' leave at home. It was expected that wives with children would leave them and go out for six months of the tour so my mother had to get her tropical outfit, including a topee (a white pith helmet), pack it in a tin trunk and leave me.

Geg gave up her job and came out to live with me in Ballydonagh. I don't believe I could have been so happy if she had not enjoyed it. I dare say I missed my mother at some time, but they must have convinced me that she would be back, and after all I knew Geg very well. One memory that must belong to that six months is letter writing. I am sitting on a three-legged stool in the sittingroom, holding on my knee a writing pad with lined paper. Geg is sitting on a chair to one side. I tell her what I want to say, she tells me, letter by letter, what to write. I make capital letters two lines tall, drawing a careful little circle at the end of lines and where two lines meet. The letter E, for example, would have six such ornaments.

Another bright memory is a discussion about a robin which — whom — she used to feed. There's a fragment of teaching of Irish dancing, there's an important moment when I have grasped the idea that God gave us a tongue for the purpose of speaking the truth. I'm sure this had nothing to do with my having said anything untrue. Why would I? It would have been just an observation about the nature of tongues, rather like the explanation that one's taste buds change, so that it was quite probable that I would like celery when I was grown up. I do quite like celery now, and I can't tell lies.

No particular memory that I can report can imply the atmosphere. The God who had so kindly given me my tongue was someone she knew and He was on our side. And on the robin's side. When I read some other people's memories I realise how fortunate I was never to have met the confrontational God, who's always trying to catch us out. And if someone had suggested to Geg that it might be as suitable in this context to say 'She' as to say 'He' she would not have contradicted them.

I understood that she had had an encouraging experience when she was about three. In the garden of her childhood there had been a well, used for watering the garden, approached by steep steps. Small Gertie was by herself in the garden, came back in to the house completely soaked. There was naturally excitement, worry and relief. She admitted she had fallen into the well. How could she have possibly managed to get out? She said, a man in a long dress had come down the steps and put out his hand to her. She told them he looked like the picture — the standard picture of Jesus as the Sacred Heart, standing with both hands held out.

One thing I like about this is that her story was accepted, but no fuss was made. No pilgrimages to the new Holy Well. Neither was I told about it with over emphasis. If anything, an assumption that we all knew that Gertie was the kind of person who was likely to be looked after that way. No licence to the rest of us to be careless about wells.

There were ten brothers and sisters in my mother's family, so there were plenty of other stories. Her elder brother and sisters used to ask her to 'hear' them their poetry, so when she went to school herself she already knew it all. Indeed, she could still recite Goldsmith's 'Deserted Village'. They had their problem uncle, who would turn up to live with them from time to time and try to teach the children Greek — when he was reasonably sober. He had painted the reindeer who hung lonely in the sittingroom; not, I think, from life.

And then my Uncle Frank — her brother — who was so dark and handsome that he had only to wear a fez to pass for an Egyptian with a smattering of English and, visiting the Post Office, could insist on buying, not any ordinary postage stamp, but one from the very middle of the sheet. When Frank was a student at the School of Art in Kildare Street (in the same class as Seán Keating) he seems to have had many requests to draw something in young women's autograph albums. Result, a pile of books with padded covers and multi-coloured pages for me to draw on that had drifted into our attic. There were some sheets of gold-leaf there too, between worn tissue; nobody else needed it, I inherited it, feeling privileged. No doubt if I had had brothers or sisters near me in age that gold-leaf would have had to be shared. You win some, you lose some. I did not feel the lack of children to play with.

It seems that there were a couple of small boys, the children of a Mrs Earnshaw, who lived within walking distance. They have left no image on my memory, neither names nor faces. Their mother's name is set in an anecdote which tells how she came to look for my mother in the afternoon, the time when I was brought for my walk. She looked in the window of the sittingroom, saw on the dark blue plush table cover a tray with a lace tray-cloth set for tea. Set, of course, by my mother for herself when she would return. The point of the story is Mrs Earnshaw's surprise.

In fact I had just one peer in my peer group and we did not encounter each other very often. Denis's father had been a colleague of my father in the Post Office. The two wives became friends and had their first babies six months apart. Denis was the older so his outgrown jerseys were passed on to me. Whenever we went to town it was to stay with his family, in Clontarf. There were still trams in those days. The overhead cables ran at the level of the bedroom where I used be put to sleep and every time a tram passed a junction in the cables there would be a brilliant blue flash outside the window, lighting up the ceiling.

I loved these visits and remember much more than there is any need to record here. True, memory of the first meeting of Denis and myself when we were both mobile is faint. I am hunkered in the corner of his playroom, the return at the top of the first flight of stairs; facing me is this other small child. I have no picture of anything behind me, but I have been told that he brought me his toys, one after the other, and one after the other I pushed them behind me into a corner and looked expectantly for the next. I don't know whether that says something about the stereotype of male and female children or just something about me.

This is why I have written from the point of view of the child I was and I have to say that my mother and my aunt between them provided me with years in Paradise. I was free to come and go, and when I came be certain I was welcome. Anything I asked was answered affectionately. I believe that for a time I was called 'Miss Fy?', Fy being Why, but no one ever made me feel I was a nuisance.

I was shown and told about flowers and birds and books. I can see myself, still quite small, twoish?, threeish?, lying on my tummy in bed with a large book open on the pillow; double columns with blocks of small print on each page and a scatter of tiny pictures, presumably an illustrated dictionary. I'm looking at this while waiting for breakfast. I can't say I remember the morning when I asked my mother about one picture and she told me it was a differential thermometer; it seems that when breakfast was ready she came to bring me out and chanced to ask me what the object was. 'Differential momemeter.' The point of that story is not that she proceeded to explain the purpose of a thermometer, but that we were pleased with each other.

Mornings waiting in bed were happy. There was a large picture of St Philomena in her prison cell with a ray of sunlight shining down on her. She was my saint. I was Máire Philomena. At the window, white muslin curtains — they must have been starched and ironed — billowed or fluttered, according to the weather. I could curl up and think. Think about whether there could be colours that we couldn't see, and, if so, could we imagine them? I must have heard someone say that dogs and cats see colours differently from the way we do. And God could do everything. So, a round triangle?

Bed in the evening was not so secure. Outside those white curtains there were sometimes witches who would know I was there if I moved so much as a toe; I must make myself lie as stiff as a stick. No question that this was a threat, something I had been told. I believe it belonged to a certain illustration in silhouette of the witches that enchanted Finn and his companions so that they were caught in a cave unable to move. At other times I was really frightened by the thought that my mother might be sitting in the chair by the fireplace, the other side of the wall, dead. The end of a conversation, overheard '....when they came in, there she was in her chair....' Whoever it was stopped speaking when they realised I was within hearing, but they stopped too late.

But once I was up and about the day was full of one satisfying thing after another. One that happened, or rather, that I achieved every day was a bowel movement. Aunt or mother would give cheerful encouragement to hurry to 'Miss White' — a handsome chamber pot — when I indicated an interest. I now realise that they conferred a life-long benefit. I know of a contemporary who used to be put sitting on the pot with a stick beside it to remind her what would happen if she didn't perform. A well-intentioned but frightfully misguided mother.

Mind you, mine made some mistakes. She did not want me to be spoilt or greedy, so if anyone happened to give us a box of chocolates I was allowed one a day, after dinner. And I was allowed to choose the one for the next day. She could have been planning to make me a chocolate addict. [In fact, I'm not too bad, provided I have my Dime bar after lunch. I stock up, one per day, when I'm travelling, even to Belgium.]

Another mistake I regret was her decision that I wouldn't be able to sing. It seems she asked me to sing — does one say 'scales' or 'a scale'

— after her and what emerged was a poor imitation. She remembered from her schooldays that the town children (Maynooth) could sing but the country children couldn't. If she had known how mothers do it in Hungary, teaching young children first two notes, then three and so on, I might never have had a singing voice but I would not have been so trackless musically. On the other hand I was never without drawing materials and spent contented hours on the floor with a pencil and the large blue drawing books that were brought back from every visit to Dublin.

I was allowed to climb anything that wasn't seriously dangerous, walk on any walls that could be walked on. My mother told me later on that her heart was often in her mouth, but she did not want me to grow up timid. I understood that if a beggar came to the door you must never send them away empty, and I rather think I picked up the impression that — no, that's wrong — I never had the chance to pick up the impression that there are different ways of speaking to different people, whether with more or less respect.

Well, I have visited nursery schools and seen children in kindergarten standing in a circle and singing and waving one hand or the other — some of them looking totally bored. Indeed, I found myself struggling with stencils and weaving idiotic paper strips when I was six. I am certain that I was much happier as things were than if I had been landed with twenty others in a child-care centre. Of course I give good marks to well-run Montessori schools or to small playgroups with five or six children, provided they take up only a small part of the day. Good as they may be, I feel my timeless childhood, with a busy, loving mother, was better. It was no small advantage in later life to be accustomed to being happy alone. If I had had to spend all day with a dozen or two dozen others, for the sake of having access to a slide and sandpit, it would have been a very poor exchange.

Luckily, I do not have to rely merely on memory. Professor Jerome Bruner has said — I heard him myself — that small children can converse best with one person at a time, one adult or one other child. It takes quite a while to learn how to join in a multiple conversation. And he was very clear that 'the best style of child-care is that which enables the child to master its own attention'. If there's nobody else bumping into you on a tricycle it is easier to concentrate on what you are doing. I have rarely seen a happy collection of small children on television without some speeding vehicle coming into the picture.

CHAPTER 2

Who likes butter?
Mother and daughter

Since I'm the one who was inside Me, nobody can tell me that I didn't have a happier time with my mother and her sister and Teddy than I might have had mixing with a crowd of other children. But there's another side to the question. Did they lose out because they spent time minding me instead of doing their proper work? When myself as mother takes out the memories of myself as small child, I think not.

It's not really original to propose that the proper work of human beings is play. Homo ludens, that's us, though these days we have managed to make work out of sport. But making daisy-chains, what could be more Arcadian? More than half the pleasure is in showing how a tiny thumb, with a thumb-nail like a rose petal, can, perhaps, penetrate the juicy stalk of a daisy, and, if not, the small hands can at least thread the stalks through ready-made holes.

You hold a buttercup under an infant chin and ask, 'Let's see who likes butter', and Time is vanquished, because the golden reflection on apricot skin is the same reflection your mother caused, in the past that becomes present, on yours.

True, the whole of childhood cannot be spent on the greensward. But my mother liked to have things pleasant about her and she always made up the real butter into butter balls. Butter used to be bought from a nearby farm. If not, it was cut in the grocer's shop from a large block, a slightly tapered cube of eighteen inches or so; I have a painted butterbox in the bathroom, holding towels. The firm butter could be divided and shaped with wooden butter-pats, large ones for the expert grocer, smaller for home, smooth on the back, a ridged surface on front, and these had to be kept in water, otherwise the butter would stick to the wood. I see myself standing on a stool, elbows on the shelf, eyes almost into the butter-dish, while my mother nicks out a small lump and rolls it between the butter-pats, first one way, then the other, until she has a neat ball, marked with crossed ridges. When all was done, the last butter-ball would pop into my mouth.

I am quite clear that it was not greed that kept me watching so attentively, it was admiration for skill, perhaps for magic. I must at some time have been allowed to try my hand because when newly married I had butter-pats myself and shaped butter-balls or rolls or, more lazily, blocks. Now I fake it, buy the stuff in half-pounds and, when I think of it, stamp them on top with a design of oak leaves, evoking a long-gone dairy.

So, when I insist that my mother enjoyed what she was doing, and enjoyed her little girl's sharing it, I am judging from my adult perspective and know that there's an element of sculpture in it, a transformation that is satisfying in a modest way. I am also remembering from further back the atmosphere of contentment, which very likely prompted me to search out almost-obsolescent butter-pats later on.

She used to go up to the common — we did not call it that, I cannot remember the word, just the space, furze bushes, rough grass, wild flowers, at the top of the hill — and collect sticks for the fire. The story about that is that she used to bring a rug and put me sitting on it and as soon as she moved away Nellie, the Irish Terrier, would race back from wherever she had been exploring and sit on guard beside the little mistress, or the human puppy, whichever way she looked at it.

Returning home, my mother would saw any branches that were too thick to break. Here I sympathise with her, because she had only a carpenter's saw; I don't know whether the efficient Swedish bow saws we have now were on the market; I do know that the last cut that allows the log to fall from the branch is gratifying. The fire from wood you harvested yourself glows with extra warmth; so does the harvester, after sawing for half an hour.

Then there were card games. Which is the game where both players seem to be bashing cards down very fast on a pile in the middle? Both my guardians and I, sometimes both of them together, when Geg was visiting, played card games. The game at which I did best was one they called Pelmanism: the whole pack are spread out upside down in a random pattern; there must not be any rows. Players in turn pick up any two cards; if they match, that's a trick gained. If not, each must be replaced exactly as it was. The first few turns are chance; after that, to turn up a three and fail to remember exactly where a three has been turned up already is to have reason to reproach oneself. Get a match, and you have another turn, without limit.

This is a lovely game, where children have a built-in advantage over adults, whether because they still have eidetic memory or because they have no distractions. But it is real play for the grown-ups also. In 'Pelmanism' there is a challenge; there is a feeling of satisfaction if one can 'place' that three of clubs that was turned up a couple of minutes ago. However, this feeling is mild indeed compared to the triumph of a small child.

The adult wins either way. If she collects a pair herself, well and good; if she fails, the child's excitement bubbles, because she's certain she knows where it is. At the end, when the child turns up pair after pair and 'clears the board' it would be a very strange mother who didn't share her delight.

Indeed, my mother used to talk often enough about those years in Ballydonagh to assure me that they were happy years. True, she had to pump her water from a pump in the cobbled yard. (One of the stories is of adult amusement when Denis and I were brought to the zoo and my principal interest was the very low pump in the elephant's domain, a pump not as tall as myself, with a pretty curly handle. Used the elephant pump her own refreshment? I can see the curved top at eye level, because I have squatted down to look at it properly.)

Sometime my mother mentioned to me that in those days she once counted the little dresses she was ironing for me; there were fourteen. Apparently I had a clean dress in the morning and another one for the afternoon walk. Note that there are no remembered warnings about keeping them clean.

Now her willingness to do all that ironing with an iron heated in the fire remains remarkable to me, but she had made all those dresses herself and certainly enjoyed making them and enjoyed seeing them running past the window or sitting down with Teddy. I know that she enjoyed the making because she used to tell me how, when she was a little girl, she used to copy the pattern outline shapes from her mother's pattern book and enlarge them so that they would fit her doll. She used to make charming dresses for my dolls as well. I liked putting them off and on, though the wearer had, for me, none of the vitality of Teddy.

So, was my mother penalised for giving me a happy childhood, or did she get a lot of fun out of it herself? Well, now that I have one daughter a sculptor, one a textile designer and painter, one who for a while was a dress designer, I feel I have standards for comparison. The dress designer enjoyed making clothes and planning them but after she had worked for a while in couture workrooms and then went on to be a designer for a company making children's clothes she decided to get out. The anxiety at the top level, the cheeseparing or clothparing at the mass production level, took the good out of it. She went into gardening, 'amenity horticulture', which she found more rewarding at its best, but with employment drawbacks.

Come to think of it, one drawback deserves mention here. She was selected for a responsible job in the Parks Department, but the Department of Finance would not sanction equal pay and the Parks people would not consent to pay a woman less than a man for the same work — so they felt they had no option but to give the job to a man. She is a member of the Institute of Landscape Architects now and such differentials have been made illegal, but she says she had always hoped to live as I did, with house and children and her own garden. She has son and house and a large garden, but has to fit them all into her spare time.

Contrast that with my mother. During the years I am writing about, her weeks were her own from morning to night. Well, it seems I used to wake rather early in the morning, might waken her by jumping on her face, but she did not have to hurry me into some clothes and get me out so that she could go somewhere else to follow someone else's decisions. If she sewed, washed or ironed small dresses, wasn't she dealing creatively with colour, somewhat as her granddaughters would do later, but having no need to think about what the market would fancy? I can't seriously compare butter-pats with sculpture, but they have something of the tactile pleasure of pottery and the only person they have to please is their maker.

Then there was the garden. Some people do not understand its allure, just as some people lack musical sense. For those who feel it, there is no room for discussion; to be free to work in their own gardens is all they ask.

> How vainly men themselves amaze,
> To win the palm, the oak, or bays,
> And their incessant labours see
> Crowned from some single herb or tree,
> Whose short and narrow verged shade
> Does prudently their toils upbraid;

While all the flowers and trees do close,
To weave the garlands of repose!

Marvell seems to assume that flowers and nectarines and melons disport themselves without human help, but the final stanza acknowledges the 'skilful gardener' and I do not doubt that the poet could observe a parallel pleasure in work.

To compare my mother's experience with that of her contemporaries is probably more relevant than to set it beside that of my daughters. She kept in touch with several of her friends from 'the office' right up to the fair old age that most of them reached. One, her special friend, married and went to the United States and was unhappy; they wrote to each other every week until they were in their nineties. None of the others married. One, (to me 'Auntie Mon') was always happy, involved in Catholic organisations, her perspective-setting comment on any complaint, 'Well, seen in the light of Eternity....'.

In the 1950s she still dressed just as she had in 1920: a flat velvet Rembrandtesque cap sitting over her square, benevolent face, white blouse under long-skirted grey 'costume' — we call them 'suits' now — and a wide blue ribbon over the blouse, held by a starry silver brooch. It occurs to me that it may well have been a Child of Mary ribbon.

The two others whom I knew slightly in later life each owned their own homes, had Civil Service pensions, went on holidays.

Were they better off than my mother, who gave up her job for marriage and me?

I am inclined to think that Auntie Mon was very well off; I shouldn't think she found her job boring, and all her spare time was filled with good things and good people. The trouble is, you have to be born like that.

As for staying all your life in one job, same place, same people, rewarded with a roof, I can see that in comparison with not having a roof at all it's a benefit, but, as may appear, Addie, my mother, had a more interesting time, a marriage that was one long challenge, but that stimulated her resourcefulness. Those years in Ballydonagh that I have been writing about were a treasure — note that the office crowd were glad to come out and share it — and in the end she did have a place here that was more agreeable than many alternatives. She had me to argue with, but also the shared delight in the garden flowers, a collection of grandchildren to whom to tell stories again, though not as a duty. Her room, with three windows looking on the garden, was directly beside the front door, so it was easy for friends to visit her, and I think it is to be noted that she made new friends when she was more than ninety. They assured me that they visited her for pleasure, because she was so interesting. Maybe she was interesting and interested because her experience had been various.

So far as that goes, it does not seem evident that 'her child could not make full use of all her abilities, and the consequence (was) that something was still being wasted', as Radcliffe Richards argues in her *The Sceptical Feminist*. After all, if Addie had stayed in 'the office' her story-telling ability would have been wasted and her colleagues would not have had somewhere so pleasant to visit at weekends.

There are two sets of comparisons to be made. One, between what Addie was doing and what she would have been doing if she hadn't married and had me, the other between marriage and remaining single. They overlap, because it is only within about the last twenty years that it has been possible for a woman to remain in the Civil Service after marriage (widows were sometimes found a job).

I should say that what she and her friends were doing was socially useful, more than can be said for a great many jobs. They were involved in the early stages of National Insurance. Addie, like most of her sisters, was 'good at figures' and enjoyed that side of the work. She was also good at guessing, which was helpful, since contributors were quite likely to spell the same name in half-a-dozen different ways.

So, she was quite happy in her job, knew it to be useful and enjoyed the company. I never thought of asking her, but I can remember her tone of voice when talking about Ballydonagh and I have no doubt that that is where she was happier.

The other comparison, between marriage and the single life has, in general, a different result. Observation of my parents' marriage left me determined to remain single — I thought any woman who got married was mad. I remember telling my father — I must have been about twelve — that I'd rather be a *peon caminero* — road workers with pick and shovel whose lock-ups were clearly labelled along the highways of Spain — than get married.

CHAPTER 3

Shades of the prison house...
Even Teddy is taken

To marry or not to marry is a question for the remote future. I am still taking a child's-eye view. What I am viewing at the moment is the rocky road up the hill to our home in Ballydonagh. I am about five, standing outside the gate in the sun, dressed in my best, facing the Sugarloaf, looking down the hill, full of excitement, waiting for Daddy to arrive.

When I was younger I had been a sailor, swarming up and down the open stairway to the attic, happy in the collar of my sailor tunic, made, of course, by an obedient mother. Now I know that the thing to be is an Indian. I don't know where the notion came from, but it remained for a long time. My 'best' is my Indian suit, not home-made this time — in fact, rather a tight fit — but properly fringed as regards tunic and trousers and complete with feather head-dress (war bonnet would be decidedly an exaggeration).

But a war bonnet or some weapons of defence would have suited the scene well enough. I am greeting a half-remembered face when I realise that it is a very angry face indeed. The Bible, it seems, has strong views about women wearing trousers. Never let him see again...and so on, and on.

It really was extraordinary, this drive to disapprove. Here was a father who can't, good heavens, have been much more than thirty, a man who had a lot of fun in him, who enjoyed Stephen Leacock and Beachcomber and Belloc, and the first thing he can think of, or rather, do without thinking, when he meets, after at least a year's absence, his small, cheerful, open-hearted daughter, is to convey to her that being a girl, which she hadn't noticed, and being an Indian, in which she took all her pride, were causes of wrath.

Of course I do not know what followed. I am sure that my mother, who did not like cooking, had exerted herself to make a welcoming meal. I dare say she had placed me at the gate to encourage good feeling. When this had just the opposite effect she is certain to have defended me, and the next six months together, which she would have vowed to keep peaceful, was off to a bad start.

Mind you, it could be argued that she had known him long enough to guess that trousers would annoy him. Before they were married she more than once had to stand up and leave a theatre because something on the stage had offended him, though she never knew what. I suppose whatever it was would have been too indelicate to mention. But guessing — you could call it empathy — was something in which both of my parents were singularly deficient. So often, when we were all living together, I would hear one saying something which I knew was going to strike sparks off the other, sparks which seemingly took the speaker quite by surprise. Maybe a marriage counsellor would have heard it differently. But whatever strategy may have developed later, I am certain that she had no notion of causing trouble by letting me wear my Indian suit.

Certainly, their backgrounds were different. This explosive father of mine was born in the Argentine of parents from the Glens of Antrim, Bible-reading Catholics. They returned to Scotland when he was very young, but those first few years on the pampas, living on roast sheep meat, with some Spanish savour to it, seems to have coloured the rest of his life, just as my infant Paradise in Wicklow solitude has been the foundation for mine.

His father seems to have been very fierce, sometimes locked his wife out of the house in that Argentinian wilderness, wouldn't let females (wife or daughters) speak unless they were spoken to.

Alex, my father, was good at school. One of the few things he told me himself about his boyhood in Glasgow was that he used to deliver milk in the morning before school, and every house left out a small jug for cream, for the porridge, as well as a large jug for milk. At the age of fourteen he passed an examination for the Post Office, went off to London, taught himself French by reading only French for recreation, passed more exams, moved to Dublin which was still under the British Crown. He must have studied accountancy because when he had to choose between Irish citizenship and the British Empire he was able to take up a place in the accounts department of the Post Office in Lagos.

During his years in Dublin he had spent many evenings in the house in Clontarf where my mother lived with her widowed mother and all those sisters. Other young men found it attractive too. My impression is that the drawingroom carpet was very frequently rolled up for dancing. This was not what Alex did best — one of the sisters said he danced like a piano — but he and Addie must have spent years of Saturdays walking in the Dublin mountains and talking about books.

Just what I and my future husband used to enjoy, some thirty years later, perhaps having tea in the same cottage, on the way up to Killakee or Kilmashogue. What went wrong for them? Afterwards Addie said that one of Alex's friends, who did not know that there was any attachment, remarked to her that that chap was always changing his digs; it should have been a warning.

There probably would have been problems if she had gone out to Lagos with him but there could hardly have been the chiaroscuro of contrast that enveloped them when he came back to Ireland. He had been transported from 'digs' in Dublin to a fully furnished bungalow with staff, Ibo or Yoruba 'boys'; houseboy and helper, cook and cook's boy, a gardener or so, four to six attendants for one white man. Clap hands, call for a clean shirt. Clap hands, call for a drink. Then an invigorating argument about how much the cook had spent.

Return from that to spend six months in an isolated cottage, with one wife cooking and ironing on a coal range, doing the washing in a tin bath outside, pumping the water, digging the garden, minding the baby. Delight for mother and child, but not ideal for a man who has recently been revelling in Imperial Service.

Later on he used to say that he only married her out of pity; if he had known that another acceptable young man had proposed he would have detached himself. I more than once heard the classic phrase 'a meal ticket for life'.

I can only guess at the circumstances of his first 'leave'. They used to drive around in a motorcycle and side-car, with me down in the 'boot' of the side-car, and while I can't remember the sensation I can see the side-car itself. This suggests that they were able to have some fun together. To balance that there is quite a clear recollection of being in the hall in Ballydonagh, in my mother's arms — hence, still quite young — and someone asks why I am making such an odd face and I reply 'I'm fwowning like Alex'. There must have been a marked negative response, to imprint it on my memory. I can even feel the effort to make my forehead obey me, rather like trying to make my ears wiggle, which I understand my Uncle Frank could do.

From the time I remember more clearly, probably the next leave, two incidents present themselves. There's anger about Teddy. Some nun has said that it is wrong for children to give affection to mere objects instead of to human beings. Something about 'idols' came into it. Teddy is banished to the top of a wardrobe where I cannot reach him. I now diagnose jealousy. It must have been evident that I loved Teddy. Alex had never had a 'personable' companion when he was a child himself, so he didn't understand. Still, he must have been lacking in imagination if he thought that to separate me from Teddy would bring me closer to himself.

I should think that Teddy found his way back by bedtime. Daddy made another mistake during this interval. I say 'interval' because for some short period we were not at home in Ballydonagh but living with different furniture in a different place in an atmosphere of uncertainty. So much so that Daddy seemed to have some responsibility for food, and he asked me did I like mayonnaise. There was lettuce on my plate, a swelling yellow bottle of that nice stuff Denis' family called Heinz Salad Dressing in his hand, so I said I loved it. A big blob on my lettuce. Take a mouthful. Spit it out.

'I don't like that at all.'

Believe it or not, there was an explosion, a sermon on the wrongness of telling lies. This was shattering because I knew that I wouldn't tell a lie, that I hadn't told a lie, and that a responsible grown-up — a Daddy — should know that.

I believe I cried, something I wasn't in the habit of doing. I think I was put outside the door; perhaps I retired myself. I wasn't used to anything more than a mild scolding. Men are larger and louder than women anyway; a man in a temper is alarming enough and when God, with whom you think you are on friendly terms, is brought into it on his side it is altogether too much.

Doubtless poor Addie had to explain again. Messrs Heinz used to package both their Salad Dressing and their Mayonnaise in identical bottles; you had to be able to read to tell the difference. The Mayonnaise of course contained olive oil and had quite a different taste from the sweetish dressing. But that left us with another problem. My father was ashamed to find that he had a child who would prefer imitation 'salad cream' to real mayonnaise, made with real olive oil, the food of real Spaniards, real people.

This olive oil problem would recur when we were living in Gibraltar. Naturally, the Spanish cook used it constantly. In some contexts — frying chips or eggs, for example — I found it acceptable. In others, as in a loathsome slimy dark green soup Isabe called minestrone, which reminded me of the sea in the Ancient Mariner ('The water, like a witch's oils / Burnt green, and blue, and white') I did not. Then there would be trouble. Once, oil was poured purposefully over hot boiled potatoes and daughter ordered to stay at the table until she had eaten them. Did she? I doubt it.

The irony of it is that it seems as likely as not that the dislike of oil had its beginning in that unjust accusation of lying about mayonnaise. Even still when I visit any of my children, who are all devout and inventive salad eaters, they say, hesitantly, 'But you don't like olive oil, do you?', and I can reply truthfully that I like salad the way they make it. When I'm at home, though, I eat lettuce, tomato, cucumber and peppers just as nature left them, with no more addition than a little salt.

When I describe my father's outbursts I do not look on my former self as a bullied or badly treated child. Fortunately, I had had so much more of confidence-building care that I believe I was not affected — just distressed. What I must have learnt from them is to believe that a child means well until it is absolutely proven otherwise — which I have not known to happen. I'm thinking, of course, of a child in its natural surroundings.

Strangely, a great many people seem to think that schools are children's natural surroundings. I cannot accept that notion in general; the human race has lived through tens of thousands of years without them. In particular, I did not find it in any way natural to be uprooted from Ballydonagh and sent to a convent boarding school when I was just six.

My mother was due to go to Nigeria for another six months. Geg was quite willing to take charge again but my father did not want me to be under the influence of the Rigney family. The choice was between going to live with his mother in a dark Lancashire town or going to boarding school.

This was a long six months of misery. At least I was among women and escaped the horrors we have all read about as indigenous to boys' boarding school. I was lonely. I was baffled. It was hard enough to know where one was supposed to be at any time, but the times for going to chapel were the worst. Twice a day a stream of girls hurried along a corridor. One side was lined with numbered pigeonholes in which each girl had a black veil and a white veil and on each veil a name tape. I know my trunk had held the two named veils, as it had held a knife, fork and spoons with my name, Máire P. McCormick, engraved on the handle of each. Sometimes I found myself early in the refectory and I could go around the tables and find a knife or a spoon that identified itself with me and exchange it for the one allotted by chance, but veils were different. There never seems to have been a chance to arrive before the swarm, and even if I had, most of the holes were too high up to explore.

It's not that I was anxious to have my own veil. I just wanted something to put on, like everyone else, not to be asked impatiently where my veil was, but my pigeonhole was almost always empty. What used to happen? I have no idea, but I can be fairly sure I would not have been allowed to pray with my head uncovered.

So long as I had Teddy there was some comfort. There were three of us younger than the rest of the school, all daughters of exiles. The other two were sisters and had each other; I had Teddy. In the mornings, after the classic wash in cold water, teeth brushed with mandatory pink tooth-powder, the dressing modestly inside our nightdresses, the hair-brushing, our beds must be made. I think big girls helped the three of us. The statutory eiderdown had to be folded with its corners turned back towards the centre; in that nest I would place Teddy to wait for my return.

One evening when we had been sent up to bed, Teddy simply wasn't there. I looked in the bed and under the bed and all around the dormitory. I believe I spent three days looking for him, crying most of the time. The most vivid memory is that someone suggested that perhaps he had been thrown into a wastepaper basket, so I went around the school looking in wastepaper baskets. One large hall had, instead of a basket, a corner beside the door boarded off to make a tall triangular container. I had to climb up to reach the top, then I struggled upside down to investigate the bottom; I remember the strong smell of discarded orange peel.

But no Teddy. I think the lay sister who looked after the dormitory must have burnt him. If it had been possible to restore him someone surely would have done so.

One solitary pleasure remains from that miserable interlude. Out beside the tennis court was a hedge that held the flowers of Aaron's Beard (*Hypericum patens*), the yellow flowers with a sheaf of ruby-tipped stamens in the centre. A kind big girl showed me that if I were to hold a plump, plucked bud in my warm palm and let the sun shine on it, it would slowly, slowly uncurl its petals and open out. I have a bank of Aaron's Beard at my disposal now, sought out because of this recollection, yet how rarely I repeat the golden experiment.

There were other things that helped a little. I found that the nun who taught embroidery, whom I was convinced was a witch, was really friendly and let me sit with her class of big girls. There was the fudge made for me by Auntie Mab, sent all the way from New York, a box full of massive brown delicious lumps, doled out after dinner.

Mostly I was baffled or sad. I cried in bed every night. What little I remember of lessons is not positive. A nasty little square of card, once white, with a curly shape on it which they said was 'a'. I knew 'a' was A. Instead of painting we were supposed to fill in the holes in stencils, using a sort of scrubbing movement with blunt, squat paint brushes. There were unmanageable weaving exercises — small sheets of shiny paper in rather nasty green and red, each one sliced into narrow strips, held together at one edge. We were instructed to weave one into the other. I would love to have them again because I don't believe proper weaving was possible unless one set of strips were cut free. I would not be at all surprised to find that the teacher had not understood how the material was meant to be used. The gymnasium class may have been quite sensible but all I could see was thousands of girls in lines stretching in all directions, all knowing what to do, and myself trying to copy them, too late.

Luckily my failure in all the skills proposed did not quite remove my confidence. It does not seem that I thought any of the skills attractive. I remember rather clearly one class, or at least some sort of discussion, where we were with some older children. A large picture of Our Lady, St Joseph and the child Jesus had been unrolled on the wall. I was asked, what country did Our Lady come from — they would hardly have used the word 'race'. I answered that she was English. No one could convince me otherwise; Geg had told me. She was reliable; others were not.

Years afterwards I sorted the problem out. I remembered sitting at the table in the kitchen in Ballydonagh, Geg telling me that my name, Máire, was Irish for Mary, but that Irish people used a different form for Our Lady, who was called Muire. That name wouldn't be used for an ordinary person. And what language was Mary? English. There you are.

Which goes to show how important were fortnightly visits from Geg. She had not been allowed to take charge, but she knew I needed her. Every second Saturday she made her way down by bus or train from Dublin. The time-table (or could it have been the convent?) allowed only half an hour or so. I always howled when she left. Doubtless people told her, as they used to tell parents of children in hospital, that I would settle down better if she didn't come. Geg understood. She was real life, she enabled me to keep in touch with my real self. I'm glad I was able to thank her when I was grown up, tell her that I would have become a quite different person without her; later again, when she grew old, I was able to return her visits, let her know I loved her. The evening before she died, among kind nuns in County Wicklow, I made much the same journey as she used to make to visit me, sat beside her and held her hand. They asked me to read the lesson at her funeral Mass and I chose the one where Mary meets Jesus in the garden.

The time in boarding school naturally seemed endless. There were two interruptions. Once several of us came out in spots, probably chicken-pox, and had to stay in bed, which was an escape. The other interruption was my First Holy Communion. It had been arranged beforehand that this should take place on the 8th of December. My mother had ordered my dress from Mrs Valentine who lived near Kilmacanogue and did smocking. The dress was in white crêpe-de-Chine, smocked at the wrists and somewhere below the waist. In the darkness of the morning some Big Girls helped me into this and arranged my special veil. I think the three small children were making their First Communions together so there was a quiet fuss around our beds. Probably the others in the dormitory were being allowed to sleep a bit longer because of the holiday — the 8th of December is the feast of the Immaculate Conception — hence the darkness and the hush. I remember nothing else except a sort of conversation with an elderly nun out in the garden near the grotto with the statue of Our Lady and the lights burning under blue glass covers.

Is 'mistake' the word? Or 'misjudgement'? Ineptitude or simply bungling? Either one or both parents must have decided that since I would have the good fortune to be in the care of holy nuns I would have expert preparation to make my First Holy Communion of lifelong value. Well, they did try hard to get me to remember how to recite the Confiteor, which in those days had a complicated ending, and I had plenty of practice in holding the cloth attached to the communion rail. This will mean nothing to any reader aged less than about fifty and it is not worth elaborating. My point is that since I did not love anyone who was dealing with me it would not have been possible for any of them to foster in me the love of God.

On the other hand, Geg showed unmistakably that she loved me, and if she knew that God loved me, then so it was. My father's effort to remove me from the Rigney influence was fortunately ineffective.

Most ironic is the fact that the clearest memory of all that time of exile is the moment it ended, that glorious moment when I was sent for to go to the Parlour, the door opened and They were there. Truly I can still feel the sensation of being in mid-air as I shot like a little cannonball into my father's arms. My mother told me later that she had stood back, to let him have the pleasure...he who was solely, pointlessly, wilfully responsible for every hour of unhappiness.

CHAPTER 4

The Kingdom of Kerry;
blighted by mixed bathing

When my seventh birthday arrived we were living in Kenmare, County
Kerry. I had a playroom of my own. Nothing in it except a large table
and space, but on the table I could spread out my new cooking set,
with its four-inch rolling-pin and impractical cake tins. I was not at all
disappointed by the inadequacy of the rolling-pin; I had also been
given a real tomahawk. The shopkeeper doubtless supposed he was
selling an ordinary small hatchet for chopping sticks. It is only now
that I come to write this that I wonder which of them bought it. My
mother knew what an Indian needed, but she must have been
hampered by the presence of my new brother, Frankie.

Daddy was around, but uninformed. Perhaps he wasn't there for the
birthday, but it was he who had found the house and enjoyed it. It was
a hunting-lodge of the Earl of Kenmare, it had reasonably reliable
running water and locally generated but somewhat erratic electricity
and it had enough rooms to leave one for Maggie, our housekeeper,
and a spare one for me. Two front rooms had bow windows looking
out on a garden which sloped down towards the estuary and, only a
couple of hundred yards away, the towers that held up the beautiful
suspension bridge. The postcards of the bridge included a corner of
our house.

Here I met Daddy at his best. We explored the garden together,
were charmed by the discovery of a rapid secret stream, delighted to
find, after a couple of weeks, an enclosed orchard that we had not
noticed. In the mornings he would enthusiastically pick raspberries for
breakfast. He decided to keep hens because we shouldn't waste the
outbuildings. They never laid, but when it was decided to cook them
the miserly creatures were found to be full of egg yolks.

I cannot guess how long Daddy was with us. There is a vague patch between boarding school and Kenmare. We must have gone back to Ballydonagh because I saw chairs there rather badly chewed up by the dogs of another aunt, Jo, who must have taken over the lease. Kneeling beside these we for the first time said the Rosary together as a family. The parents had a surprise. I, now aged six, could take my turn at giving it out — saying the first half of the Hail Mary, to which they would respond, for one decade — but when the five decades, with the Hail, Holy Queen, were finished, I stayed on my knees, on and on and on. It must have been after two or three evenings like this that they asked me what I was doing. They found that whenever anyone said 'Say a prayer for me, that's good girl' I dutifully tacked yet another Hail Mary onto my night prayers. Fortunately I remained obedient and when told that one prayer would be enough for everyone I consented.

Were we already in Kenmare when Frankie was born? If so, who looked after me? Of course, hospital was not thought to be as necessary as it is nowadays, so it's probable he was born at home. Whatever about that, Alex was in very good form; quite likely pleased that he was negotiating a transfer to Gibraltar, where he was going to be Postmaster General, and no doubt pleased also to have a little son.

When a baby like Frankie is born in hospital now it is diagnosed at once as being or having Down's Syndrome. All my mother noticed was that he was very slow to suck. Breast-feeding must have been unsatisfactory and she had to give him a bottle with an extra large hole in the teat. Even with this feeds took hours. I had no idea there was a problem and I rather doubt that I was any help at all. Well, we had Maggie to help with the house and I suppose Frankie slept a good deal. My mother found time to teach me to hem the skirt of a blue check dress for some doll. She tried to teach me to knit — I remember sitting up in a tree struggling to sort out stitches — but that didn't take.

I was able to read for myself. I remember reading a large illustrated *Peter Pan* and a handsome *Grimms' Fairy Tales* — not unfrightening — but of course my mother read to me as well. There was Stephen Leacock's *Frenzied Fiction*, which we both found almost too funny to get on with, *Three Men in a Boat*, and a full-length *Robinson Crusoe*. She knew I was paying attention: when Crusoe is going to swim out to the wreck he takes off his clothes; on board, collecting useful objects, he puts something in his pockets. 'What pockets?' I have never looked up that detail, even when reading Defoe to the next generation, but the notion of contriving to make the best of a desert island remains.

Clearer than any fiction is a conversation as we sit in the same window seat where she used to read to me. My mother has a prayer book open and is showing me that on the left-hand pages are the hymns I have so often heard during Benediction, on the facing pages a translation. *Tantum ergo sacramentum veneremur cernui...* So great a sacrament therefore let us venerate... It's not that I remember attaching a meaning to every word, but the notion that a set of words that sounded entirely different could have a meaning explicable in the words I knew gave me a new slant on language.

A pity nobody thought of explaining that Irish was another complete system. Even more of a pity that they didn't let me stay at home and ask Maggie to speak Irish with me; she came from Castletownbear and I feel sure she was a native speaker.

Instead I had to walk every morning over the bridge and through the town to the convent of the Poor Clares which ran the National School. Mother Abbess interviewed myself and my mother; they got on well and corresponded for years afterwards. It must have been claimed that I could read, because the nun took a black book out of her deep black skirt pocket and opened a page. I read, 'It is truly meet and just, right and availing unto salvation that we should at all times and all places give thanks....'

When we left Kenmare Mother Abbess gave us a good missal each, edited by Abbot Cabrol, a daily one for my mother, a Sunday one for me. Hers, as was usual, had the full Latin text with English beside, mine only some parts in Latin and some extra explanations.

My birthday is the first of September, so I may have just reached seven when I started in that school. At boarding school I had been miserable; here I was merely frustrated. The boredom of standing in a half circle holding a Reader, the glossy pages fading to yellow, waiting forever for my turn to read a sentence, was simple boredom; I sympathise with guards who have to stand outside the residences of diplomats.

Arithmetic does not seem to have made any impression; I suppose we recited tables. I liked the look of Gaelic script; I may have sometimes even made the right sounds because of hearing the others, but I truly did not grasp that it was meant to mean something. There was a sort of 7 that reached below the line of print; when you came to that you said 'agus'. I had no idea that it was a relic of scribes in a hurry and corresponded to &.

Many of the other children came barefoot from miles away; I suppose now that they may have had better Irish than the nun who was teaching them, so that they were not learning Irish, but learning to read. I wasn't learning anything, except to know what it is to be baffled. I liked best the 'headline copy' in which I had to copy such sentences as 'Aitneann ciaróg ciaróg eile'. The modern Irish reader will note that I do not put in 'h'. What I was copying was a strange hybrid, a copperplate version of the Irish manuscript hand. The capital 'A' had a lovely wavy line at the base. The headline proverb says, 'One beetle knows another beetle'.

Singing class was conducted by a nun who twanged a tuning fork. I would stand prudently silent. Most of the other girls were marvellous knitters; they used to knit doll-sized socks on four fine steel needles and even turn the heels. Since I couldn't succeed at home, trying to make a simple scarf on large needles, there was no hope for me. I have a notion that I was allowed to go home early. Just as well, since, like others I have met, I found it impossible to use the three-seater lavatory, three circular holes in a wooden bench.

Though in classtime I didn't fit in I had no sense of being an outsider at playtime. Play consisted mostly of running around chasing each other, making up for the strict order of the classroom. One girl from the town, Peggy, came home with me from time to time, but she wasn't any good at climbing trees. I in turn had tea with her; her family had a shop and made lovely ice-cream with raspberry sauce, using a sort of hand-churn with ice around the outside. Delicious stuff.

School took up too much time, but there were still hours and hours in the garden and walks with my mother through exquisite woods, the ground all moss and small ferns. It was here that I was given that satisfactory answer about Teddy in heaven. No wonder we were talking about heaven. Then there were other walks to fetch butter from a farmhouse that had passion-flower growing around the dairy door. Had we a baby in pram?

Much more profitable than school were hours spent with Mr O'Shea. I rather think he farmed the land that belonged to the house. Anyway, he showed me how to sharpen a scythe, let me watch him cut a field of hay, help turn over the swathes when the sun had partly dried them, build it up into haycocks. He brought me to the boggy land up behind the house, demonstrated how to move fast from one fairly solid tuft to another. I remember him now whenever I sharpen a reaping hook for the garden.

Visitors came too, though of course not as constantly as in Ballydonagh. Madeleine, one of the office friends, gave me valuable advice; I was alone with her, sitting on tawny rocks beside a stream, cooling our two pairs of feet. It was true; hers were misshapen, in fact her toes were practically plaited. She didn't exactly say that she had been foolish, when young, to wear pointed shoes, but she did say feet were ugly and I took in the warning.

The Great Visit was when Denis, his younger brother Noel and their parents, Sid and Florrie, came down to stay. That summer is on record as having been out-of-the-way sunny. To spend it in Kerry, with friends, was uncommon good luck. I rather think they came down while Alex was still with us, so he had Sid for company and then they stayed on.

Noel was not too young to swing on the swing Alex had put up — a rope tied to a high branch with a cushion for a seat, or to explore the garden, the hidden heights behind the stream, the so-called hot-house full of musty smelling geraniums, the junk-filled outhouses around the yard at the back. The potential of the place for sheltering Indians was endless; the grown-ups must have been tired of being ambushed. On the other hand, perhaps not; it is very agreeable for grown-ups to have their children happy all day without requiring adult intervention.

When the sun slowed us down we lay on the lawn, spears of brilliant orange montbretias blazing above us. A few times we all crossed the suspension bridge and scrambled down the bank on the far side to a skimpy beach for a swim. Since the Dublin family lived on the sea front and had the miles of pale sand at Dollymount at their disposal this was not attractive unless we were feeling very hot indeed. That it happened I know, because of the photograph. 'Snaps' were what we called them then. Sid took a snap of Denis and Noel and myself. A copy was sent to Alex. Another thunderbolt out of the blue. What had happened to 'his little Carmelite'? *Mixed bathing.*

I can explain the little Carmelite. Someone must have asked me what I was going to be when I grew up. People will ask that when they can't think of anything to say. I apparently answered, 'A Carmelite.' Maybe Alex put this together with the lengthy trimmings to the Rosary and decided that he had produced a future saint. The facts were much more mundane. Geg had said something about a Carmelite convent in Greystones; I think she used to go up our hill and down the other side to get to Mass there. Anyway, it was mentioned that they didn't eat meat. What instead? They ate turnips. Now I was specially fond of mashed swede turnips, with butter, so saw how to plan a well fed future.

By the way, I find that I have begun to refer to my father as Alex instead of Daddy. I was used to calling Denis's parents Sid and Florrie, Denis similarly called mine Addie and Alex, so when we discussed them with each other, as we did for years, these were the names we naturally used, the names that float up when I am remembering time spent together.

Another set of snaps that survived for a long time provoke recollection of a game that kept us occupied for hours. Denis would wear a beach wrap that fastened round his neck and came down to his feet, and some kind of cap or hat. The three of us would process out to the steps at the front door, where Denis would reverently take off his biretta and celebrate Mass, with myself and Noel as acolytes. Noel had the job of pulling an imaginary rope to ring the bell in the steeple. The other highlight was the sermon, preached from a tree pulpit. Acolyte or no acolyte, I insisted on having my turn at a sermon, a forecast of things to come and, I gathered later, vastly amusing to the grown-up congregation.

The sun shone on Kenmare, but not all the time. There was winter, long knitted stockings for school, a fire in the bedroom, my mother in bed asking Maggie to put some hot turf from the fire into bed with her because she was shivering. She had a bout of malaria, was delirious and it was frightening. Even more horrible was a nightmare I had, the memory of which recurred for years: a girl made of dust sitting under my bed, arms stretched out straight in front. 'Remember Man thou art but dust and into dust thou shalt return.' The priest putting Ash Wednesday ashes on our foreheads used to say it in Latin then; a pity anyone translated. Now nobody says it in either language.

Maggie's insistence that on Hallowe'en we move all our beds away from the walls, so that they wouldn't be in the way of the dead going through, might have been frightening but it wasn't, because she was so matter-of-fact.

Winter was over when we sailed to Gibraltar. The sun shone and I had a lovely time climbing little ladders, helping sailors to paint, playing pushing things around on deck with grown-up passengers. I had most of my meals on my own. Breakfast from a menu a foot long was an experience. So was rice as, so to speak, a vegetable. I knew rice only as a pudding. This was a Japanese ship and fluffy white rice was there for lunch. I must have been eight by this time and I only hope I was more help to my mother than I remember being. She had had to do all the packing and moving, to Liverpool and then to whatever port we sailed from. She had Frankie to look after and she was always seasick for most of our voyages. We sailed to and fro several times and I decided that I wanted a career at sea, as a cabin boy.

CHAPTER 5

The warm south
and Africa across the Straits

Our house in Gibraltar went with my father's job as Postmaster General. It had four balconies, with arches and wide balustrades. From those at the back, belonging to the drawingroom downstairs and two bedrooms upstairs, one of which was at some time mine, you looked down on the dockyard and port and across the bay to Algeciras. Behind Algeciras were low hills, every evening black against rosy sunsets. Sunsets might be a few minutes early in winter, a few minutes later in summer, but there was never occasion to remark how nice it is to have the evenings getting longer again. I preferred my other room. It was in the front, to one side of the main part, so without balcony, but with a morning view of the mountains of North Africa floating across the pale shining straits. O fortunata....

Did I notice these views from the very beginning? How can I be sure? I do remember long before that being on Howth summit with the usual quartet of grown-ups, hearing them talking about the marvellous view and wondering what on earth this thing, 'a view', could be. I must have been pretty small, probably not able to see over the gorse bushes, but my parents greatly valued a rewarding vista so no doubt I absorbed awareness.

Four similar houses made up North Pavilion Road. Called a road, it was really a series of wide steps. The shape of Gibraltar is fairly well known; a peak rising perpendicularly at the Spanish end, a descent almost as abrupt on the Mediterranean side, sloping a little more gently on the Atlantic side, providing some habitable space for a small packed town and a spread of houses toward the south, all strung along two or three roads and a network of various steps.

Our house was topmost of the four, with the best view of Africa.

The steps in front were not only wide but new, or at least in the process of being renewed. Spanish workmen were engaged in laying smooth new concrete all across. They are the first people I really remember meeting. One of them had cigarette cards and he taught me to count them in Spanish. We usually had two or three Spanish maids, a cook and a housemaid, and Carmen who brought Frankie for walks or down to Rosia Bay to the tiny beach inhabited by nannies and mothers. A washerwoman came once a week and boiled things in the copper cauldron in the laundry. This was purpose-built in the basement, with a tiled floor sloping to a drain, two deep sinks or troughs, plenty of light and space. The rest of the basement was taken up by the tank for holding the winter rainwater through the dry summer. The main water supply, used for baths, washing up, probably for laundry, was sea water but there were freshwater taps in bathroom and kitchen for hands and faces and cooking. The water for these had to be pumped up every day, about seventy strokes of the pump. A job for me, though Alex would sometimes do it himself.

The other watering job was harder. Alex arranged a zinc tank standing on the floor beside the water gauge of the large tank and siphoned the rainwater into it, for the garden. A two-gallon zinc watering can had to dumped in, filled and heaved out. Then I had to carry it, water slopping over my sandals, a dozen yards or so to the basement door and out into the enclosed garden at the back. A dollop on each of the arum lilies which stood around the edges of the flowerbeds, each one behind its own semicircle of rooftile. A whole canful on the roots of the Morning Glory which ran a deep band of essential blue all across the top of the further wall. Alex really enjoyed the Morning Glory. Each morning he would pick a handful of chalices to be put all by themselves, no leaves, no mixtures, into a small vase and admired. In season now I often pick flowers from the Convolvulus that rambles the other side of the road, the same flower but white, not blue, and put them on the breakfast table, but I trail some of their elegant leaves along with them.

As for the watering, Alex may have done some himself at first, when he was excited about having a garden, but before long he found that he could achieve two ends with one watering can — keep the garden in flower and find work for daughter; I think my task required twenty cans full. His amusement came from refilling the tank from which I heaved the water. This was done by sucking the end of the rubber tube that he had fed into the top of the main tank until water flowed, then showing me how to stop the flow by lifting the end above the invisible water level, thus finding out how much we had left for the rest of the summer.

What I liked best about the garden was the Nesperus tree in the middle. I have never come across the word or the fruit anywhere else. The thing was about ten feet high, with disproportionately large, leathery, fuzzy-backed, dark green leaves. I could get into the middle of it and crouch there eating the funny fruit; three seeds the size of small chestnuts fitting neatly together and wrapped around by yellow skin and a modest layer of juicy pulp. That was about all I could do in the garden; it wasn't a garden for sitting in. Chairs and tables were on the verandahs. Fun was outside.

At the top of the steps was a flattish space of tarmacadam onto which our side gate from the kitchen opened. We had a small front garden, the only one on the road, with pale blue Plumbago and great white pendant Datura. Above this, level with our upper balcony, was the Garrison Church, where troops from South Barracks, another fifty feet up the slope, paraded with their band on Sunday morning. It was pleasant after breakfast to sit on the upstairs verandah and listen to them.

During the week the trees around the church grounds were at our disposal but they were not as satisfactory as the collection of similar knobby, low-branched trees that surrounded the racquet court a couple of hundred yards away, below the barracks, as it were balancing the church, with a row of non-commissioned family quarters in between. Those trees were designed for easy climbing, or rather monkeying around. I found that it was possible to climb from one to another taking in five of them without coming down to the ground. We competed to see who could spend longest hanging upside down by her knees, until we found that there did not seem to be any natural limit and nobody wanted to spend all day in suspension. When we played there we addressed each other by the names of the characters in the William books (by Richmal Crompton) but I cannot recollect that we tried to copy anything done by William and the gang of Outlaws. We simply were a gang and there must have been four of us because there were four Outlaws, and Joan Strivens' mother crocheted badges for us. We spent hours there and nobody seemed to mind, though the space was fenced in.

Who were *we*? We were available children. Joan lived in the dockyard flats below, Ena was Gibraltarian and lived on Scud Hill. I don't remember who the fourth was. I should think we met playing hopscotch or Tom Tiddler's Ground on that flattish space at the top of the steps. The son of the Chief of Police, who lived two houses below, would have played there some of the time. I remember sharing with him the modest acrobatic possibilities of the double handrail that ran down the centre of our steps. He was very likely sent off to boarding school in England so doesn't much feature in my recollections.

I do remember meeting his mother at an early stage of my colonial life. I was coming from the town and walking up, she was walking down. I politely said, 'Good evening, Mrs Garood.' She explained to me that it was, as yet, only afternoon, and that it would be more appropriate to say 'Good afternoon'. Now, why do I imagine that there was any implication that Irish people in their funny way say 'Good evening' at any old time? Mrs Garood was Scots, and quite nice and was probably just a grown-up explaining something to a child. However, I absorbed the fact that being Irish and Catholic was faintly odd.

At this point I want to explain, feeling a little ashamed of myself, that though I have so far written 'my mother' whenever I wanted to refer to that parent, I had never thought of her by that title. She was Mammy. In some forgotten way I learnt in Gib that one didn't have a Mammy, one had a Mummy. What can I do? I cannot now bring myself to use either word. I encouraged my own children to call me Mama, which most of them shortened, as they grew older, to Ma, not an improvement. By now many of them call me Máire, as do the grandchildren, coming full circle.

So, there were trees to climb, roads and steps for a game in which one ran alone, marking their track with arrows drawn in chalk and the others followed. The same chalk served to draw lay-outs for hopscotch. There were fortifications all over the place, leaving stone slopes to walk on, the gardens of the Alameda with old cannon for ornament and play. These were all pleasant, but secondary. The true delight that returns was the sensation of running, having left appointed duties behind me, out the gate, around under the church, along the short level stretch towards the racquet court, then flying downhill, swimsuit and towel under my arm, hot sun melting the tar and activity melting me, along by some fortifications, down a wooden spiral staircase, running along a narrow plank over the water, under the walls, changing in a flash and diving into cool, cool transparent green.

When I say cool, I mean at the right temperature for people, not the sort of water that surrounds these islands. From mid-April or May you could swim or float or dive comfortably all day long. The *Gibraltar Chronicle* printed daily the temperature at two or three locations, Rosia Bay being one. The corner to which I used to direct myself had a stretch of sand for nannies or mothers and toddlers, changing cabins above, a rock projecting into deeper water with a diving board and smooth cement patches for sitting on. Beyond the sand, backed by the tall fortifications, a relic of rocky shore, untouched, where we independent children sometimes played 'follow-my-leader'.

Helpful advice soon taught me to swim. Someone told me to pick up a heavy stone, hold it in my arms and walk out waist deep, then hold my breath, lean over and let the stone pull me down to the bottom. As soon as I was down I naturally let go of the stone — and realised that I was popping back up to the air. Once one has recognised that humans tend to float it's a matter of graduating from dog paddle to breast stroke to crawl and so on. The diving-board pointed towards a raft. Most of our time was spent between the two, perhaps trying to swim the whole way under water or asking each other whether we'd kept our knees straight when we dived.

The higher diving-boards were on the enclosing pier, on the outer side of the bay. That was the men's side. They didn't come round to the ladies and babies, but we could go over there if we liked. The first time I swam all the way over I was proud. Then I found that I could go backwards and forwards indefinitely and there didn't seem to be much point. A difficulty did arise, but not yet.

I now find it interesting that I do not seem to have been aware of something I might have questioned. When I say 'we' climbed trees and 'we' spent our time in the water between diving-board and raft, the two sets are different. Of my climbing companions one was Gibraltarian, the other had a father who worked in the dockyard in some non-commissioned capacity. Rosia was an officers' bathing place. Naturally; it was much the most agreeable and accessible. I went there; the others probably went to the Baths at the other end of the town.

Of course we went to different schools. There was Brympton, for the children of officers. The Loreto nuns ran three schools: Europa Convent, where I was sent, a small one near St Joseph's where Ena almost certainly went, and another larger girls' school down in the town. Irish Christian Brothers looked after the boys — the boys, that is, who were not sent 'home' to school. The better-off Gibraltarian boys were also sent 'home' to Ampleforth or elsewhere. Perhaps that is why my remembrance of the set who used to swim in Rosia is so cloudy; the boys among them were probably summer visitors.

I would run down to Rosia in the morning, sometimes bringing a snack for lunch. Carmen would quite possibly bring Frankie along in the afternoon. She could sit on the sand and chat with the other Spanish child-minders and I would spend some time playing with him. He was always happy, would put his hands over his eyes to hide just as long as you could go on saying 'Where's Baba? Ah, *there* he is'. At home he would place Daddy's shoes in a wandering line on the floor and lie down beside them in mysterious play. Of course like any toddler he loved to be chased.

The trouble was that he so often needed to be chased in reality. He found out how to get up on a chair and open the Yale lock on the front door and vanish down the steps. If found by a stranger he certainly could not have explained himself. Uncle Frank had given him a pleasing silver-gilt baby spoon and pusher — a useful object I have never seen since — but little Frankie could not feed himself well and it took adult guesswork to know when he needed to go to the bathroom. He sometimes played out on the steps with whoever I was playing with. It was Peter, the son of the Chief of Police, who laughed at him and said he was a parrot. I objected firmly. I did not recognise that he was at all unusual; I supposed that that is how babies are. Photographs show that he was quite evidently what we then called a Mongol.

I loved Frankie and helped when we were out together but I did not seek opportunities to look after him, as Daddy thought I should. When he (Alex) was a boy he was delighted to have the chance to play with a baby, or so he thought. I was upset when Frankie ruined the camera Auntie Mab had given me by dropping it in the water tank. I was much more upset when Mummy gave me a half a crown — one eighth of a pound, must have been equivalent to well more than a pound now — and let me go shopping in the town by myself. This was almost the first money I had ever had. I bought myself a wooden Chinese pencil box with a lid that had a picture of an elegant tree and was made of thin slats that rolled away when you wanted to open it. I thought I had found a treasure. Mummy was disappointed that I had not thought of buying a present for Frankie. I felt really badly about that. It dawned on me that I had been selfish, but at the same time I had a parallel awareness that there was no point in buying things for Frankie when he would get more enjoyment out of a shoe. Looking back I suspect that it was just this that neither parent wanted to acknowledge. I know that they brought him to see a Spanish specialist. I gathered that he slept very little at night and my mother had to be constantly alert to hear him climbing out of his cot, so she really needed to have Carmen, or someone, look after him in the afternoon while she had a siesta and the someone would sometimes be me, but between school and swimming I eluded too much involvement.

(Reading the last paragraph a few months after writing it I notice that I have used 'Mummy' even though I wrote a little earlier that I could not use either that or 'Mammy'. It seems that while writing I was living in the past; I am sure that pencil box hasn't surfaced in my memory for decades.)

Europa Convent was a boarding school, the boarders being Spanish children and young women of good family, with a scattering of titles. Boarders wore a dress or overall of navy with small white spots, day pupils wore navy with pale blue collars. Some of the day pupils were Gibraltarian and Catholic, quite a few colonial, like myself, but not Catholic. I had the distinction of being Irish, having shamrock sent to me on St Patrick's Day, but not such a postbag-full of shamrock as used to cover the breast of Sister Lorcan, the porteress, the giver of welcome.

To reach school in the mornings I would walk up towards the barracks, leave the parade ground on my right with men in uniform stamping their feet, turn towards St Joseph's Church, climb some narrow steps beside it and reach one of the proper roads. An adult would walk north along that for some distance, then zig-zag back south towards the convent; a child would naturally climb the bank between the roads and cut off the zig-zag. This child would nibble the sorrel that grew on the bank; she also preferred to walk on the pleasantly rounded tops of the low walls that bordered the real roads. I don't know when the nuns became aware of this habit. They didn't approve. It was not correct behaviour for a young lady. They probably knew that quite often a military band would be marching euphoniously in the opposite direction. I argued that within the school I kept fairly well to school rules but outside was different.

Once inside, past Sister Lorcan's little room and the parlour, was a wide, bright, well-polished passage with tennis court on one side, shoe-rooms for changing shoes on the other. The tennis court had a few weathered marble classical statues at each end, and a line of date palms, whose sticky fruit would fall on the court in season, towering above the road below. Across the further end of the tennis court was another wide passage onto which opened the three or four junior classrooms, the last one having windows that looked out above the road and over the bay and let us see ships coming and going.

This meant that classes were pleasingly punctuated by the clunk of tennis balls and the calls of the players. One did not attend to them, but they were a reminder that life was not all work. Since there was only one court people had to take their turn to play for half hours throughout the day. Timetables and notices hung up, showing who was due to go to music practice or tennis at what time and who would get a red or a green or a purple ribbon to wear if she did not get too many 'crosses'. Unacceptable behaviour earned a cross, but after a certain length of time and perhaps an apology it could be rubbed out. By second year we were all equipped with diamonds of ribbon, held by a pin between the shoulder blades, passing over the shoulders and weighed down by a medal in front. A nun who was really displeased could take this ribbon off; its absence would be remarked. Even if one didn't so very much care, social pressure more or less compelled an apology and a request for its return at the time appointed.

The system seems to have worked rather well. We talked a bit in class, passed notes to each other written in code, sometimes skimped our homework, but must have been fairly easy to manage. We stood up when the nun or lay teacher came in, said a prayer together before sitting down and got on with the subject. We learnt definitions of the Parts of Speech: 'an Adjective qualifies a noun. An Adverb qualifies a verb, adjective or another adverb.' In more senior classes we spent hours and hours in parsing and analysis. Our teachers must sometimes have been puzzled about how to account for anomalies in English grammar, but they didn't let us know they were puzzled.

In First Year we also learnt off definitions of archipelagos and peninsulas, drew maps of the main rivers and mountain ranges of the world, the mountain ranges looking like blanket stitch. I think that is all the geography I was ever taught and it seems to have served any purposes I have had. We memorised our catechism, too, and the parables told by Our Lord. With my mother's example behind me, I enjoyed learning poetry; all that remains from that class are fragments of *The Wreck of the Hesperus*.

The introduction to algebra I remember. Our teacher wrote on the blackboard a line of lower case a and b, x and y, some with a little 2 on their shoulders, some with a 2 or a 3 in front, at the same level. An x or a y with a 2 above it was to be called x or y squared. The task was to arrange them in lines so that 3b, for example, would be under another b, not under an x, and not on any account under b squared. When they were tidily arranged, you drew a line underneath and added each column, like ordinary addition. It was quite a disastrous introduction, yet I always loved algebra and that teacher was a friend for years and my bridesmaid when I was married.

Gibraltar was a haven for Loreto girls from Ireland who wanted a year or so away. Some might go to the convent in Sevilla; the less adventurous would take up the offer of Gib. Naturally, they had to have time off. What could be more satisfactory for the nuns than to have an Irish Catholic family within easy reach? Tera, who introduced me to algebra, came straight from school. She confessed years later that she had, to everyone's surprise, failed her Leaving Cert. She came out to study and take it again, which she did, and then trained as a nurse, and that probably influenced me to do the same. Others who spent a year or so were older. My parents were happy to have them around, just visiting, or to keep us company on 'runs' in to Spain.

My father re-organised the running of the Post Office and everyone agreed that he re-organised it well. It was a significant source of revenue for the colony. And he organised it so that he could take one or two half days a week and spend them on a 'run' to the cork woods or to Tarifa or to the beach at Estepona. We were sometimes McCormicks alone. Funny, I haven't thought of mentioning my parents' name, which I fairly early decided to spell for my own use as MacCormac. Anyway, the afternoons that I remember best, Daddy recklessly lighting a fire in the cork woods, in a clearing among trees that looked, with their smooth chocolate-coloured trunks and nubby beige branches, like shorn sheep in reverse; the stony beach near Estepona so hot that it was painful to bare feet running down to the sea, then Daddy dispensing bread and butter and a tongue from a glass jar, all cut up with his penknife; longer runs to Malaga to eat *riñones al Jerez* and buy big boxes of Muscatel raisins; these were family outings.

Those were grand, but I think that fairly soon I got into the way of making myself scarce. I felt I could be excused if parents had someone else, teacher from the convent, or nurses (who all ranked as officers) from the Military Hospital, or visitors, anyone to serve as a sort of insulation.

At home I was not very effective insulation. There may have been some things Alex didn't say in front of me but plenty came through. 'A meal ticket for life' for example. He felt that a wife should be physically serving him, scrubbing floors, washing clothes, cooking — good Spanish cooking. It was very frustrating for him. He had landed the job he enjoyed in the place that suited him best, but the job itself implied that its holder's wife didn't scrub floors. Cooking might have been socially acceptable, provided there was a maid to clean up, but there was no hope that Addie could produce Spanish cooking.

Instead, a Spanish cook would bargain every morning with the vegetable man who would bring to the kitchen gate a donkey-load of tomatoes and grapes and melons and oranges — a whole melon for breakfast suited Alex very well — and peas and peppers. Addie would try to plan with her what to have for lunch and dinner. I might be around to interpret, but it was unlikely to satisfy el Señor. She and I were quietly amused when on one occasion he asked the kitchen staff to produce for us what they liked best themselves and it turned out to be bacalao — the salt cod that hangs out to dry under the eaves of thousands of whitewashed houses. The smell was so strong that we didn't even try to eat it, but it defeated Alex as well. I rather think he laughed about that effort himself.

The choice of food was one theme. Not that Addie was trying to provide what she would like to eat herself. Her favourite meal was always fresh brown soda bread and a fresh boiled egg. No; she had to try to outguess him. Eventually we found a cook, Isabe, who insisted on walking from La Linea every morning in time to make breakfast and going home at night to make sure her daughter was not left alone. There you had a strong-willed woman, and she would have a hearty fight with the Master nearly every morning. I would hang over the banisters of the upstairs landing and listen. But even when the choice of food was taken out of my mother's hands, she was still foolish enough to try to get him to come to meals at some foreseeable time. Let it be one o'clock or two o'clock or three o'clock for lunch; let it be six or seven or eight for dinner, couldn't he just decide which suited him best, so people would know what to do? His view of this was that she wanted to make him obedient, 'like a little dog.'

This is just a sample of the simmering tension from which I tended to absent myself. I could see that it was the notion of control that gave him an excuse to bluster. Maybe if she had decided to have a boiled egg (without brown bread) every day at one o'clock and let him sort out his hours with the cook this particular row would have fizzled out. But there were plenty of other excuses. An ongoing one was Irish Catholics versus Spanish Catholics. Irish Catholics go to Mass regularly but tell lies; Spanish Catholics are just naturally Catholics, they are good, it is not relevant that they do not feel bound to go to Sunday Mass. Addie would hold to what she had been taught; to miss Sunday Mass without valid reason is a mortal sin. This argument was pursued by two people who went to eight o'clock Mass every morning, expected me to go too and knelt in different places, so that I had to decide which to choose. Yet it was Alex who would insist that resident Spanish maids should head out in time for Sunday Mass. Carmen at least used to take her veil and go somewhere, perhaps to Church.

There was the recurrent decimal of St Paul; St Paul said women should obey their husbands; St Paul said women should be silent in church, which meant they shouldn't argue. This young woman argued, said she would sooner be a *peon caminero* than a wife. I think Alex was non-plussed; a lovely word, that.

A ground bass to all these contentions was Alex's decision to believe that he wasn't really married. He tried several times to get a case for annulment; we had not only our parish priest but two bishops involved. Addie's account was that when they first met this newly acquainted young man asked her what age she was, which was very bad manners; she answered, but subtracted two or three years. Having said it, she felt she had to stick to it. In his version, by the time marriage approached — after years of friendship, hill walking and talking about books — he was doubtful. If she were younger than he was, he felt he had a duty to marry her, but if she were older he had no such obligation. He could not believe that anyone would lie in such a serious context, so when on some application she wrote the age she had first thought of, he accepted it. When he found it was not accurate, he decided that the marriage was invalid. An ironic aspect is that he himself did not know, within a year or two, how old he was; his mother had been living in such isolation in the pampas of the Argentine that she registered several children at the same time. Neither parish priest nor either bishop — one of them a longtime friend of both parties since their time in Nigeria, a man of lovely wit and tolerance — could see any case for annulment.

For my part, I used to ask in my prayers every night that Mummy and Daddy would be friends. One night — I'm kneeling with my elbows on the brown silky bedspread of my bed in the room that looked towards Africa — it dawned on me that this was one prayer that wasn't going to show results. Perhaps I had some inkling that God doesn't 'make' people do anything. I am not sure what age I was — ten or eleven — but I am sure of the feeling of relief. I was clear; I wished them both well, but if they would go away, singly or together, and not bother me, that would suit me nicely.

Probably it was not so long after that that they did go away. The friendly bishop I have just mentioned was staying with us (saying Mass in the house, to avoid the hassle of full episcopal ceremony if he went to the parish church).

It was planned that Alex should drive him up through Spain and France. It was also understood that sometime later Addie and myself and Frankie would go by ship in the ordinary way with the intention of being in Dublin for the Eucharistic Congress. (At that time the Catholic Church had organised massive devotional gatherings in different countries, centred around High Mass in the open air, very like the celebrations associated with the travels of Pope John Paul II. The Irish Congress was the first large-scale undertaking in the twelve-year-old Free State. It went remarkably well: huge crowds in the Phoenix Park, John McCormick singing during the High Mass, emigrants returning from all over the world. And as it happened, a boy scout named Seán Mullarney was one of the Guard of Honour around the altar.)

With about two days to pack, it was decided that Addie and Frankie would go in the car and I would go to school as a boarder; Alex would return in time to put me on a ship to travel home alone.

I was not enthusiastic about being a boarder — no swimming, no library, but I was quite delighted by the prospect of travelling alone. So, for a term, it was back to sleeping in a dormitory, but in a cubicle with curtains around. As far as I remember, at home I was expected to go to Mass every morning. In school you could ask for a late morning once or twice a week. That was a luxury; lying inside your curtains, listening to the others scurrying around, but of course you still had to be up for breakfast. The daytime was as usual, without the walk on the walls. We played elaborate games of hopscotch — you called out 'Gloria!' when you reached the end of a sequence without fault and earned the right to stand at the far end of the pitch, with your back to it, and lob your stone over your shoulder to land on a square which you marked with your initial. Henceforward you had the right to hop on that square but no one else might. Gain two squares beside each other and you had as good as won the game.

It was the evening — well, the afternoon and evening — that I found irksome. Boarding schools as a matter of course allot a solid block of time to homework. We were allowed to read when we had finished. Read what? At home I had my own bookshelves, books numbered and catalogued and loved, Andrew Lang's *The Arabian Nights* and his Blue and Green fairy stories; the Pooh books and *Celtic Fairy Tales*; a series of beautifully produced and illustrated collections called No. 3 or 4 or 5 Joy Street, edited every year by Eleanor Farjeon and given to me by Auntie Mab; some William books and some collections of poetry that I'd love to find again.

In a red cover with a martyr's palm, the Life of St Philomena. This I read many times. My name is Máire Philomena; because of my mother's reliance on her she seemed very familiar. 'Life' was not the best title, because the only evidence for the life of the young girl whose bones had been collected from a Roman catacomb came from dreams that three women remote from each other dreamt on the same night. However, Philomena showed herself lively and humorous once her relics were claimed, arranged to have prayers answered not only punctually but with amusing extras, and when the small container of relics reached the church in Mugnano where she intended them to remain, they became so heavy that they could not be carried any further. Some years ago revisionists in Rome removed her name from the list of saints; another Roman bungle. I was pleased to see it recently in a list of higher degrees awarded in Trinity College Dublin.

Downstairs, the grown-up bookshelves with Belloc and Chesterton, down town the Garrison Library. There must have been books for me there because I remember so well my astonishment and delight when I had to stay in bed with a cold and Daddy brought me a William book from the library. Astonishment at his condescension, at his knowing I loved William, and above all at his finding one I hadn't read.

The convent had a children's library in one classroom press. You could have one book at a time. While they lasted, I took one for each recreation and brought it back at the end of the hour. The nun in charge seemed at first to find it difficult to believe that I had finished them and quizzed me about them. Then they unlocked a press in the parlour which had more variety in it, respectable magazines of a certain age and one discovery, a book by E. Nesbit about the Mouldiwarp. I did not meet Nesbit again until I was reading her books to my own children, but I remembered.

I had expected to be a boarder for less than a term. The date appointed for my father's return and my departure drew near. My trunk was packed. I was in that end classroom from which we could see the port and I watched the stubby, compact black and white liner with the Italian colours on her funnel, the *Roma*, gliding in. Everyone knew that when she sailed out I would be on board.

I was called to the parlour. He had made it just in time to tell me I wasn't going. Mummy and Frankie were in Ireland, but they would be coming back later on and I was to be a boarder until then, but he would take me out at weekends.

The impact of the announcement does not come back to me. I remember standing in front of him — he is sitting down — and being asked why I was making such a peculiar face. I was twisting my mouth to one side and must have looked like an illustration to Belloc's *Cautionary Tales*. I didn't cry and in a way I feel that I was not so very much surprised. That was how things were likely to turn out. There had been the promise to go and see the fireworks in Algeciras and Daddy changing his mind at the last moment. There were plans to bring us to the pictures which held until ten minutes before the starting time. I don't believe Alex ever found himself with his own TV but he would have been a master channel-changer.

It's only when I look back on it now that something else strikes me. We were a small class who got on well together. As I said, everyone knew that I was going to travel by myself on a ship and go to the Eucharistic Congress in Dublin. Then in a moment it was all off. I am sure my friends sympathised with me, but I had no notion that I might have been let down in front of them, that I might have lost face. Those early years alone seem to have left that sensation undeveloped. No. It was in bed at night that I realised how disappointed I was. Not so much about missing the voyage, not about missing Mummy and Frankie, but just feeling homesick for Ireland.

CHAPTER 6

'Yes, and back again.'
Wild flowers, Euclid and debates

Daddy kept his promise about bringing me out at weekends, whether to a beach in Spain or to a fair in the Alameda Gardens, where I went on a roundabout and ate waffles for the first time. There may not have been many weekends before the end of term. I found myself back at home in North Pavilion Road with Daddy and a maid. At times, perhaps on her day off, we did our own cooking. When I told him I needed a pair of shoes he gave me some money to buy them myself. I felt quite triumphant going into the Post Office and upstairs to the PMG's room to show off my white and blue striped purchases; they had (relatively) high heels. He was perfectly genial about them; glad I was pleased. I felt rather differently when I began to walk home. A girl needs a mother to stop her buying fool shoes.

It was a light-hearted interval. Nobody was expecting him to be in on time for anything. If he decided to take me for a run it was the decision of a moment. However, he felt some responsibility. Watering the garden in the evening was not enough to keep me occupied. There was a writing-table beside the furthest French window in the sittingroom. I was to sit there for an hour in the morning and work my way through Hugo's *Spanish in Three Months Without a Master*. Then I was to spend an hour in the garden, filling a bucket with stones and pitching them over the wall at the end, to slide down the cliff beside us.

I kept time conscientiously, but I don't suppose the next occupiers of the garden found it smooth and sandy. Stony soil is stony soil. The other hour was more effective. I found a framework for the Spanish which I was already speaking with the maids and in the shops and of course I found this framework much easier, in respect of vocabulary and pronunciation, than would someone beginning from scratch. Read the explanations, translate an exercise in one direction or the other, turn to the back of the book and correct it. Look at the clock and do the next if there is time. It was not so different from the puzzles one tackles for fun. My eleventh birthday was approaching.

Day by day I knew more. I was learning that I could teach myself. Perhaps everything we learn we teach ourselves but when we are at school we are aware only of being taught. Daddy checked my corrections occasionally but the active exchange was between me and the book. Since I was living with the language, naturally it did not take three months to work my way through Hugo. Then Daddy produced a standard Spanish primary school book, an attractive little volume with five or six subjects bound together and thickly scattered with faintly archaic illustrations.

At the same time he arranged that I should have credit to buy books at the only bookshop/stationers in the town. I had permission to buy as many as I liked —provided they were in Spanish. He explained that when he was a boy he had taught himself French and then Spanish by reading for diversion only in the language he was learning. I don't believe I relinquished English reading but supplies were sufficiently limited for me to appreciate a quantity of little books about Sexton Blake in Spanish. These were, of course, translations from English; Sexton Blake was a very elementary Sherlock Holmes, with a boy Watson. The next step, or steps, were the colourful historical novels of Rafael Sabatini, which I supposed to have been written in Spanish. An error; in spite of his southern name he wrote in English.

Sabatini reminds me vividly of toothache. The memory places itself somewhere at this stage in my life, myself in bed in that front bedroom. I have found that the novels are available in English and I have two of them, in red board covers. It's the middle of the night. I finish the second one and immediately start to re-read the first. My front teeth have been throbbing more and more intensely for two days. Sleep is impossible, I am trying to forget myself in print. Next day my mother convinces the head of the family that something must be done. He brings me to the dentist near Main Street. I sit back in the high chair. One quick whizz and life is miraculously lovely again. I have had an abscess in the root of a front tooth. It is drained and filled; the tooth is dead and gradually turns darker and darker but it cannot give me any more pain. Complaints are heard that my several visits have cost ten pounds. Perhaps prompt treatment would have left me with a live tooth, perhaps not.

The head of the family had a respectable salary, with house provided and no income tax, but he did know his income was his. I didn't get pocket money; when he had had a good run on the fruit machines down in the Grand Hotel he might load me with a couple of handfuls of sixpences. I have no reason to think my mother got reliable pocket money either. After all, she had all her meals. He bought the furniture, mostly at auctions when other colonials were leaving, but for the drawingroom he got his sister in England to choose and send out a three-piece suite. It was not uncomfortable but neither was it beautiful and Addie did not care for it. She made bedspreads and curtains from the cheap but well-coloured silks one could buy in the Indian shops in the town — artificial silk, with damask flowers. However, they did not stock good quality cotton, so when summer was due to return my mother would send away for little packs of patterns in different colourways, we would choose three or four to make dresses for me, little suits for Frankie, perhaps something for herself. Then I would have to ask Daddy for the money. I remember one confrontation in his study when he demanded to know how often I supposed he got a new suit.

I had a party dress, too; pale green with lace panels, passed on from Uncle Frank's step-daughter. I remember two parties, one in the Rock Hotel, one in Government House and I remember not enjoying them at all. The fact that I was not allowed to attend dancing classes in school may have left me feeling rather fish-out-of-waterish. To be fair to a father, of whom a sister-in-law had said that waltzing with him was like waltzing with the piano, I might have remained quite incompetent even if I had had dancing lessons.

And to be fair to him, and to myself, I shall mention two observations of mine in different contexts which I remember because he was both surprised and pleased by them. One was a suggestion in respect of tourists, who were said by some of our neighbours to be over-running the town. I thought that everyone should live in a place so agreeable that they did not feel eager to hurry through other places. The other observation arose from my casual remark that I had said a Hail Mary to find a needle I was using. He made it clear that prayer should not be used for trivialities. I asked, would he say a prayer to find a lost five-pound note. That would probably equal fifty pounds now; he agreed that he would. I expressed a belief that in the eyes of Heaven a needle, which could do something useful, was likely to be more valuable than a bit of money. I dare say I was a right little eleven-year-old prig, but I am still inclined to agree with my former self and to be grateful to my father for being pleased.

It might be more prudent for me not to mention that he was also pleased when I quoted something from a book he had bought, a book in Spanish of speeches by Benito Mussolini.

Government House, where I did not enjoy the party, was in the centre of the town, where the Main Street opened up into a small square. The Loreto Convent, the town one, faced it across the square, the stationer's shop took up one corner as you entered the square; there seems to have been a dress shop at the other. From Government House, every evening at sundown a detachment of soldiers with officer and keys and some music would march down to lock the gates in the wall that guarded the town from Spanish invasion. I do not believe they were locked against residents but the long procession of Spanish workmen for the dockyard had to be out by then. When we had a Welsh regiment, their mascot, a smoothly groomed white goat, would march in front of the guard.

Further along on the right was the Courthouse, set back behind a courtyard roofed by the most beautiful pendulous Wisteria you could find anywhere. A little further on, the dark Spanish Catholic cathedral did not quite face the pale bright Anglican cathedral which had a suggestion of a mosque about it. Higher up, behind the Catholic cathedral, stood the Garrison Library of which I shall have more to say. Then, towards the far end, the General Post Office.

The spaces between seem to have been occupied almost entirely by Indian shops and a few bars. These were designed to capture the tourists who flowed through the town two or three times a week. The shop windows were filled with bags made of creamy camel skin, leather slippers, ivory carvings, especially those baffling globes within a globe within a globe, each surface carved so ingeniously with roses. From our end, at that time, grown-ups reached the town by the lower road, where pale, light horse-drawn carriages called *gharris* — not a Spanish word, possibly Indian — waited near the bottom of our steps, or by a rackety bus. Of course they could walk, as the younger heat-proof generation did, and pass along the casemates where on the upper side of the road was a green field sheltered by pepper trees and nourishing the Governor's cows. Only Government House tasted fresh milk. The rest of us relied on tins of Cleeves evaporated milk with its trio of Irish cows on the label. The pepper trees waved bunches of almost iridescent pale pink seeds. A little further on you passed below the Alameda.

Then came a small, sad cemetery with the graves of young soldiers of two centuries ago and at once you went through the gate in the wall built by Charles V. This defence reached away up the side of the Rock and was a likely place to see some of the rather famous apes. Pass through that and you were almost in the Main Street.

While I had Rosia Bay, our space of trees, the stretch of scrubby wild open space down near Europa Point where we could chase each other, even have harmless battles of stone throwing, all unaware of the heat that drove our elders to take their siestas behind closed slatted shutters, Main Street was not important. However, the Rock was all of a piece and it was my background until I was more than eighteen, so I have tried to block it in now rather than after the interlude which takes up the rest of this chapter.

I did not have the pleasure of sailing alone on the *Roma* but there was another voyage home with my mother and Frankie and I enjoyed it as much as ever. It may have been intended as a holiday but it seems more likely that it was the result of a row.

We found ourselves living in a newly-built bungalow in a place called Glencormac, near Kilmacanogue, with one of Addie's sisters, Jo, and her husband and son and dog and cats. Kilmacanogue is the village on the road between Dublin and Wicklow where I used to be brought to Mass when very small. At that time we had lived two or three miles nearer to Wicklow. Glencormac was inland on the Dublin side. Delightfully, Geg was there some of the time; sometimes she was looking after two young American nephews, aged about three and seven.

When I try to put the scene together I realise I must have been one of the least curious young people you could find. The little boys' mother, Margaret, one of Addie's many sisters, died when her sons were quite young. Was she ill at this time, all the sisters rallying round? Margaret had been in Ireland for the Congress; she painted climbing flowers on the walls of the small sittingroom. Was she still there when we arrived? How did we all fit in?

I must have found myself with more responsibility for minding Frankie than I had been used to. I remember wrapping a blanket around him and persuading him to sit quietly beside a pretend camp fire and be a squaw. With whom was I playing Indians? Probably with Denis and Noel who remember a wild time when we dressed up every day, put plenty of war paint on our faces — greasepaint from Woolworths — and chased around ambushing small groups of hikers, who seemed quite willing to play up. Greasepaint tended to linger in the bath. I doubt if we knew any other way of taking it off. Denis knew they would never have got away with making such a mess at home.

There were plenty of hikers because the countryside around was real countryside. Instead of two or three acres of scrubby land at the foot of the Rock there were fields and woods and free rocky outcrops, stretches of furze and bracken, to explore. As for trees, a tall sycamore in the field facing our house demanded the development of quite new climbing skills. The bungalow adjoining ours belonged to the Whyte family, who came there for the summer and provided me with two companions, Jacqueline Whyte and her cousin Mary who lived not far away.

Jacqui, Mary and I found it convenient at times to identify ourselves with the Scarlet Pimpernel and his band of helpers. It was decided that Jacqui and I could take it in turns to respond to the title of Sir Percy Blakeney (the Pimpernel himself). Since we used to spend more time trying to walk on our hands and do somersaults in the air than doing anything else it does not seem that we took the French Revolution very seriously. We also climbed that fine tall sycamore. At first it did not seem possible to go more than twelve or fifteen feet up, then we found a way to get over as it were a hump in the main branches and the rest was easy. I made a point of waving my hand above the highest leaves and managed to do so in a few other large trees as well. Rather a silly idea, to trust myself to the weakest branches, but I knew I must be attached at three points —two hands and one foot or two feet and one hand — and there were no accidents. I used to enjoy going up in that tree just to be alone and invisible. Nothing prevented grown-ups from doing the same, but you never saw them up trees; I could see no point in becoming a grown-up.

For all this climbing and handstanding the other two girls wore flannel shorts and I tucked my dress into matching knickers. My mother always made some of these when she was making my summer dresses, and they were just as convenient for climbing as the shorts. They didn't get preached about either. One Sunday the sermon at Mass in Kilmacanogue dealt with the scandal given by young women going around in public wearing trousers. We rather thought Jacqui and Mary might have been the intended targets, but decided that more likely it was mixed troops of hikers that were being reproved.

The two bungalows, ours and the Whyte's, were rented from the substantial farm above us on the hill, Heatley's. The son who stayed at home had built them. During our time there he had begun to build another similar pair in the neighbouring field. He did the work himself, with the help of an experienced carpenter. Foundations were dug and walls made by pouring concrete between large fixed panels made from boards. I'm sure there is a technical term for the process; when the lower level has set hard the boards are moved up and supported by wires running through, resting on the completed section, and another few feet of concrete are poured in. I greatly enjoyed being allowed to give a hand, mixing sand and cement seven times before pouring water into a hollow in the middle, sloshing the mixture around as you might mix a Christmas pudding, but with a shovel instead of a spoon. I liked to see how they planned to leave the openings for windows, and how the carpenter would make the window frames on the spot.

I had good times in Glencormac. I remember one morning finding myself near a little stream in a hollow the far side of the big field, the sun glowing on my face and on the little flowers we called milkmaids and realising how happy I was.

The stock of books in the house was not satisfying. Someone, long before, had bought a set of a dozen or more volumes bound in red with their own bookcase. They contained extracts from literary works — but only extracts. I have never found out what happened to the Man with the Broken Ear, and I am not likely to, because I do not know whether he lived in the imagination of Victor Hugo or Jules Verne or some other. Around the time of the siege of Moscow he froze solid and the usual experimental scientist put him somewhere safe, just chipping off a chunk of iced ear by mistake. Clearly, he was destined to be thawed and surprised at some later date, but where and when? There were also three very thick instructive volumes from which I learnt a little about mechanics, but only a little.

But some occasion, probably a birthday, if so my twelfth, allowed me to go to a real bookshop in Dublin. What I picked was a set of four neat, boxed, pocket-size *Nature Rambles* by Edward Step, a volume for each season. From these I learnt to identify some more birds than I knew already, found out what the thousands of black and yellow striped caterpillars on the ragwort in the field opposite would turn into and was able to get even better value from country living. I was bothered for some time because I could not get any information about a hairy plant with lovely star-shaped blue flowers that I found in a ditch. Years later I grew borage in my herb garden and it seeded itself very readily, so I cannot blame Mr Step for not mentioning garden escapes.

How I came by *Celtic Wonder Tales*, retold by Ella Young, with illustrations by Maud Gonne, I do not know. It is just what Geg might have given me. These Wonder Tales about De Danann, about Brigit and the Dagda and Angus the Ever Young, about Mananaun and Lugh the master of all crafts, enchanted me and made Ireland an enchanted island. I have that book still, the only one from my childhood. It was reprinted by Dover Books a few years ago and I gave copies to each family of grandchildren, but with so much noise around from television and radio and news, news, news I don't think there is much chance that any of this generation will have had as good value from it as did mine.

Good fortune struck. The big house at the corner where we turned off the main Wicklow road, Jameson's Corner, belonged to the Jamesons, makers of whiskey. They had a Steward, the Steward had a house and in his house a tall press or cupboard filled with paperback books ready to tumble out. I do not know how we met, but it was a lucky day. For some time I gobbled up three cowboy books a day — Hopalong Cassidy and Max Brand. Then I turned to his store of science fiction and liked it even better. It was a bit of luck to be able to wallow in SF because the Nature Study I met in school in Bray was harmless enough and I never had a real science lesson. In fact Mr Edward Step made me a star of that class. We had fine big playing fields and for one class our teacher brought us out to see who could find and name the greatest number of wild flowers. My catch was twenty-nine or thirty; the next best was eleven.

And one day a School Inspector turned up in that class and simply chatted with me. I also made my mark by coming first in a class test in Irish at the end of my first term. We were given beforehand the answers to all the questions so that we could learn them off. I was neither confused by any previous knowledge nor bored by repetition so I learnt them almost perfectly. I don't think my classmates minded at all, probably thought it a joke. As far as they were concerned I was a bit of a novelty and I was good at painting pictures in autograph albums. And then I disappointed the kind nun who was teaching us; we had in our poetry book 'The Castle of Dromore', in Irish of course. She asked did anyone know the song. My mother used to sing it for me in English and I loved it, but I could not produce even a squeak to hint at the tune. But that was just Irish class. We also had a class in which history and geography were taught through Irish and here I was a complete dud.

I have with me still evidence of boredom in maths class. It seems to have consisted of sums which did not take very long to do. I filled time by drawing in my blotting book and by tattooing the Saint figure on the back of my left hand, with a needle and ink. Yes, we had inkwells in every desk and were still writing with pens, wooden handles into which one could fit new nibs of various sorts. I must have met the modern Robin Hood, Simon Templar, who used a stick figure with a halo as his trademark, in the Steward's grand store of paperbacks. Anyway, his head, with halo and one elbow are still just visible on my hand. Leslie Charteris wrote the books; there were some in my local library.

My blessings on the teacher, Sr John Berchmans, who noticed that I was bored. She put me at a desk at the back of the class, gave me Hall and Stevens' *Euclid*, proposed to me that I learn one theorem each day and write it out and check back to see that I had understood it correctly. The first couple of days were a struggle. It is hard to see why you need to prove something so obvious as that vertically opposite angles are equal. Then the system clicks and you find that each proof depends on the whole chain before it. If I had been born to be a scholar no doubt I would have rushed ahead and learnt one theorem after another at full speed. I did not, but I experienced the charm of mathematics.

In fact, instead of going on with geometry, when I had dealt with the day's theorem I would quietly open the lid of the desk at which I was sitting. This must have been the second or third year classroom and their French Reader could be found in every desk. It was a good Reader; the stories in it were really funny, at least to someone of eleven or twelve. How I found I could read French is unclear, because there had been some, brief, French class in which I was quite lost. No doubt Spanish was the key.

Our English Reader was also well chosen. After the family custom, I learnt off all the poems in it as soon as possible, including Poe's 'Bells' which is a challenge to the memory. Browning, Keats, Shelley ('The Cloud'), but best of all several pages of a verse translation of 'The Death of Hector'. One day no teacher turned up to take English class, which we had down in the Science Room, perhaps somewhat cut off from the other classrooms. I persuaded willing classmates to divide up into Greeks and Trojans and shouted the narrative while we chased each other over and around the desks, waving rulers as swords. We did not go so far as to drag the dead Hector around the walls.

I look back with satisfaction on another day when I took it upon myself to lead the class. Our teacher was Miss Eva Garty, a slight young woman whom it was possible to tease, and the class got into the mood to tease her. It dawned on me that she was really suffering so I got up out of my desk, went to the front of the class and said I thought it was time we realised that we were being a very nasty crowd, or something of the sort. It worked. And, quite unexpectedly, when I was back at school in Gib again she turned up there and became a family friend.

There were no walls to walk on along the road to school in Bray. I must have gone by bus at first (though Geg used to run to Mass in Bray every day) and then it was decided that I should have a bicycle. I loved it, I loved the winding road with its swooping curve downhill as it approached Bray, just before I was to turn left for the Loreto Convent. I believe I could find some verses that I made up on the way. And I found it possible to cycle for longer and longer distances without touching the handlebars, until I was able to go the whole way along the main road freehand, so to speak, getting up such speed downhill that I could usually get right to the top of the following hill without touching. After all, nobody ever told me not to.

Cycling in winter was a different story, toes icy, frozen fingers bloodless inside tight leather gloves, warnings against chilblains if you tried to warm up against school radiators.

Then came a shock. It seems that my mother and Frankie and I were alone in the house. Geg must have gone to New York to look after the little cousins some time before. One day Frankie, who was five, suddenly went pale and silent, his hands white and the tips of his fingers blue. Someone — probably Reggie Heatley — drove all three of us in to Dublin to one of the children's hospitals. My mother and I waited, were told they were doing a tracheotomy, told to come back in the morning. I suppose we stayed with friends. I remember waiting again when we returned, then a doctor came down with the news. No more Frankie here; he'd gone to heaven. Well, he was much loved while he was here; no one ever said a cross word to him. I was sad for a while, but there were distractions.

Before long the two of us had left Glencormac and taken rooms in a house in Monkstown, a Dublin suburb, and I was taking a tram every day to school in Dalkey — another Loreto Convent, of course. I also took a tram in the other direction a couple of evenings a week to classes in the College of Art in Kildare Street. (The classrooms are now an extension of Leinster House, the old board floors all covered with carpets; I was in one of them a couple of weeks ago in quite a different capacity.)

Our landlady was a character from Molly Keane's world, quite ripe in years, who stayed up all night once a week playing poker, drove down to Seapoint every morning for an early swim, her car of the sort my children would call a banger. She was good company, cossetted her grown-up son, taught us to play poker and was proud of her apple tree, an Irish Peach. They were a lovely little apple, quite early, and since we had the chance to eat them it seems I must have started school at the proper time, in September, when I was thirteen.

I liked the school in Dalkey. I cannot work out whether I spent more time there than in Bray, or vice versa, and it is not important. Unawares, I risked getting a bad reputation. During the first Assembly, Mother Superior listed three offences that had been committed in the school, behaviour not at all suitable to young ladies. Someone had climbed over a certain wall. Someone had been found in the orchard; the nun who noticed her had closed and locked the tall gates and gone to find someone to identify the culprit. When she returned there was nobody inside. I had climbed out over the gate. I was the other two offenders as well, but I was still unknown so I behaved more properly from then onwards.

After maths, the classes I most enjoyed were sewing, where we had a whole afternoon of conversation with a well-read nun, and Christian Doctrine, where we had a Church History which went into a fair amount of detail about the principal heresies — those of the Manichees, Arians, Montanists. There is a saying, 'oportet hereses esse' (heresies are necessary); Christians didn't find out what was implied or involved in their beliefs until someone tried out something that the rest agreed did not fit in. Some acquaintance with the unaccepted proposals gives the modern believer a firmer picture of what they themselves do or do not accept. I'm rather a Pelagian myself; I think people are inclined on the whole to be good.

It could be simply that I naturally enjoy argument. There are a fair number of Loreto schools in Ireland. They used to arrange an annual debating tournament among themselves, with a clear-cut plan. Six girls on each side; a leader made a ten-minute prepared speech, the next spoke for five minutes, the other four for two minutes each, and when both teams had had their say they then took it in turns to undermine the other team's arguments. I think everyone enjoyed it. It took time out of class. It does not seem to have occurred to us that it *was* class — considerably more productive than most classes. I found myself leading our junior team, not only setting out my own arguments but helping to plan the order in which the others would make their points. Someone noticed that I was a year younger than the next youngest in the class. No danger that I would get too big for my boots; it was acknowledged that I had a good head for debating, but I almost cancelled this out because few could understand what I was saying. An elderly nun with free time undertook to drill me, marked my paper with pauses, / or // or ////, and would hear me read it through at odd moments in any corner she could find. I came across one of these marked papers years later and recognised echoes of Chesterton.

We were staying in the flat in Monkstown when the news came of G. K. Chesterton's death. I cried when my mother told me. I have never cried before or since for the loss of a person I did not know, and rarely for anyone I did.

To return to the debates. We had practice runs with our own two teams and mine was picked to challenge the other schools. This meant meeting visiting teams and going off in buses to be the visitors. Commonplace for hockey players but a novelty for me. Our team got into the finals. They were held in Loreto, Stephen's Green. I remember the hall quite well, our two facing rows of six tables and chairs, the judges to our right, the blurred audience to the left. The leader on the other side had red hair and a remarkably easy, confident delivery, but our arguments must have been good because the result was a tie.

The interim result. The final victory must now depend on extempore debate by the two leaders. We were each put into a room by ourselves with a topic — and, I suppose, the side we were to take — written on a slip of paper and given *five minutes* to think of what we would say.

If we had ever had a shot at extempore speaking I might have managed something; as it was, I was surprised into paralysis. When I was summoned half a minute later and given a chair to hold onto the back of I could not open my mouth, even to apologise.

I wonder have I since then met the leader of the winning side. She may well have gone into politics, but I don't suppose she remembers that final debate any more than I remember the others leading up to it.

School did not overshadow that year or so in Dublin. We saw more of our friends, including Denis and his family. One day Denis and I took a boat out and explored Dalkey Island. In season I could go swimming. Dún Laoghaire library was only about ten minutes walk away and I went every day. On my way I would visit the church and make the Stations of the Cross. I did not like doing this; you are not meant to, but I felt it was the least I could do when enjoying myself the rest of the time.

I have a diary dating from that period and I think it contains little more than notes of books read. If I were to consult it this chapter would grow out of proportion. I cannot be sure whether it was then or a little later, in Gibraltar, that I made a sort of pact with myself to read one serious book for every two fiction, fiction meaning Saint books and Edgar Wallace, very possibly Dorothy Sayers' Peter Wimsey. I know it was in this library that I found *The Wallet of Kai Lung* by Ernest Bramah which continued to charm me for many years, and also *Murder in the Cathedral* by T. S. Eliot. It's possible that I borrowed this supposing that it was concerned with detection. It delighted me. I read it many times. And then the company, or at least the chief actors who had performed it in Canterbury Cathedral, came to the Gate Theatre in Dublin.

Tera, who had taught me algebra in Gibraltar, was back in Dublin by then and she brought me to it. This was my first experience of theatre. It has not been easy to find anything to quite live up to it. By the end, when the murderer-knights come out on stage to make their casual, low-key explanations, the tension had built up so far that I was overcome — I hope our neighbours were tolerant.

If my mother did not come to the theatre too it was probably for lack of money. The stuff was very tight. Rather too clearly I remember a fair held in school to raise money for some good cause. Stalls of all the usual sorts. It might have been better not to go, since I had one single penny to spend and had to move around looking as if I might buy this or that but changed my mind.

A typically sudden change. Alex turned up in Dublin. I was to drive back with him to Gib. In two days time.

CHAPTER 7

Civil war in Spain;
relative peace in Gibraltar

He whisked me away, brushed aside talk of missing exams, bought a glossy new car from the Austin works somewhere in England, drove it onto quite a small boat to go over to France. I have a vague impression of something with sails, possibly a ferry that could carry half a dozen cars.

The clear patch in cloudy memory comes when we are sitting at a round marble table at a bar on the quay. A glass of red wine is in front of me. Naturally, there is one in front of my father as well.

'Now take off that little badge of yours and drink this.'

The badge was a silver shield with a heart on it, a message that the wearer does not take alcoholic drinks. My conscience didn't bother me. I cannot remember how I had found myself in church with a great many other girls 'taking the pledge'. Not Confirmation, because I had been confirmed in Gibraltar, where it's done to much younger children. Whatever the reason, I had said the words and promised to abstain from alcohol and I felt stuck with it. But when obedience conflicted with the pledge, I warmed to obedience.

The next significant memory is Beauvais. Another towering brown cathedral. I knew Sevilla, with pillars as massive as houses, I had prayed in other large, dark churches dominating the houses around them. Even our own little cathedral in Gibraltar was of the same family. We went through the usual door-within-a-door. I looked up, was bemused by white, bright enclosed pillared space going upwards forever. I have never been there again but since that revelation I have understood the point of the Gothic arch.

We drove on down the straight poplar-lined roads of France, the sun shining all the time. I wound down the car window on my side; my left arm rested on the ledge and became a darker brown day by day while the right arm retained its Irish pallor.

We hurried, saw little by the way. We reached Chartres too late to get into the cathedral. Somewhere in Gascony there is a statue of D'Artangnan in a square. Then the Pyrenees. Because of some familiar essays by Hilaire Belloc I was prepared for magic; we were not on foot, so the magic escaped, but we drove up and up through brilliant flowers between sheltered remnants of snow. We stayed the night in a small hotel where a river rushed under the window. I promised myself that sometime I would come back and stay in Eaux Chaud. Perhaps it's not too late.

Next morning, climbing on again, then that astonishing hard-edge transmutation; everything behind us green and growing; everything in front, into the far distance, range behind range of crimson and purple desert.

That was an impression. Once we were travelling through Spain we found it alive, even familiar, but oddly empty. For once I am sure of the date. We reached Gibraltar two weeks before La Dieciocho de Julio, the 18th of July 1936, the day of Franco's arrival from Morocco, and the name of a street in every town. That is, the name of streets a few years later, after the insurgents had won. Not so long ago during a convivial evening with Green Party friends and acquaintances I remarked that in my youth I had not only been pro-Franco but had worn the kind of badge then on sale in his part of Spain — a narrow black strip with the 'rojo y gualda', the old red and gold flag of Spain, before the Republic changed to a tricolour with purple, and also the flags of Italy and Germany. I could sense a wave of shock passing around the circle. Most of them were too young to know that Catholic Ireland had been on Franco's side anyway.

We were much closer to the war. We knew and loved our parish priest, Fr Grech. The parish priest of Marbella, whom government supporters had roasted to death over a fire, had been a friend of his. We had admired at a distance the parliamentarian Calvo Sotelo who had been assassinated. From our point of view this rising against a bad government was akin to our own 1916 Rising, or the venture of Bonnie Prince Charlie. Indeed the legend shimmering around young Jose Antonio Primo de Rivera, son of a remarkable Prime Minister, made him resemble the bonnie prince, or the young JFK of the future.

There are, I suppose, two sides to any civil war. We knew one, we listened to the Spanish radio — both sides; we looked at the newspaper maps and rejoiced when a new district rallied to Franco. I doubt whether any others in colonial circles, civil or military, read or spoke Spanish well enough to be in touch. The British establishment believed in supporting an established government, or so it seemed. Later on I met suggestions that London's policy of non-intervention was not all that a favoured government might have hoped for.

My father was able to drive in and out of Spain without impediment — the region near us had welcomed Franco. I visited the front near Malaga, which was held by government forces for a long time. I had the honour of sitting in the studio while the radio General, Queipo de Llano, was giving his daily broadcast. I treasured a gold Falange badge given to me by a star aviator. If Italy and Germany were willing to give some help, good for them.

I was fourteen when the civil war began, sixteen or seventeen when Madrid fell. Not an age when one looks with serenity on both sides. It was a bloody war. I have preferred not to read books about it. I believe we were not entirely mistaken in backing Franco; in the Mezquita in Cordoba I have seen marble panels with very long lists of names of priests and canons of the cathedral who were executed by the government forces. And, after all, if Hitler damned one side by supporting it, it was Stalin who supported the other.

We were living beside the war, not in it. I had many other preoccupations. Now that I have mentioned Fr Grech I must say a little about him, because I think that, next after Geg, he is the reason I adhere to the Catholic Church. He was Maltese but spoke Spanish well and English also. He could put DD (doctor of divinity) after his name, but his manner, his sermons, his way of living were transparently simple. He lived with his sister or sisters and their families in a house near St Joseph's church. I remember his look of love when a tiny brown-eyed nephew who cannot have been more than four processed in with the slightly more mature acolytes. But he seemed to love anyone who called on him. He listened patiently to the marital arguments of my parents and tried to bring harmony. At Christmas he used to arrange a simple crib on an altar beside the High Altar. Just Mary and Joseph kneeling at each side, a straw roof over them, a shallow dish of fresh green grass, specially sown, growing in front. Between the two figures, a square white cloth. When the many bells rang for the Gloria at Midnight Mass Fr Grech would come down the steps, over to the crib, and happily take away the cloth to reveal the holy Baby.

I used to enjoy the Masses for the dead. Even if there were only a handful of people in the church for morning Mass, an older priest, Fr Andrews, might be up at the organ, ready to play it and chant *Dies Irae*. There are some splendid musical settings of this hymn, tremendous trumpets and shivering penitents, but what I like is to hear the words.

> Rex tremendae majestatis
> Qui salvandos salvas gratis
> Salva me, fons pietatis.

I love the transition from 'King of dreadful majesty' in the first line to the gentle 'fount of pity' in the third; the compact Latin which says 'those who are going to be saved, you freely save' in four words.

There used to be an Easter sequence which is even better poetry; there's the wonderful Lauda Sion of St Thomas, 'praise full of delight and beauty'. You can, if you search, find them on disc or cassette, but I hardly ever hear anything that is just right, and listening at home is not the same as hearing the words as part of the action to which they belong.

There you are; Fr Grech, with no resources — the church collections brought in enough for candles — and a small, plain church, passed on the riches accumulated during hundreds of years. No wonder I'm grateful to him.

No queues for confession, such as we had in those days in Ireland. If you went into St Joseph's and knelt near the confessional at the back of the church, before long Fr Grech would look out from behind the altar, look enquiring, and if you nodded yes he'd hurry down the aisle. My instructions were to go to confession every two weeks. Always the same; distracted at my prayers, disobedient. Well, how could you help thinking of other things when you were saying the Rosary? But you weren't supposed to; the point of it was to think about the Nativity or the Coronation of Our Lady in Heaven. I was happy to do so for the length of two Hail Marys, but the repetition of the remaining eight would lull me off. It was relief, many years later, to find that the Rosary had been introduced as a substitute for reciting the psalms.

I suppose I was lucky not to have other problems to bring to confession. I don't think of myself as a late developer, just as someone who had plenty of other things to interest her besides girl/boy complications. I had already made up my mind not to marry, so what would be the point of interesting myself in some boy or man. Well, I was not completely untouched by charm. There was Leslie Howard, who played the Scarlet Pimpernel to perfection and was also Romeo. Between Dublin and Gibraltar I managed to see *Romeo and Juliet* five times. Then — towards the end of this chapter — we saw the same film in Madrid. Dubbed. Without the words of Shakespeare and the voice of Howard, the man on the screen was quite elderly and without attraction. I can say 'towards the end of this chapter' because I have realised that this section of my life in Gibraltar was not as long as I had supposed. I was fourteen, going on fifteen, when we drove down on the eve of the civil war; World War II broke out on my eighteenth birthday and we left a few months later to stay in Spain.

I was not technically a late developer. When I was twelve, back in Glencormac, my mother told me that I would at some time find my knickers stained; that she would provide me with pads to deal with the problem; that it would recur every month. Well, it did; of course it was a nuisance. I thought it was only going to happen for six months or so, but that must have been a misunderstanding. That it might have any purpose was not mentioned. As likely as not my mother didn't know. In Gibraltar I could use the family account with the chemist to buy sanitary towels. I saw an advertisement for Tampax, asked the chemist for them instead, found that they solved most of the problem. No discussion, though I gathered that it was inadvisable to go swimming. Isabe, the argumentative cook-housekeeper, had to tell me that it was not correct to put stained pants into the washbasket; these one washed oneself.

I once heard a psychologist say that anyone who reaches late teens without knowing 'the facts of life' must have decided not to know. Well, back in Glencormac Jacqui's cousin had explained to both of us that babies emerged from the mother's belly button. I knew that 'navel' would have been more correct; the succulent little flowering plant, Venus's Navel-wort, flourished on the sides of the stone walls round about. As for babies, I didn't plan to have any, let them come out wherever they liked.

The funny thing is that all this time my reading was quite extensive. The Garrison Library had become my lodestone, as swimming had been before. I had already made that rough-and-ready rule for myself, one solid book for every two frivolous. In the second category came all the Saint books and one hundred and twenty (listed) by Edgar Wallace. The solid books were a mixed lot. Many of them turned out to be more enjoyable than Edgar Wallace; it was not out of a sense of duty that I read all Shaw's plays and prefaces. On the other hand, it is hard to know out of what sense I read a series of James Agate's memoirs (Ego 1, Ego 2, etc) which consisted entirely of theatrical criticism, discussion of plays that I had not seen and never would see. Some I found on the highest shelves in the lending library: *Amadis of Gaul*, an influential romance of chivalry, the only book that Don Quixote's parish priest did not blame for setting him astray in his head, came in five volumes; I drew and painted the knights' shields. I must have learnt much more from the memoirs of Tallyrand, also in several volumes, but they would have been more valuable if I had known a little more history; my school course was confined to Britain and ended in 1688.

The Garrison Library was a substantial building, a club for officers and gentlemen. My father could sit in the classic leather armchairs, but children and possibly women were limited to the one-room lending library. I ventured through one door when the armchairs were empty and found a whole set of stories by de Maupassant, Gautier and others; good for my French and broadening to the mind; left me with the impression that mistresses were as usual as wives; nothing to do with me. Then my father found me reading *Salammbo*, a story about, if I am not mistaken, decadent Carthage or perhaps Alexandria. This he decided was unhealthy. He forbade it, but I think he understood that I had just been taking his advice to read French. I handed it over without regret.

I found another room with glass book-cases, no inhabitants; here there was an old set of Molière, old enough to have the long s, like f, and a faint musty smell. I enjoyed these, and lots of more up-to-date literary criticism which suggested further reading. But none of these had a fraction of the influence of another five-volume biography that I found on those shelves, the Life of a man who said that the best way to educate a girl was to let her loose in a good library.

If Johnson had known that in the future any good library would contain Boswell's account of himself and his conversation, would he have conceded that this, too, might contribute to a girl's education? Surely, yes. I have opened a page at random, to see if I can find what used make me laugh out loud so many years ago while at the same time infecting me, I think, with good sense. Listen to a page headed 1783, Aetat. 74:

'A man cannot tell *a priori* what will be best for government to do. This reign has been very unfortunate. We have had an unsuccessful war; but that does not prove that we have been ill-governed. One side or other must prevail in war, as one or other must win at play. When we beat Louis, we were not better governed; nor were the French better governed, when Louis beat us.'

On Saturday, April 12, I visited him, in company with Mr Windham, of Norfolk, whom, though a Whig, he valued highly. One of the best things he ever said was to this gentleman; who before he set out for Ireland as Secretary to Lord Northington, when Lord Lieutenant, expressed to the Sage some modest and virtuous doubts, whether he could bring himself to practise those arts, which it is supposed a person in that situation has occasion to employ. 'Don't be afraid, sir (said Johnson, with a pleasant smile), you will soon make a very pretty rascal.'

He talked today a good deal of the wonderful extent and variety of London, and observed, that men of curious enquiry might see in it such modes of life as very few could even imagine. He in particular recommended to us to *explore Wapping*, which we resolved to do.

Boswell's footnote reports that they did indeed explore Wapping, but were disappointed; either because uniformity has spread through every part of the metropolis, or from their own want of sufficient exertion. That Boswell made me laugh I know, because my father, who had firmly suggested that I do my reading down in the sittingroom instead of lurking in my bedroom, was driven to ask, what was I giggling at?

Amusement naturally prompts laughter. Once, in school, in the senior year, I was sitting alone in our small upstairs classroom and I surfaced to realise that a nun had been standing smiling on the step above me; she said it did her good to hear anyone enjoying a book so much. Anthony Trollope died while overcome by laughter while reading *Vice Versa*.

While I believe that the library, and especially Boswell, was the most important influence on my education at least at that stage, home took for granted enjoyment of Chesterton, Belloc, Ronald Knox, the towering Catholic writers in English, and my father frequently ordered books from the Catholic publishing house of Frank Sheed and Maisie Ward. One of their authors was Christopher Hollis. His *Noble Castle* put Christianity in the context of earlier and later religions in an imaginative way and broadened my faith; his *Breakdown of Money* laid the foundations for scepticism in regard to the present financial system.

I have just looked at the date, in my mother's hand, in the flyleaf of Chesterton's collected poems. 1936. The book was on the end of my bed when I went up after Midnight Mass (and cake and a glass of Muscatel from Malaga) on Christmas Eve when I was fifteen. I loved the poems, and I was glad to be beginning to have some books of my own again. My father had given away all my collection while I was in Ireland. I found it hard to believe that anyone could dismantle someone else's books while they were still alive, but I suppose he thought they were childish. I would have had to leave them anyway. He gave them to Mr Mifsud, the head driver for the Post Office, for his children; I hope they enjoyed them. An estimable, good humoured man, who later on very calmly taught me to drive.

One famous poem of Chesterton's, 'Lepanto', about that decisive sea battle in which Cervantes fought, could have been heard very often by anyone who happened to follow us about. I had a new friend in my class, Gabrielle, not only Catholic but half Irish.

We had *Henry V* for English class that year and I don't know that Shakespeare has anything to beat it for challenging speeches — the one about the feast of Crispian and 'Once more into the breach dear friends, once more / Or close the walls up with our English dead.' There's another one about bees. These, and some others, Gabrielle and I used to declaim without inhibition, striding along the roads leading to Europa Point. 'Lepanto' is splendid for such an exercise; I have to restrain myself from quotation.

Gabrielle and her sister and brother had grown up in the Canary Isles and spoke Spanish from infancy; during Advent and Lent we spoke Spanish together, not exactly as a penance but as requiring some slight effort. That was in the colder weather. Gib could be quite cold and wet in winter, and it was pleasant to have coal fires instead of Spanish braseros with charcoal. When summer returned there was a new rule. My father did not intend me to go to Rosia Bay any more. Mixed bathing. Now I had suitable companions I could swim in Camp Bay, the non-commissioned military bathing place. It wasn't too bad. During the morning we had it more or less to ourselves. It was small, the beach was stony, but the sea was just as delicious and supportive as around the corner in Rosia.

Hanging around Rosia was a way of life. Girls from school who spent their time there would have been among those who found life more interesting when the Mediterranean and Atlantic fleets, with their complements of midshipmen, converged on Gib in the springtime. Perhaps if Rosia had not been forbidden I might not have gone so often to the library or spent so much time painting. Drawing and painting had always been encouraged at school and when I returned I found they had built a new art room looking out over the playground. For years, however, while I was younger, it had been wiser not to be noticed drawing and painting under my father's roof; it was the sort of thing the Rigney family did (Uncle Frank was, in fact, very prosperous by now, art editor of the US Boy Scout magazine, which came to me regularly, and author of several books, one about magic, one about origami.) Well, I wished I had an easel. My mother managed to hinge some laths together to make one and one day my father walked into my room and found me unmistakably painting. But my subject was some flowers in a blue and white equally unmistakeably Spanish jar; painting was suddenly quite acceptable.

The rest of my time in school was agreeable. There were only two or three of us in the examination class (Oxford and Cambridge Senior). Maths was a pleasure, as was art; French and Spanish no problem; history annoying, because our text was a History of the British Empire; religion, a sort of compendium of the Gospels; Latin was the only difficulty, because there was no Latin class and Mother Colette had to try to find odd moments when both she and I were free to consider Livy and Horace, who wrote such very different Latin to the language I met in church.

These few years seem to have been more peaceful at home. The Spanish war was a distraction about which Addie and Alex were in agreement. We had people coming and going, sometimes staying for a couple of months. There was a row about Christmas one year; my father gave me a portable typewriter but took himself off and moved into the Grand Hotel for the duration. I may have provoked another row by falling down a cliff. It was only a small cliff, twenty feet or so, not deserving the name, tucked away near Governor's Cottage at Europa. A few of us had been looking over the protective wall at the top, wondering whether we could get down. We were joined by a very young aircraftsman who said that if we came back next day he'd have some rope. We did; he had strong but thin twisted cord, like seagrass. Who would try first? Me. The cord was too slippy to hold, so I wound it once round my hand, found some slight footholds for my feet, let go of the wall and tried to hold the cord with my other hand, only to find myself speeding downwards at pretty well normal falling speed. I got a crack on my forehead which poured blood, and the friction had cut the hand which had had the cord wound around it. They got me up with the help of the butler from Governor's Cottage, and supported me as I limped home, where I expected sympathy for my wounds — I still have a bit of a scar over one eyebrow. I expected wrongly. Somehow the aircraftsman was mentioned in the account of the disaster and from that moment my father was concerned with nothing else. No good protesting that I was with a group of my usual friends, that we had barely met this youngster, who didn't seem to be much older than we were. I could not be trusted not to involve myself with strange men. I was thoroughly annoyed at such wilful misunderstanding.

The same sort of mistake cast a faint blight over my final exam. Gabrielle and I were doing it together. There were so few students that we all had to go to the examination centre in the Christian Brothers' school. There we met two boys, friends like ourselves. At least, Gabrielle met one of them, a rather good looking chap. They wanted to talk to each other during the gaps between papers; this left the friend and myself to make the best of being left out. I cannot remember that we had anything to say to each other, but whatever word got back to the nuns resulted in a lecture to me not to go off in company with male examinees.

By the way, the examiners in history accepted my non-conformist answers to questions about the Empire, but the Latin people were less flexible; if I couldn't scan Horace or put some sentences into half-way-correct Latin, I failed. I did not realise how much this would matter.

The summer that followed was one of uncertainty. The Spanish war was over but it was understood that Germany was likely to provoke something on a larger scale. Gabrielle got a job in the library, something I thought I would have loved to have, but I was not permitted to apply. Instead I became a V.A.D., a sort of trainee nurse in the Military Hospital. Neither hours nor work were arduous, but I learnt to put on, artistically, regular bandages — which won me a certain respect when I became a real nurse a year or so later.

On my eighteenth birthday, it happened; Hitler invaded Poland. A couple of days elapsed before Britain declared war. We listened to the radio in half a dozen languages and expected such an important fortress as Gibraltar, the key to the Mediterranean, to be bombed within hours. Instead there were six months of 'phony war', nothing happening. Unfortunately for me, several of the Loreto nuns were on holiday in Ireland and couldn't get back for the beginning of term.

This was very bad. A message came asking me to come up and teach until they returned. Two years earlier my turn had come to change the various coloured ribbons for the broad pale blue of a Child of Mary. I protested as long as I could. A Child of Mary was the equivalent of a prefect and could be called upon to keep order if nun or teacher left the room. If I cannot remember how they prevailed upon me it is probably because I want to forget, just as I am pleased to realise that those horrible weeks of being a teacher have almost wiped themselves from my memory.

Usually when I waken in the morning I work out what day it is, what I'll be doing. If I do not quite live up to the Duke of Wellington's wonderful certainty, 'If a man wake to turn in his bed, depend upon it, it is time he were out of it', I can usually find something to which to look forward. Not during those weeks. I would wake to a feeling that the ceiling, or the sky, black and heavy, was only a few feet over my head. I think the worst class was a bunch of newcomers of mixed ages, speaking only Spanish, who did not know what they were doing in the tiny room we'd been given any more than I did. The classes with girls who had known me on the other side of the fence three months before were as bad in a different way. They thought it was a prolonged joke. There was a little consolation in finding that the Gibraltarian girls to whom I had been told to teach Spanish had a rather poor grasp of the language, even though they usually spoke it at home. This information turned out to have some value later on. As for the rest, it made me certain that teaching would not be my career.

At last the nuns came back and we went away. My father had applied for a vacancy in the accounts department back in Lagos; this would permit him to retire at least five years earlier. He got what he wanted and was more fortunate than he could have guessed. The house in North Pavilion Road sustained a direct hit when the war warmed up; the frontier with Spain was firmly closed and it seems life in Gib became so stressful that the new Postmaster General shot himself at his desk, formerly my father's.

CHAPTER 8

Conspiracy in the Old Castile; submarines evaded; safe in Dublin

My father had arranged to take a slice of leave in Spain before going on to Nigeria. Some oddments were boxed to send to Ireland; they must have been, how otherwise would I have the fat green salt jar on the kitchen mantelpiece or the set of painted nesting tables my mother liked? The three of us drove off to visit places we hadn't seen before. We were in the Austin car Alex had bought from the works three years earlier. That had been quite noticeable even in Gib, where cars were handed on from one batch of colonials to the next; our first car, ten years before this, had been a high-up primitive Ford, if not a Model T, then very much the same. A few years later, driving through snowy peaks to visit Granada, I had huddled in a rug on the back seat of a Renault with only canvas sides to protect us from the weather. In 1939, after three years of war, to drive through Spain in a private car was itself a privilege; to have a still glossy saloon must have given much satisfaction to its owner.

We had time enough to go further north than usual. Madrid, of course, and the Prado. We visited the Irish ambassador, no doubt to clear our neutral position if the war with Germany should escalate. (My father had both British and Irish passports, and switched nationality according to circumstances, preferring Argentinian; no Argentine passport, because if he should go back there before retirement age he'd be called up for military service.) The room in which we sat had a Paul Henry on the wall; I looked at the ultramarine mountain, quite close to the viewer, and decided that it was fantasy. Eighteen months later I was in Connemara trying to catch the same colours.

I think it was in Orense we saw women doing the washing at natural hot springs and ate delicious partridge in a casserole.

75

Everywhere we stayed in modest hotels and I'd be sent out to buy *churros* from the vendors in the street. These are crisp strings of batter, deep fried and eaten hot with sugar. Where did my father find a suitor for me? I seem to see a long street and a young man with crutches, perhaps wearing a medal. I can quite see how gratifying it would have been for a hispanophile like my father to have a Caballero Mutilado as a son-in-law. An officer wounded in the war would have a pension as well as an honourable title. Very possibly an agreeable young man; if I had known and liked him I would not have been much bothered by a missing leg or arm (perhaps both) but I had to make it clear that I did not intend to marry anyone.

A principal aim was to visit Castilla, inaccessible during the war years, Avila, Salamanca, Segovia. We arrived at the Irish College in Salamanca for Christmas, bringing with us a Christmas pudding in a tin. Two Irish priests, the rector and vice-rector, had been holding out without students during the war. They showed us their exquisite building, in the same brown-gold stone as the major buildings of Salamanca, their library with incunabulae, the portrait of the O'Neill who had been first patron of the Colegio de los Nobles Irlandeses. We all wore outdoor clothes all the way. They had both been students there and told us that in winter they had always had to wear the heaviest available tweed coats while studying. Now even the diningroom was freezing. There was a brasero under the table and during the dinner a smell of burning; the sole of the rector's shoe was smouldering. But all was good humour; three Irish guests for Christmas were a treat.

We drove on towards Segovia. On this trip I shared the driving with my father; one night climbing a hill in fog, we each in turn fell asleep at the wheel, but avoided disaster. When trouble came it came at a convenient place. We had got rooms in Casa Corrales, a very simple fonda and hotel facing the railway station in Segovia. My father had gone for a drive but come back on foot to report that he had got out of the car for some reason, and perhaps forgot the handbrake, perhaps just left the car too near the edge. It had slid down the bank at the side, rolled over and remained upside down in the snow. Luckily there was an army school of engineering based almost on the spot. They heaved it up, diagnosed a broken rear axle and undertook to repair it, whenever possible.

A singularly fortunate place to be shipwrecked. There are Spanish tourist posters that show other attractions but I doubt if a brochure is ever brought out that has not one view or another of the Alcazar, that Frenchified arrangement of turrets sprouting from the summit of a cliff, the old cathedral shouldering it from behind. That's the further end of the town; the street that runs up to them begins under the enduring aqueduct of Trajan.

I rather think that if my father had had the means to travel he would have gone on and on. Since he was caught he settled for enjoying Segovia. Long discussions were necessary at the College of Engineering. Every evening there was a *tertulia* around the wood-burning stove in the diningroom. There was at least one permanent resident, a small brisk man who reminded me of a water wagtail, director of road building for the Province of Segovia. A businesswoman who stayed a night at intervals showed me how to knit efficiently with the needles tucked under my elbows and told me I could at least tidy up my eyebrows — *al menos se puede arreglar las cejas*. A younger military person, either student or lecturer at the College of Engineering, was always there for the *tertulia*, sometimes during the day as well; possibly a resident. A few locals and other military persons regularly joined us from the bar outside. The star of the gathering was without question Don Juan X, at any rate without question in his own mind. (It's true that the risk of a writ for libel at this distance in time, space and language is not grave, but I had rather be on the safe side. No names, they say, no pack drill.) We would be seated in a circle around the cylindrical black stove in the centre of the room. Señor Corrales would come in, take the lid off the stove, drop in a few more logs; he was never seen to do anything else. The atmosphere would warm up. The door would open, and there would stand the confident figure of Don Juan in his hunting boots.

'Que tal?'

It is a quite ordinary expression, 'How's things?', but for me it belongs to the Squire of Segovia. I have no idea of his importance in the town itself; we were based outside the walls, a mile of so from the aqueduct. Don Juan had a factory, tiles or something, further down the road, and here he reigned.

He was company for my father. Possibly as a matter of custom, just possibly because of the presence of my mother and myself, Don Juan sometimes brought his entourage, his wife and two daughters. I rather admired the dark sheen and the regular waves of the Señora's hair; the daughters were equally controlled. We did not find anything to say to one another, but the fathers got on very well. Mine seems to have invited the other family and the roads engineer to dinner one night. I remember sitting at a different table and taking part in wine tasting, a comparison between the Marques de Riscal and some other Rioja, that was prolonged to such a point that I noticed an odd sensation in my head; the knees, when I went upstairs to bed, were less reliable than usual. The young ladies drank their wine watered, like the Greeks, and were not asked their views. Another evening we residents had a memorable dinner; Don Juan had been hunting in the mountains and had provided wild boar. It is as far beyond ordinary pork as good brandy is from modest table wine. Asterix and Obelix do well for themselves.

That is not the only meal I remember in Casa Corrales. This is a region of good food and good cooking. A restaurant at the foot of the aqueduct is famous for roast sucking pig. We could not afford to go there, but we did very well where we were. Señora Corrales had ways of doing white beans with parsley and a few cockles (no shells, not like those untidy seaside paellas), or a piece of roast veal sliced as thin as flower petals that made Don Manuel (the roads engineer) send in messages of warm appreciation to the kitchen. He believed it was best for the digestion to remain upright for some time after a meal so he would walk around the diningroom and chat and tell us how fortunate we were. A very agreeable fellow guest, later to become a fellow conspirator; he saw that I had been painting in watercolours in a sketchbook and he thoughtfully had a proper board made for me so that I could paint on stretched paper.

We had to sit around the stove, not only in the evening, but during the day if we were indoors; there was nowhere else to go, no heat in our own room save from the chimney of the diningroom stove running up through it and the self-generated heat in featherbeds with embroidered sheets. My mother and I went to Mass in the mornings in the nearby church. The snow was sometimes quite deep. I am puzzled now to know how we managed to dry our shoes or keep ourselves reasonably warm. When we would come in from Mass (often the only congregation in a small freezing stone building) Antonia, the maid, would have warmed our heavy delph coffee bowls before pouring in the coffee and we would wrap our hands around them and long for the newly lighted stove to build up a little heat.

This would have been after Alex had gone off to Nigeria. I am not clear about our plans. He had suggested that I might become an apprentice to an artist who made ceramic pictures, spread over a large number of tiles; this fell through. There was a notion that I might study in Salamanca; meanwhile, we were doing very well where we were and we could hardly abandon the car, still awaiting repair.

It's true that I was not badly off; I had an exceptionally lovely place to sketch, a place to which I could not do justice. I had plenty of reading because there was a great range of European classics translated into Spanish, printed like newsprint and sold for a couple of pesetas. I still have a properly bound Xenophon which I seem to have read with care, and which must have occupied a fair amount of my time. I found a couple of school textbooks, a two-year course in German, which I completed during the five months we stayed. I was able to compare notes about this with the military person who was sometimes with us at lunchtime; he had learnt by heart a pocket Spanish/German dictionary. (This young man provided me with a problem of conscience. I must have passed some of my time writing letters; one of them must have mentioned some minor grumble that he had made. The censor picked it up; I was interrogated by two uniformed officials. I said I could not remember who had said whatever it was. Next time I got to confession I confessed that I had told a lie; the real problem was that I did not regret it, and would say the same again. This no longer bothers my conscience.)

So, I could amuse myself, but how very tedious it must have been for my mother. We went walking together and she would wait while I sketched. We had four or five paperbacks in English, two of them so bad that we got a fair amount of fun out of them: a spy story by William le Queux and *Rogue Herries* by Hugh Walpole. You have to be stranded with a book like that, be driven to read it again, to realise how cockeyed it is. We made up crosswords for each other, something at which she was much better than I. She wrote letters, but she had, in effect, no conversation except mine. Antonia was very friendly, Don Manuel always courteous, but conversation could not go very far in limited Spanish.

Of course, I could translate. That is how the 'conspiracy' was possible. The car was at last repaired. Whatever arrangement Alex had made, it turned out that Don Juan would give shelter to the car, apparently while waiting to purchase it. Meanwhile it was not his. By this time the snow had melted and we had to make our way through mud to get to the town. It was galling to have Don Juan, with wife and daughters, wave as they sped past in *our* car. When we told Don Manuel what was happening we realised that we were not alone in finding Don Juan obnoxious. Don Manuel arranged that I should have driving lessons from his chauffeur in order to pass the Spanish driving test — presumably what I had brought from Gibraltar was not sufficient. There was suitable level ground in front of a church directly under the cliff that sustains the Alcazar. Here the chauffeur would lay out twisted paths marked by stones to train me to reverse properly. Then we progressed to reversing in real life around the narrow and complex streets of Segovia itself, where I noticed that practically every street had one or two churches. I had to have lessons about the working of the internal combustion engine. While we were doing this, of course, Don Juan couldn't swan around in the foreign car, but he was confident that it would be his before long. I got my test, drove to Salamanca, where we found a cheap hotel nothing like our classic friendly fonda, but within our means.

When we returned to Casa Corrales we developed our plans with Don Manuel. It seems to have been understood that it would be necessary to visit Madrid to arrange for the sale of an imported car. No need to bother Don Juan; Don Manuel could make everything clear and he would lend us his chauffeur in case I should have difficulty finding my way around in Madrid. And so he did, and all was arranged — and when we returned, the chauffeur was the owner of the car. I don't think we were going to get much out of it anyway; the cost of repair probably ate up most of the sale price, or was set against the limited amount of money we were allowed to bring in each month. The satisfaction of selling at a modest price to the amiable chauffeur who brought us to Salamanca, instead of to the boisterous Don, was considerable.

I did not particularly regret handing it over. I suppose, since the days in Gib when I used to vanish in order to stay home and play rather than 'go for a run into Spain', I had seen cars as a mixed blessing. Since we got back to Gib, private cars were scarce enough, 'new' cars much more so, the same driven by a girl of eighteen so unusual as to provoke far more attention than I cared for. We could not have afforded to use it anyway, since the money we were allowed to import was barely enough to pay full board at the skimpy hotel, leaving nothing over for petrol. The letter from Don Juan that followed us, warning us of the anger to be expected from our Husband and Father — *el Marido y Padre de Vds* — was compensation. We showed it to the Irish fathers, who already knew the story and they shared our enjoyment.

Here in Salamanca my mother had the possibility of conversation but it cannot have been a way of life she would have chosen. She still had no occupation, we were still living out of one suitcase, we had no money to replace clothes or even to buy a cake to supplement the stewed goat standard in our hotel. When Alex was with us money was more elastic; I think we must have counted as tourists then, residents afterwards.

I went to classes and lectures at the University. At first I was disappointed to find that I could not matriculate because I had not done well enough in Latin. (Only this moment has it occurred to me that I might have passed an exam on the spot, since it probably would not have been tied to scanning Horace.) Instead, I joined a class for foreigners. There were only three of us, one Japanese young man, one German girl and myself, with a round amiable teacher.

I was jealous of the German girl. She was by herself, had been there for quite a while, spoke Spanish she had learnt on the spot, indistinguishable from the Spanish students. It was a faint consolation when one of these presumed that I came from Andalucia, gratifying when our teacher complimented me on the style of my essays, but I still regretted that I must return to speaking English every afternoon. Our lessons took only a few hours a week. I spent the rest of the time sitting in on lectures, especially those on the History of Art, and reading in the library. I was consoled for non-matriculation when, talking with students, I realised that, following a distracting civil war, the whole system was geared to turning out a new generation of teachers as quickly as possible. I mixed sufficiently to know that the real students were not enjoying themselves very much.

Nevertheless, I felt that since I was in Salamanca anyway, it would have been an advantage to experience total immersion in Spanish. Ironic, when no doubt my mother would also have preferred to be somewhere else. But there was much to please: the buildings of the University, all golden and adorned in relief, enriched here and there with centuries-old graffiti; the great arcaded plaza, where young men and women would walk *en masse* in opposite directions in the evenings; the plains of Castile in the springtime. I know we arrived in the spring because we were just in time for a special sort of tart made for picnics at the beginning of May, stuffed with pork and chicken and hard-boiled egg.

In a square among the University buildings is a statue of Fray Luis de Leon. I bought a compact leather-bound edition of his *La Perfecta*

Casada; it is a commentary on The Good Wife, that passage at the end of Proverbs which was probably written by a woman. A dangerous man, Fray Luis. His language is so seductive that he persuades you to accept his view of life. I still believe he was right in his praise of the rewards of early rising — *madrugar* is the lovely Spanish verb — but he gives rather more space to the evils of make-up. *Afeites* is the word he uses for cosmetics; since *fea* means ugly I associated the two ideas, and I dare say he made the most of the assonance. He set a high standard for working with one's hands, spinning and weaving. He must have influenced me for years, though I still had no notion of marriage.

While writing this, I have looked in vain for *La Perfecta Casada*; I know where it ought to be but it seems I didn't put it back. Instead I am going to quote a few verses from the source, the last chapter of Proverbs, in the RSV Bible:

> A good wife who can find?
>   She is more precious than jewels.
> The heart of her husband trusts in her,
>   and he will have no lack of gain.
> She seeks wool and flax,
>   and works with willing hands.
> She rises while it is yet night
>   and provides food for her household
>   and tasks for her maidens.
>
> She opens her hand to the poor,
>   and reaches her hand to the needy.
> She makes herself coverings;
>   her clothing is fine linen and purple.
> Her husband is known on the gates,
>   When he sits among the elders of the land.
> She makes linen garments and sells them;
>   she delivers girdles to the merchant.
> Strength and dignity are her clothing,
>   and she laughs at the time to come.

Fray Luis wrote a chapter about each verse; there are several references to her business ability, but I think he must have downplayed this side of her character, because I have not, unfortunately, imitated it.

Being a university town, Salamanca had more and better bookshops that Segovia and so I spent what small funds we had left from our hotel bill on literature. This was not as selfish as it may sound; I am talking of thin pocket-size paperbacks of Tirso de Molina, Calderon, Lope da Vega. The few pesetas they cost would not have bought anything that my mother would enjoy. The two of us would look into the windows of one special cake shop, but to look was all we could afford. Sometimes we managed a block of chocolate, but it was the cinnamon-flavoured kind that is intended for making chocolate to drink. Its influence remains; when I make cocoa I usually add a suspicion of cinnamon.

We splashed out once. It seems probable that my mother felt she had to have her hair permed; she wasn't fussy, but she was in the habit of having it done every six months or so, just to keep it tidy. I had hitherto had mine shingled, that is, cut straight across about ear level and cut very close with a special sort of clipper up the back of the neck. By the time we had been a couple of months in Salamanca we must both have been feeling pretty shaggy. I decided to have a perm as well.

This I report because it had even more influence on my later life than had Fray Luis. The little sausagey roll all around the end of my hair was so hideous that I vowed I would never again cross the threshold of a hairdressers. As soon as the hair was long enough to make it possible I tied it up on top, later I made two plaits and for longer than I can remember I have made one a bit to one side and wound it round. I must have saved hundreds of pounds, not paying for cutting and setting like other people, but where are they?

Well, our stay in Salamanca cannot have been more than a few months; news came of the real start of the war, the fall of France. My mother hurried down to Gib by train — it seems strange now that she could not get what information she needed by telephone — and was back in a couple of days with the news that if we hurried we would get places on a ship leaving three days later. I have to admit that I relished being on my own for that short time; so unfair of me. We packed whatever was worth bringing, books included. The Irish fathers invited us to tea in the admired cake shop, and a very amusing tea it was, with lots and lots of little saucers like a Chinese meal. We entrained and travelled through the night down to La Linea. Do passengers on Spanish trains still pass around bottles of wine?

There was some fuss with the police about letting us out; I cannot remember just what the problem was, but I admire my mother for having got through on her own with limited communication. Perhaps she had made them understand that she had left a hostage and must go back. Anyway, we found ourselves on board a cruise ship, P & O I think, with only six passengers. Two of the others were from Dublin, a honeymoon couple who had taken a chance with Spain. I think it possible that we met at the aduana in La Linea and that I had done some interpreting; whatever about that, they were wonderfully enjoyable company. And no wonder — Tommy and Máire Doyle were to be notable contributors to the culture and fun of Dublin.

It really was a strange experience to have dining saloon, bars, smoking room, all the provision for a few hundred passengers at our disposal to wander around, not that the bars were open. We learnt afterwards that we had been very fortunate; the Loreto nuns were evacuated on the next, and last, ship and conditions were very different, with hundreds more people than the ship was designed for, water rationed, a real refugee voyage. In ordinary times ships mark their location on a chart at midday, even boast about how many knots they are making. In war time, dodging submarines, passengers have no idea where they are, so I am vague about how we got to Dublin.

One morning early we are near Butt bridge, in sunny, almost empty streets. I am not sure whether we have come by train from Rosslare or by boat to Dún Laoghaire or the North Wall; the latter seems most likely. The really extraordinary thing is that there are some small boys about and they are speaking English with Irish accents.

CHAPTER 9

The Royal City of Dublin Hospital: sterilising by 'glimmer'

Dublin meant seeing friends again, especially Denis and his parents. Then we headed west to Tera, who had introduced me to algebra in Gibraltar, to theatre in Dublin and was now a district nurse in Kilkerran, with her own cottage on the edge of the Atlantic.

It was summer, a good summer; sea to one side of us, heather to the other, hidden in it sky blue pools and lakes. My mother and I would go out in Tera's car when she went on her rounds. I would bring my paints and Don Manuel's handy little board; I still have a few watercolours to remind me. I learnt various useful things that summer, how to make soda bread and apple cake in a pot-oven, how a nurse on her own could deal with accidents, how she must insist on being called promptly to a birth lest the local 'wise woman' should have different priorities. I cannot now commend Tera's way of disposing of the contents of the Elsan — we used to dump them over the edge of the rocks straight into the sea — but it did introduce me to an alternative sanitary system.

Tera used to tell us amusing stories about her training; it seemed to be acknowledged already that I was going to be a nurse. Well, I was going to have to be something; my father, backed by a book on psychology, limited the female field to teaching and nursing. (The book was *The Psychology of Character* by Rudolf Allers, published by Sheed & Ward, and if I were to read it again I think I would find a good deal in it that had influenced me.) I had had more than enough of teaching; my father had, one Christmas, given me a typewriter but had warned me not to learn shorthand because I might find myself trapped in an office. As for going to college, it is possible, though not certain, that he would have paid my fees, but as an intending student in Dublin I would have fallen between the horns of a dilemma: two universities; born in Ireland, I could not go to UCD unless I had passed Leaving Certificate Irish; an obedient Catholic, I could not flout the Archbishop's ban on going to Trinity College.

When we returned to Dublin it must already have seemed probable that I would train at the Royal City of Dublin Hospital, usually known as Baggot Street Hospital, because we looked for a flat in that district. We did very well, with three large rooms on the top floor of 76 Morehampton Road. True, the kitchen was one end of the landing, the only water was a cold tap one flight down, the shared bathroom was almost in the basement, but we could see out to Dublin Bay from the sittingroom and up to the mountains from the rooms in front; what's more, the noble chestnut tree in front reached up to our windows.

At last my mother had a reliable, if very small, income because it had been agreed that the Colonial Office would pay her direct. She also had her own space to furnish, something she could do well for a few shillings. The only real expenditure was a pointillist carpet of blues and black for the sittingroom. With pale lemon walls and curtains made from lining material of exactly the right grey-blue, the little tables salvaged from Gib painted to match, she had a room everyone admired for the next twenty odd years.

I had some months to spare. I joined a Gaelic League evening class which had an inspired teacher, Proinnsias mac an Bheata; if I had been able to continue I might have become reasonably fluent. My decision to attend the School of Art as a day student could have been critical. I never had any fancy for nursing; I believed that it was useful to society and that I would pay any future debt in case I should need at some time to be nursed; it seemed also to be a sharing in the job of the Good Samaritan's innkeeper. I had, too, Tera's example; as a nurse one could acquire one's own house, and eventually arrange one's own time. More than the house the notion of a ship appealed to me. If I did midwifery I could become a ship's nurse, compensation for not being acceptable as a cabin boy.

But these future plans were vague; I am pretty sure that my real intention was to qualify as an SRN, as an insurance policy in this world and the next and get back to painting as soon as may be afterwards. At the School of Art I was having lessons from people who had known Uncle Frank; Seán Keating and he had been in the same class. A few years ago I was fairly furious to hear that discontented students had thrown the classical casts out of an upper window, to shatter below. I doubt whether I would be enchanted even by the original Discobolus; I presume that what we had was a cast of a Roman copy. There was the Dying Gladiator, a Venus of Milo and some other reliables. One didn't have to like them; it was drawing that was satisfying. It was not until I read *Drawing With the Right Side of the Brain* that I understood why I had found myself so contented; while I concentrated on my pencil the anxious left side of my brain was silenced.

I did well enough for Keating to promote me to Life class before anyone else in my set. Once he gave us a theme for composition, to be displayed anonymously, and he said mine was the only one that was, properly speaking, a composition. I had doubtless read more books about art. And one day he asked the class to put their hands up if they had been to look at the pictures in the National Gallery (in effect, under the same roof, but entered on the other side of the building) twice during the term. I had been there three times but I hesitated to put up my hand; others may have felt the same. No hands went up, and he stormed.

Just possibly, if I had owned up on both occasions he might have advised my mother when she consulted him that it would be worth the risk of trying to make a career out of art. What he did say was that it was very hard to make any money. At the same time I had come to feel that, though I loved the act of drawing, the world would not be deprived of anything special if I went no further. Before I became a student I took it for granted that if I had a blank surface and a pencil something would present itself to be drawn. After a couple of months I noticed this was no longer so. As far as I remember I decided that if I were destined to be an artist such a blank could not occur.

Of course I was still reading. I remember a heavy dark green volume with unsophisticated engravings in the footnotes, the *Chanson de Roland*, medieval French on one page, modern French facing. Influenced by Belloc, I read the whole. I had earlier got through most of the *Cancion del Cid*, similarly updated. Both tend to be tedious. Wonderful what a digestion one has at nineteen. I note from a bookplate that my copy of Pope's translation of the *Odyssey* was bought at this time, though I would have thought I had read it earlier. Not tedious. I had so much liked 'The Rape of the Lock' that I had accustomed myself to read heroic couplets with much the same pleasure as their original readers. I can understand the criticism that they do not mould themselves to Homeric action.

I can also see that such reading did not mould me to sink imperceptibly into a flock of student nurses, but they were a friendly group and did not tease me. Only six newcomers were taken in at a time. One of our batch was a Jewish refugee from Germany, Helen Deutsch, with whom I paired off as much as I did with anyone. We spent several weeks in the Nurses' Home with Sister Tutor, getting used to our new uniforms, learning some anatomy, how to make a bed properly and how never to carry a bed-pan uncovered. The physiology and the graduated bandaging that I had learnt in the Military Hospital in Gibraltar proved valuable.

The uniforms were classic. We had to buy four grey cotton dresses with three tucks around the hem, a slim shoulder pocket for a thermometer and a deep, useful pocket under the enveloping apron. This white apron came right up to the stiff collar in front, merged into straps that crossed at the back; all the buttons, which before long disappeared in the laundry and were replaced by safety pins, were covered by a wide starched belt fastened with studs. More studs for the long, tapered, stiff white cuffs. (The bill from Pyms for 1 doz collars, 1 doz pairs of cuffs, 12 aprons, the dresses and a pair of handmade shoes came to sixteen pounds, eleven shillings and three pence, the best part of my mother's monthly income.)

At first we folded each other's caps. The fine white hem-stitched linen square had to have one hem turned back, centred on the wearer's forehead, the rest of the material neatly pleated at the centre back, then the turned-up hem brought back and pinned to hold everything in place. When you got the knack you could do the pleating yourself, pressing your forehead against a wall to hold the hem in position. It was as becoming a way of keeping hair covered as I have seen.

Once in the real world of work we found that the cuffs were worn only for doctors' and Matron's rounds and for handing out meals. Sleeves were rolled up out of the way the rest of the time. On night duty in winter, with the window of the sluice room always open, a sheepskin jacket would have been more suitable than rolled-up cotton sleeves. I got bronchitis, a cough that persisted so long that patients worried about me. I sat an exam while coughing once per minute. One of the ward sisters could hear me coughing all night and eventually arranged an interview with one of the consultants in his ward.

'Well, nurse, do you think you could carry on?' Of course fool nurse says yes. On my next day off my mother put me to bed and got the local GP, who cursed the hospital and said I was at risk of having chronic bronchitis, and kept me in bed for a couple of weeks. Another one of the six had got TB in her first year and had had to leave; I hope she prospered.

The cold was not a constant problem. We had difficulties because of the 'Emergency', sterilising instruments with only an illegal glimmer of rationed gas, poaching eggs on an open fire made with wet turf. The 'Emergency' signified the difficulties experienced in neutral Ireland during the second world war; the 'glimmer' was the small flame that could be used, but should not, during the hours when gas pressure was low; turf, or peat, is an excellent fuel when it is dry; not so when wet. Worst was the ongoing anxiety that recurred every morning. When we went on duty at seven thirty in the morning Night Sister would be waiting in the hall with a list. Always there was the fear that she would stop you and say, 'Nurse McCormac, Female Surgical today' or 'Theatre' or 'Accident' or 'Private Patients' or whatever. Even when you had been moved the day before you could not be certain of not being moved again; even when you had been six months in the same place you might be ignored. If you were sent on night duty you got the afternoon off, to sleep. For a long time every change was to somewhere unknown and hence alarming, but on the other hand once you knew your way around and were unhappy with your lot you might long in vain for change.

As you moved around you found yourself working at some time along with every other nurse on the staff. There were two or three whom I thought I did not like; after a few days of working side by side with them I found that all but one were quite acceptable company. That one was not disagreeable, she merely had a notable ability to look elegant and leave work to other people.

Time off was similarly uncertain. Notionally we had time off either from 12.30 to 4.30, back on duty until 9.00, or from 4.30 for the rest of the day, but when Sister had looked at her rota she might easily tell you that you would have to take the afternoon instead of the evening. Or vice versa. Towards the end of training I was back on the Female Landing, where Sister had been very fierce and seemed to want to make probationers cry. (No tears from this one.) Now I became something of a favourite and on Sunday after Sunday she kindly changed my afternoons (which on Sunday were from 10.00 to 3.00) to evenings. This was unfortunate because I had usually arranged to meet someone who has not yet appeared in this narrative and I could not get in touch with him by telephone. It was a good thing that he knew all about the ways of the hospital.

On the whole the worst of the changes was to night duty, and the worst part of that was the cooking. Every week the probationer from one of the landings had to cook for all the rest, a dozen or so, and for Night Sister. It was alarming enough to be alone with a huge Aga (having been warned that someone had once left the lids up and the whole hospital had been without cooked food the next day). The real trouble was that you had to produce meals from whatever food was left out, and do it twice, because naturally nowhere could be left without staff so there had to be two sittings, and get your own ordinary work done as well. Some nights, if you were on medical wards, might be fairly quiet, but I know that there were eleven-hour nights when I did not get off my feet at all. We had two nights off per month.

I had complicated things further for myself. When on day duty I soon found that the church beside us welcomed nurses to receive Holy Communion before seven o'clock Mass. We could hurry back for breakfast at seven, and very pleasant it was to see mornings getting brighter and brighter and the flowers opening up in the lovely little garden beside the church. The thing was, having got into the way of it, I didn't see any strong reason for not going to Mass when we got off night duty, just in time for eight o'clock Mass. Our morning meal, normally dinner, was at half past eight. This would be no problem nowadays, but then you had to be fasting from midnight to receive Communion, not even drinking water. Complicated enough to plan according to whether you were on first or second sitting, always taking into account that real time in Dublin is twenty minutes later than GMT, while when summer time is on you have the bonus of an extra hour. I could, if I were not busy, run up to the kitchen and have a last drink of milk at twenty minutes past twelve or even twenty past one, but must take care to avoid food after that; not easy when I was on the cooking rota.

It is only fair to say that night duty had its good side. It was very busy when we came on duty, getting reports, settling patients in; a mad rush in the morning, giving non-ambulant patients washing water in an enamel dish, collecting these, distributing the wretched breakfast of white bread and butter and tea, doing some dressings, reporting to staff nurse, tidying up and making some beds before day staff came on.

The good part was that in between there might be quiet hours for reading. In this old hospital there were no offices for nurses; the three of us — for four wards containing fifty patients — would camp behind screens with shaded lights, and make rounds at intervals. Most of the nurses risked a light snooze on quiet nights and talked of 'night nurse's paralysis', of waking up when Night Sister arrived on inspection and finding they couldn't move a limb. I found it hard enough to adjust to sleeping in the daytime, sometimes with the sounds of tennis outside the window; I knew that one night without sleep could leave one wide awake next morning but deeply sleepy later, so I made it my plan to switch over at once, not to close my eyes during the first night, so as to foster the ability to remain awake, reading, whenever I was not busy. I hoped that if I could keep this up I would be able to sleep more soundly in the daytime. I found that a rapid cold bath, or rather, cold plunge, when I got up in the evening was helpful.

My first month's pay, one pound, had been spent on the Temple Classics edition of the *Divina Commedia*, three neat little blue volumes for Purgatory, Hell and Heaven, Italian on one page, prose English facing; T. S. Eliot recommended this edition. These fitted in the pocket of my dress with room to spare and gained for me the gratifying nickname, Dante. Not that we used nicknames very much; it was surnames all the way, but a good many nurses, including myself, were addressed simply as 'Mac'.

I had the pleasure of reading the last cantos of *Purgatorio*, where Beatrice manifests herself to conduct her charge to Heaven, while sitting on grass on the penitential island in Lough Derg, St Patrick's Purgatory. There, the night-long vigil in the church, with set routines of prayers, had been desperately difficult, but on the second night pilgrims were allowed delicious sleep, and this was the third day, all duty over and we were just waiting for the boats to come, bring a fresh batch of pilgrims and row us over to the train. It used to be said that if you 'do' Lough Derg once you do it three times. Once was enough for me, but I'm glad to have done it, rather in the same way as I'm glad to have 'done' nursing. Everything afterwards has seemed like a holiday.

Nursing did me good; I think the understanding most deeply implanted was that the world is divided into two parts: that which is sterile and everything else. Gauze, cotton wool, dressings, towels were packed into drums and sent off to be sterilised. Instruments, including syringes, needles and long-handled Spencer-Wells forceps were boiled in the steriliser in each ward, or in the Theatre. We learnt a routine for different routine requirements, just what was needed for particular kinds of dressings or transfusions. One put a metal tray on a trolley, released the catch on the sterile drum, washed one's hands, took one of the Spencer-Wells from the container where it rested in disinfectant, carefully lifted the lid of the drum, removed a towel and spread it over the tray, using the forceps, turned to the steriliser and extracted the required objects, took out another towel and covered the tray with it, still without touching. When oneself, or Sister, or a surgeon, was doing a dressing, one took the dressings out of the drum with the Spencer-Wells and kept the lid shut the rest of the time.

It seems to have worked; if cross-infection had happened there would have been holy murder, as there was if any patient was found with a bed-sore, so I think I would have known. I have spelt out the routine in some detail because I gather that it has been displaced by pre-packed trays of sterile disposable syringes, disposable tubes, disposable plastic covers and that they all have to be disposed of by incineration, which is hideously wasteful, with toxins in the smoke which may in the long run cause as many problems as the procedure, whatever it was, was intended to cure.

Then there was a lesson in punctuality or reliability. Because you knew how important it was to get off duty on time you knew that nothing must permit you to be a minute late in going on duty and relieving your opposite number. I usually ran along Morehampton Road and down Waterloo Road, in to the Nurses' Home, up to my room, and could then change into black stockings and uniform with all its fastenings, slip on pre-pleated cap and run over to the main building inside five minutes. Of course there were also lessons in reliability in the training itself, giving the right injection or the right tablets at the right time, not giving an ordinary dinner to a diabetic, but that can be taken for granted as the purpose of training. I'm thinking of the side effects.

I should think we all found that we were capable of working much harder than we had ever imagined. That's what I mean by saying everything since has been a holiday. I discovered for myself — probably read it somewhere — that I could manage better if I spared ten minutes of the midday dinner break to lie down on my bed and relax, limb by limb. I would get up revived. I have continued ever since, when possible taking a good deal longer than ten minutes.

Of course we also learnt to take responsibility. For the first six months we wore those grey dresses and were understood to know practically nothing and spent a great deal of energy and Vim on the sinks and locker tops and in speeding without actually running with piles of bedpans. Then suddenly we were into our Stripes — dresses in blue and white stripes made by the hospital's sewing woman — and we were in charge of some new probationer, letting her take the temperatures of patients who were not at risk, working up her speed in bed-making. I know I did not bully my charge as much as I had been bullied and I made sure that when making beds we talked with the patient, not over his or her head.

I cannot have been very long into my stripes when an emergency arrived during lunch time, when Sister was off and I was in charge, for three-quarters of an hour, of the surgical end of the Female Landing. A houseman had already phoned the surgeon; we just had to get the patient up to the theatre full speed for an appendicectomy. We did, but it was an ectopic pregnancy, already too late. The patient died, the surgeon was depressed. The chaplain, coming from the church next door, was furious with me because I had not summoned him to hear her confession. I didn't have the nerve to point out to him that women who die in childbirth — and that should cover her — are known to go straight to heaven. The fact was that he had not crossed my mind; I was not senior enough to be warned about things like that.

It's worth mentioning here that Baggot Street was technically a Protestant hospital, with, in my time, a Church of Ireland Matron (voluntary hospitals had been set up by one denomination or the other), but I doubt whether the Catholic hospitals could have been more respectful when Holy Communion was brought to the patients or more careful to have a nurse in full-time attendance with anyone dying. This was my job several times and I found it encouraging. At least once the other patients in the ward said the Rosary together. Later on, when I was employed as a 'special' by a private patient in a different hospital, I discovered that an elderly man was on the point of death, quite alone. I deserted my proper patient to keep him company.

Was I already sceptical of authority before I began my training? It must be evident that I did not have total faith in my father's good sense, but how far would that transfer? From the beginning it seemed to me that the obsessive tidying of lockers — which had nothing on top but a drink — and the exact squaring of counterpanes in honour of Matron's 'rounds' in the morning was not fair to patients, though they played the game if they were well enough. Other hospitals seem to manage without so much drill. Still, it did not do any harm. Much more unfair to patients was the absurdly early awakening. One thing of which I immediately disapproved was the routine of white bread and butter for breakfast, white bread and butter for tea, then a staff nurse making the round with a tray of varied aperients. Even then I used to say that most Irish people were familiar with brown soda bread, wholemeal or almost, and it could have been made every day in the vast Aga while it wasn't making dinner. That, in fact, was the snack I usually had when I came off duty and went round to my mother's flat: brown bread and cheese and a glass of cider. Even dinner was not all it might have been. Sylvia Roberts and I discovered that in a pantry off the kitchen there were a couple of zinc baths filled with leaves of cabbage floating in water. We were delighted to get a nibble of raw cabbage but we felt that the patients were missing something, say, those vitamins we were being taught about in nutrition lectures.

The non-planning that most affected student nurses was the scheduling of the lectures required for our examinations at a centre in town that we shared with other hospitals. They were in the afternoon and ward sisters would try to arrange things so that nurses who had to go to lectures would be off duty at that time, so you had to chase back to snatch some tea and go on duty again. You felt even more oppressed when on night duty and you had to try to sleep some days in the morning and then get up for lectures, other days have your time off in the morning and sleep in the afternoon.

Now I must relate how I was rewarded for being a good girl. A goody-goody girl? When there was a 'hop', an informal dance, in the Nurses' Home, it had no attraction for me (remember, no dancing classes) so, if asked, I would always be willing to do an hour or so of night duty to enable someone else to stay back and enjoy the fun. Authority knew us individually. As soon as I was senior enough to have a room to myself I was given the only room on the ground floor with a window that could be used as an entry; it was understood that I would not use it myself and that I was even too right-minded to let anyone else do so.

Now the same quality, call it what you will — for my part I attribute it to not having experienced 'socialisation' in early childhood — made me suitable for work in the Accident Department, the AD. The staff here consisted of a sister and two nurses; during the afternoon or the evening one of the nurses would be on duty by herself, while sister and the other nurse were off duty. I ask myself now why they were so sparing of nurses when they had us for nothing; we had to pay a fee of thirty-six pounds for training and we got back just that much, a pound a month for three years.

Well, I shall not dwell on the tasks of nurses in the AD. It seems strange now that I used tear around polishing the board-room table and a series of mahogany doors every single morning, before mopping the WC and setting out complicated arrays of objects that each physician or surgeon was said to require for his or her clinic, different every morning of the week. In the afternoon or the evening I would be the one on duty by herself. Most of the patients were children with cuts or warts, or adults with septic fingers or minor burns. One afternoon a week Dr Carthage Carroll had his clinic for patients with varicose ulcers, mostly older women. All I had to do was hand him adhesive elastic bandages and dispose of the ones he had taken off; he did all the work himself. I remember him not only for his unusual name but for his unusual brisk goodness. The smell would fill the whole department, outside the room we used. I felt sorry for the people plagued with such a miasma around them day and night, so very slow to heal, if not impossible; healing requires good circulation, and that was itself the problem. Later, researching an article, I found that work places are legally obliged to provide suitable seating so that workers do not have to stand all day, but it is rarely to be found.

Of course real accidents were brought in from time to time, but much less frequently than now; petrol was scarce. One bit of chain-saw damage was enough to make me wary of chain-saws for life. I would ring for a house surgeon and an extra nurse from one of the landings, or more likely they would have been warned before the ambulance arrived. In short, during these afternoons and evenings on solitary duty I would be fairly busy, but since there might be quiet moments I was never without a pocket-sized book in that pocket under my apron. Among our mixed bag of patients there might be some who came in simply to have a dressing changed. There was one of these whom Sister looked after. Then he began to turn up when I was on duty.

He had had a thoracoplasty — an operation then in use for patients with TB whose lung refused to collapse when air was injected into the pleura, the lining of the cavity. I believe it was understood that if the affected portion of a lung was put out of action the disease would halt. I have no idea what current practice may be, though I know that this operation is a thing of the past. We had had another thoracoplasty in the private wards when I was on duty there and I knew that the effect of having some inches of ribs removed, and having this done in two stages, was more painful than just about anything else we dealt with. The patient had to sit up in bed to drain and it was hardly possible to find a comfortable position. So, when this thin young man, a recent thoracoplasty, would come in every few days I was predisposed to sympathy. He had a long curved scar running up beside has scapula and at the lower end it had failed to heal completely, hence the dressings. He also always had a book under his arm.

Well, one usually chatted with patients while doing whatever had to be done. One afternoon I noticed that I was wondering whether the book-carrying patient would be in; I had him bracketed among Sister's patients and assumed he missed her only by accident. Later I learnt that he was quite clear about the duty rota. I remember that the first book I admitted I had in my pocket was a prettily bound little thing by Gertrud von le Fort in German, which I only partly understood. The first book he lent to me was *Morals Makyth Man* by Gerald Vann; if not published by Sheed & Ward, it could have been.

The Sheed & Ward influence had lasting significance. Frank Sheed had written a modest paperback called *A Map of Life* which had impressed me during my teens. I even remember the room in school, an awkward little room behind the stage, known as the Dungeon, where I grasped and responded to his explanation of Being. Do not take what I write now as authoritative. It is a matter that has been discussed for centuries. The best I can do is say that each of us, and every thing, has a nature: the nature of a dandelion is to be a dandelion, or a plant; the nature of Venus is to be Venus, or a planet; the nature of one of us is to be human; the nature of God is to be Being.

And Being is generous, sharing being with a vast variety of things, but first of all, if one can say first, expressing itself in love. Love cannot just be; it consists in loving something. Hence They whom we call God are not lonely; Father, Son and Holy Breathing Forth are always Being because of love interchanged; we are the overflow.

If you want to have what I am trying to say expressed clearly, recite the Creed; if you want it illuminated, read Julian of Norwich. I did not read her until many years later; Frank Sheed enabled me to hear what I was saying when I recited the Creed. He also put together another slim volume, *A Groundplan of Catholic Reading*, essentially a three-page reading list with an introduction. In the introduction he said, very truly, that much of the reading we do is 'cigarettes for the mind', something to keep it occupied while not really working. The foundation for the Groundplan was the four gospels; as far as I remember, one section was more or less philosophical, the third section more literary, Piers Plowman and Dante and so on. I had saved up the second section till my twenty-first birthday, when I began Jacques

Maritain's *Introduction to Philosophy*. I should not really have waited; this was a text for senior classes in French schools. No matter, by the time Seán and I met in the AD we had an extensive shared background of books.

Our first meeting outside the hospital was most gratifying. One afternoon he brought himself to suggest that we should go somewhere together. Because of not being socialised, my answer was uncivil; I said, well, not to the pictures anyway. We made an appointment to meet on the steps of the National Gallery. We went in and found that we both knew it quite well, enjoyed many of the same pictures and both especially liked the gallery with drawings.

What a happy time we had. Mostly we went walking and talking. One day, our feet brushing through autumn leaves, he ventured to take my hand. I have read a Chinese writer saying just what I felt about the joy of first holding the hand of someone you love. Often enough we failed to meet because I had been moved from the AD and Sister had benevolently changed my time; Seán understood, just as I did if he failed to turn up; we both knew the failure could not be intentional. I especially remember one afternoon when I came off duty and saw him, unplanned, waiting for me across the road at a little distance. I think it was that unexpected sight that made it clear to me that I loved him.

We met by appointment because we both knew the unwritten rule that between patients and nurses there is a great gulf fixed. Indeed, there was a fair-sized gulf between nurses and men in general; at that time not even sisters or Matron could be married; most of the sisters lived in one room of the Nurses' Home, Matron had a flat somewhere in the hospital. No wonder I so definitely did not intend to make a career of nursing; I might not intend to get married, but one room in a Nurses' Home....

So, nobody knew that MacCormac was breaking a taboo, but it began to be noticed that she was getting post almost every day at the Nurses' Home, handed out at lunch time. Until then any post I had went to my mother's flat. Now I was getting mysterious plain postcards, the plain side filled with neat writing — in Latin. I can hardly have failed to look pleased when I was handed one. The teasing was entirely friendly. Then, after these had been coming for a while, the word went round. Someone had seen Mac on the top of a bus with Mullarney!

I had been in the AD, somewhat isolated, all the time that Mullarney was being cut up and looked after in a ward on male surgical. He says that I once came into the ward to deliver a transfusion stand and that he knew he would like to see me again, then someone seems to have said, 'That one's mad.' Because of the changing around it seemed that three quarters of the nursing staff knew him and liked him but they didn't grudge him to me. They saw, I suppose, that there were a pair of us in it. Which means, in Hiberno-English, that one of us was as nutty as the other.

Even before the news broke I had been an object of general interest. I had weighed twelve stone when I began training. Some of this must have worn off but I was still plump. I decided to cut out carbohydrates, eat only vegetables and meat. I must have let porridge pass, otherwise I would sometimes have had no breakfast. Anyway, the results began to show up promptly. I lost a pound a day, weighed on the official scales; I had to make new holes for the studs in my starched belt practically every day. And I had excellent support. The staff nurse who carved at our table gave me as much of the crisp brown outside of the daily joint as I could manage, and I could help myself to unlimited vegetable — no potatoes. The housemen would ask just how much more I had lost. No doubt they saw themselves assuring future patients that weight loss was simple. They could hardly have known that they would also need to prescribe being in love.

Seán and I invited each other to meet our respective mothers. I had spoken to mine about this patient who read such interesting books. The poor thing expected a gentleman of about sixty. Instead came a fairly angular young man of twenty-six who had had TB for years and wasn't out of the wood yet and had a widowed mother to support. She must have been deeply worried.

One thing she didn't know, which indeed I had forgotten myself. About half way through my third year my father had decided to pay something extra, seventy pounds or so, that would allow me to leave the hospital after three years, when I should have done my final exam, instead of working for very little pay for another year and a half. His plan was that I should go to South America and look after him. I did not rule that out completely but near enough, because I, just once, said a prayer on these lines, 'You know what it's right for me to do. If you mean me to get married, send the husband before I finish training. If someone suitable doesn't appear, I shall assume that you intend me to join the Medical Missionaries of Mary and that's what I'll do.'

It may seem difficult to believe that I could formulate this plan and forget about it. It is not so strange when you consider that most

Catholic girls, then at least, faced the possibility of having a vocation — a vocation, that is, to be a nun. I was simply specifying MMM because the foundress, Mother Mary Martin, had met me when I was in my pram; I knew they were a very enlightened set of women, and when the time came I would already be a nurse. A woman doctor had told me I should have been a doctor. In private life I would not care for that burden, but if it suited MMM that would suit me.

My father's disbursement had one especially gratifying effect. I have complained already about how lectures were squeezed in between working hours. There was no concession at all for study and there was a considerable amount to be learnt. Anatomy, the little we did, and physiology I liked. Pathology seems to have covered treatment as well as diseases and there was a great deal of it. Some of the others memorised and 'heard' each other. I just went over and over what seemed the more relevant parts of a thick book. There were practical exams, given by sisters from different hospitals, orals, with doctors, for which we had to wear hats, adding to the stress (I never wore a hat in ordinary life; always a black lace mantilla for church), and of course written examinations.

I found out that to qualify as a State Registered Nurse, as well as passing the exams, one had to have worked in a training school for a specified number of days. I got out calendars, subtracted holidays and the time I had had bronchitis. I would have accumulated sufficient time twelve days before the final exam! Instead of being summoned to Matron's office because of some misdemeanour I asked for an interview. I told her of my calculations. Nobody had ever done such a thing before, though three-year training was not so unusual. But there it was. Black and white. I would have twelve clear days to study. From my point of view it was not unfair; I thought everyone else should have the equivalent. And I did not intend to continue as a nurse anyway so, even if I had an advantage, it would not make any difference to anyone else.

That was a lovely moment, when Matron accepted my case.

CHAPTER 10

Anatomy, exercise, anxiety ...and marriage

My plans for my next potential career must have been made before I said farewell to Baggot Street and sat my finals. I did not want to go to Mexico or the Argentine. In fact, I did not want to leave Dublin. I am fairly sure it was during the summer after I finished nursing that Seán put the question into words: if we could get married tomorrow, would I? I answered 'Of course' and we kissed for the first time.

One of the doctors whose clinics I looked after while on the AD — not the same one who said I should have been a doctor — had suggested physiotherapy. I was attracted. It was not about saving life but about improving the body's functioning. I found anatomy interesting. Better still, the work was done during ordinary working hours. Someone with a child or children to bring up would be able to manage more easily than if they were trying to earn a livelihood by nursing. The very notion of a married nurse seemed strange.

Note that the question had not yet been asked, neither was I thinking of combining work and marriage; it was work in widowhood that I felt must be at least taken into account. This was realistic, up to a point. Seán had been a patient in two sanatoria, in one of which the grim joke was that if they offered you chicken for dinner it was a sign that you had not long to last. He had seen men of his own age die. His father had died of TB at the age of forty-two, when Seán was seventeen. In another way it was not so realistic; since I did not mention this aspect of my plan to anyone, nobody pointed out that he was a well-qualified accountant and a permanent employee of a statutory body, and his widow and children would have an adequate pension. Years later we discussed pension arrangements but it never crossed my mind at this time. No wonder my mother was worried.

In fact Seán's mother and I had reason to be worried during the following year or so. He went back to the office. The scar seemed to heal. Then, at intervals of a month or two, he would be knocked out with a high temperature and have to go back on the operating table to have it drained again. There was a desperate afternoon when we sat on a seat in Stephen's Green and he told me that his surgeon had said, after seven of these episodes, that he could not do any more. At the same time he had never felt ill or had any reason to suspect TB, apart from an X-ray that had been prompted by a spot of blood on a handkerchief. This never happened again. I have sometimes wondered whether he might have avoided most of his problems if he had not had that X-ray.

My chronological sense is poor, but after all, the timing of these events is not important now. If I were to ask him he would be able to tell me month by month when he went back, when he had to go on sick leave again, when even half pay ran out and his colleagues made a collection for him, when Mr Montgomery took him on in the Meath hospital, nicked off the infected tip of his scapula, put his arm in plaster and solved the problem. What matters now is that it was solved; what mattered then was that the Meath is only a few minutes walk from the Adelaide Hospital where I was working in the afternoons as a student physiotherapist, so I could go to see him every day.

Whether he was coming to see me, perhaps to escort me up to work on night duty in the Fever Hospital in Clonskea, a pleasant walk from the flat in Donnybrook, or I was going to see him, we managed to write to each other most days as well; post must have been much cheaper then. Together we read Maritain and Gilson, Eric Gill and the extraordinay Dominican, Fr Vincent McNabb. His small book, *Nazareth or Social Chaos*, was good and 'green' so long before that became popular. When asked what one could do without actually leaving ordinary suburban life and going 'back to the land' he said, don't eat anything that has had to travel more than ten miles to reach you. We worked our way through thick handbooks of logic and moral philosophy which turned out to be useful later on. We shared poetry, too, and for my part I made sure of a leavening of detective stories from the library.

I found work in Clonskea a convenient way of making some money during my free time after my nursing finals and before the term began to study physiotherapy. I could sign on for a week at a time, possibly for a day or a night. When I went for an interview with Miss Allen at the School of Physiotherapy in Hume Street I was accepted as a student. 'But, Miss MacCormac, you are a nurse; there must not be any excursions into night duty.' Of course I agreed; I had never thought of such a thing. But once the idea had been put into my head, and once I knew our timetable, it looked quite harmless. We had lectures and practice every morning — well, five mornings a week; this was a different world from hospital. As soon as we had some elementary skills batches of us would go to work in the physiotherapy department of the Adelaide Hospital in the afternoons. The other batches would be free during those afternoons. The practical work was arranged for periods of four or five weeks together, which would give me a clear run to sleep in the afternoons and do night duty during the weeks in between. Eventually this became too complicated. The doctor who had encouraged me to take up physio wanted — and paid for — half an hour of massage for herself in the mornings before class; she also sent me a few private patients. The free afternoons for some reason became more and more scarce. A time came when I had been on the go for seventy-two hours and the notes I was taking tapered off into drowsy squiggles every few lines. I recognised that night duty must be given up.

Clonskea was, at that time, a modern fever hospital, having provision for most patients to be isolated. It was built in blocks, each having a kitchen and office in the middle and ten or a dozen single-bed rooms stretching away either side, the rooms having observation windows in line so that staff could monitor them from the centre. Hanging in each room was a gown that we slipped on before attending to the patient. There was a four-bed, or four-cot ward at the end of one wing. I say 'four-cot' because when I was there the patients I encountered were almost all babies or young children. In the morning we would give the children a bowl of bread and milk called 'goody'; each baby, wrapped in a little bundle, its head on a pillow in the middle of a full adult-size white bed, would have a bottle, propped by a folded nappy, popped into its mouth. If a baby hadn't managed to suck its bottle when we returned we would pick it up and feed it, but the DIY system was normal. We felt quite fond of the poor little things, but it does not seem to have occurred to anyone that they needed to be held. Not that two of us could have held a dozen babies in one morning. I do not remember any of them crying much or making a fuss. Of course they were ill, but I suspect now that many of them must have been depressed. They certainly did not prepare me for the behaviour of well babies.

Neither had the babies and children in Baggot Street done so. The children's ward there was fortunately not large; it shared a landing with the private wards. The Sister in charge was very kind-hearted. I was not on duty there for long. I did not query the custom of the place. The nurses were fond of the children — more potential toddlers than babies — and would lean into their cots when passing and joke with them. Parents were allowed to visit for half an hour three times a week, but they had to go when the bell rang; everyone knew it was better for the children; they only got upset.

We did not actually think it was better for the children who were Dr Parsons' patients to be put sitting on an enamel potty when their beds were made in the morning and to stay sitting on it until a minute before he did his rounds. Dr Parsons must have been in his eighties. He was important. It was for his patients that I had had to poach eggs daily over the wet turf fire. He lived near the hospital and someone looking out of a front window of the children's ward would be able to see the top of his bald head as he came trotting along the path in his white coat, up the steps and in through the main door. Somebody always was looking out. The time it took him to greet Rooney, the Porter, proceed through the hall, along to the slow lift and up to us, was just time enough to slip the potties out from under his patients, leaving them with dry beds, though with a red ring imprinted on their bottoms. It was out of concern that he looked for wet beds; he did not know the cost. Years later an article of mine based on these experiences was not without effect.

The physiotherapy course I found congenial in itself and free from the shortcomings I had met in nursing. We each had to equip ourselves with a copy of *Grey's Anatomy* and half of a real skeleton. We were required not only to be famliar with every muscle but to be able to draw the bones to which they were attached and indicate the attachments. Naturally I was glad to have a reason to draw and I did it rather well. The School of Art seemed to have faded from my horizon but there are suggestions of confidence about anatomy in the very small wooden crib figures, Our Lady and St Joseph, a mixed bag of Kings and a couple of shepherds that I made one winter with a penknife and which come out every Christmas with various additions.

A major part of the course consisted of designing exercises to use the different muscle groups we were learning about, or to deal with specific problems. We did not just plan them, we performed them, and practised teaching them to each other, so we had excellent exercise every day, even without running. How easy it seemed then to stand up from sitting cross-legged without putting a hand to the floor, how remote a possibility now. We practised massage techniques on each other as well and of course we had lectures and exams on the relevant pathology. Relaxation was emphasised; stammering was the problem of one of my patients in the Adelaide and it seemed that my encouragement of relaxation was of benefit.

There was another SRN doing the course, but she was doing her post-registration spell in the Mater Hospital and had to go back on duty, or possibly work in her own physio department, every afternoon. Most of the other girls had come straight from school. Nobody else could feel quite as liberated as I did. Usually — when not involved with freelance nursing — I ran over to six o'clock Mass at the Carmelites in Gayfield, just across the road, then home, for breakfast, ran a carpet sweeper around the flat and left my room, the sittingroom, without trace of habitation. Then I would run in to Hume Street — jogging had not been invented, but the action was similar, save that summer and winter I wore sandals made by the local cobbler — pausing on the way to do that half-hour massage.

Sometimes at weekends or when I had a free afternoon my mother and I would buy a half bottle of wine and take a modest picnic up to the hills at Ballinteer. We had been doing that when I was in Baggot Street (one day off a month) and I did not drop everything just because I now had Seán. My mother sometimes had more or less professional reasons for these outings. To make a little extra money for herself she had had the idea of making stuffed toys, rabbits or squirrels or a simple horse, and making blanket pram-covers with appliqué pictures on them featuring the same animal. She offered them to Switzers and they wanted to buy all she could make. Naturally she did not repeat her designs; that would not have been any fun. So she became more creative with her animals, moving on from elephants and kangaroos to calves and lambs observed from life. When we went up the hills she would be noting which way the calves' ears were placed when at rest. Some more adventurous animals, like that splendid herringbone tweed goat with green eyes, had the honour of being commissioned by Nora McGuiness for window-dressing Brown Thomas. Even her elephants, from a standard pattern, were so elegantly harnessed that her designer granddaughter treasures one.

Then one of her friends introduced her to an organisation, the Apostolic Work, which made vestments for priests on the missions. She took this on, machined hundreds of yards of braid —heavens, maybe thousands — onto chasubles and stoles and maniples, and didn't make any more spare money. Not from sewing anyway; she made some from time to time by using my typewriter with two fingers to write stories for *The Messenger*, 'the little red Messenger'. Since I was living at home I contributed from my earnings.

She certainly did not have to depend on me for company. Back in Dublin she had not only old friends, the office crowd, and new friends, but three of her sisters within easy reach. She had even found houses for them — a cottage with an excellent garden for her eldest sister, Pidgie, who had returned after many years in the US and was now living on a Cumann na mBan pension and, I suppose, her savings, gardening, embroidering and reading Dickens and Edith Wharton. This was the sister who didn't marry because she had reared one woman's family and didn't want to rear another. Geg was back also, and lived with another sister and her husband and son in an attractive house looking down on the Dargle river, also located by Addie.

Addie and I managed pretty well together. On one matter we never agreed; she insisted that there was one right place for each thing and it was much easier to put it there to begin with. I argued that this system might make it easier to find things, but that it was obviously easier to put an object in any one of a hundred handy places than to seek out the one right one. What my mother cooked, she cooked well, but cooking had never interested her very much. Rationing was still in force for butter, tea, sugar; we drank coffee, so often shared our tea coupons. Bananas were a remote memory; it was considered a clever idea to mash cooked parsnips and flavour them with banana essence. I must even confess that the coffee we drank was usually a brown syrup out of a bottle labelled 'Irel'. This did not bother us; we had come from a country only beginning to patch itself up after a three-year civil war. When I was at home for a meal I was more likely than not to cook it, especially likely if Seán had been invited. One of my reliable dishes was a casserole of heart. Calf's heart, I think. It gave me an excellent opportunity for dissection, it was cheap and, with plenty of parsley, well flavoured. It was only after marriage that I learnt that the poor man found everything from inside an animal, save for neatly sliced liver, quite repugnant. He wouldn't mind doing without liver either.

We had plenty of time to go house-hunting. I had to finish my course, and he, we hoped, had to recover properly, though he was in ordinary health between bouts of inflammation. One of our plans was to build a house from the stones lying on the side of the Sugarloaf mountain, but it proved impossible to get a site; the whole area was held in common by fourteen owners of goats. I do not remember how we found a five-roomed cottage near the top of Carraig Olligan — a hill familiarly known as Katty Gallagher. The climb up from Shankill railway station took the best part of half an hour. The road — the Quarry Road — was steep and very rough. The view from the windows was just lovely; on our left, Killiney Head tapering out towards Dalkey Island, in front the sea stretching over to sometimes-visible Wales, to the right, Bray Head with its ancient clumsy outline making a full stop.

The owners were two brothers, who were all that was left of a family that had lived in an older cottage and had built a new one; now they were moving back into the old home and asking seven hundred pounds for this. There was a half acre of garden; rates were minute; the problem was to persuade a building society to give us a mortgage. We managed; Seán was back in full-time work; I had saved enough, with some money my father had given me, to put down a deposit of one hundred and fifty pounds.

I am not sure why we did not get married right away. We waited, spending Saturdays and Sundays breathing in dark green dust, until Seán had been a year back at work. All five rooms and the hall up the middle of the house had been distempered a dull green and it appeared to be necessary to scrape every scrap of it off. Either emulsion paint was waiting to be invented, or we did not know that it can obliterate colours underneath. Some friends of Sean's dismantled the black range and built up a raised hearth in its place. Why? Possibly the range was defective, but I suspect it was just because I detested the idea of polishing it with black-lead and I fancied using a pot-oven. It happened to be a very hard winter; snow lasted for six weeks. Whenever we paused to rest on our climb up the hill, as we heaved up cans of paint or wood for shelves, we could gaze all round at a brilliant white landscape and a shining sea. Once on our own, working away indoors, we agreed that we would not so much as kiss; too distracting.

One evening a week the two of us went to carpentry classes in town. I was the only female student and I regret to say that I did not continue for very long. Probably night duty interfered. I had qualified as a chartered physiotherapist and saw some patients in my mother's sittingroom but I found it convenient to register with an agency and let them find freelance nursing jobs for me. I should not have cared to work as a private nurse in the day time; not enough to do. Nights were not so bad; I stitched and embroidered some nightdresses for myself, in silk and fine cotton and linen.

We assembled essential furniture; first a coffee mill and two soup spoons, then a square deal table and two folding chairs, bought for half a crown each, which have been re-seated and re-painted often enough to look quite well in the conservatory, where we now have lunch in middling weather. Then the pot-oven and a primus stove, some pots and pans and an Irish-made tea set which included a square, lidded pottery box designed to hold a honey comb. Seán had learnt enough about wood to be able to make a base to fit the extra-long mattress ordered for our bed.

How did it happen that my father gave us a handwoven striped Avoca blanket? Did he choose it himself, or did we buy it with the five pounds he left when he blew off a week before our wedding? Here I need to backtrack a few years. When he retired he found that because of the war he could not easily travel north from Nigeria so he went to South Africa instead and bought a house, sold that and bought another. That did not last long either; he sold it at a loss and, I think, went from there to Mexico. I think he chose Mexico because he was not yet old enough to go free in the Argentine; having been born there he should have done military service and could be imprisoned for evasion if he went back before the age of sixty or sixty-five. At some point he found that it was as cheap to travel backwards and forwards across the Atlantic in a small cargo ship as it was to live in a *pension* or to buy a house, so he arrived in Dublin now and again.

He arrived in Dublin, then, to find that the daughter who was to go and housekeep for him when he got to his native land was entangled with an unsuitable young Irishman. He and Seán had a heated discussion in the sittingroom while Addie and I waited in the diningroom or listened at the door. The bit I remember is his claim that I was too good for Seán because I knew so many languages. Biased; Seán had good Irish and was even brushing up my skimpy Latin grammar. Denis's parents invited all four of us — Addie, Alex, myself and Seán, over to their house in Clontarf. Denis had met Seán, an encounter that he had reported back with amusement, but this was Sid and Florrie's introduction. It is to be remembered that the family

107

friendship went back to the time Sid and Alex had worked in the same office as young men.

The four of us went out to Clontarf together by bus. We got off at the right corner, walked up Vernon Avenue, went in the gate, rang at the door, which was opened at once to welcome us, and then Alex stated that he could not believe until he had seen it that he would be insulted by being invited along with that man, turned around and walked away. That left six people dumbfounded for a little while — Denis was of course there as well. Then we shrugged, said more or less 'That's Alex for you', sat down to tea and had a happy evening. Seán and I never forgot the support that Sid and Florrie gave just when we needed it. They said they only had to see the way we looked at each other.

Time had passed. We had arranged to be married in April. Alex turned up again. Was he going to stay for the ceremony? No. He made a last attempt to dissuade me, left the five pounds and went off again. We would have had a problem if he had stayed because whenever he came to the flat he took over the sittingroom as his bedroom and we needed it for our home-made wedding breakfast. We were married as early as possible — I had suggested six o'clock, but the priest's eyebrows went up. Haddington Road, where I used to go to Mass while in Baggot Street, was parish church for both of us. We both had our Latin missals, listened to and read the long blessing that looked back to Rebecca and Isaac, Jacob and Rachel. We let the rest of the party — Tera was my bridesmaid — go back to the flat by car, but we wanted to walk. We had chosen well; all the gardens along the quiet roads were bright with flowering currant and cherries and forsythia. Sid met us and took photographs. Upstairs I put the ready-measured coffee into a very large pot of simmering water and we had a crowded happy party. An aunt I have hardly mentioned had given us a wedding cake, the rest I had made myself. We had some sort of sparkling wine but didn't really need it, then the taxi came to bring us up to our hillside cottage. We had, of course, cases to unload and Seán had some mystery packages. They needed several trips between car and house. We sat down on our new hearth rug — I think that was one of the surprises — and looked at the white wedgewood vases and some other pleasing things he had chosen as gifts from friends of his. A colleague had given us a most welcome supply of large white towels.

But who had been so kind as to give us two pounds of butter?

Eventually we learnt that it had been the week's ration for the taxi-driver's family.

CHAPTER 11

Life together
with a well and a spinning wheel

That first afternoon together we were almost blown apart, but only literally. We went up the hill to collect armloads of the white sticks from old burnt furze bushes for a fire; when we reached the top we were met by an enormously strong wind on the other side which forced us to crouch in the lee of a low bank. The brothers who sold us the house had told us it was 'a great place for drying turf' and so it was.

Next thing was to make a meal. Our plan was to spend two weeks on our own in our own new territory. We felt like children playing house but knowing it was real. I had planned meals day by day and got in the supplies we'd need. The first was easy; pasta with tomato sauce; Seán made a good try; he ate some all right, but had to go out to the garden to get sick. He came back and we both apologised like anything, but I had to revise my menus. It wasn't only heart he disliked, it was the whole boiling of southern pasta and rice meals which are now commonplace in Ireland but were not so then. We could not foresee that for the next forty years whenever the children and I had that sort of meal I'd have to make something traditional for Seán.

Neither could we foresee after our first time in bed together how well we could learn to make love. In fact, we went for a silent walk, sat down in shelter, and one of us said, 'Well, I'm glad we didn't get married just for that.' We had what may seem to some the disadvantage of complete inexperience, but to my mind the great advantage of confidence, of having no misgivings. Tolstoy, deploring his own introduction by a prostitute, says that a person's first experience of intercourse will colour everything afterwards. By definition, I have no way of comparing, but it seems to me that two people who love each other and learn together, neither having anything different to look back to, may be fortunate.

Our days were full; putting the house together, digging the garden, reading separately or together, going to the top of Carraig Olligan when the wind moderated. From there we could see another view of the Sugarloaf that had filled the landscape of my childhood. We were so happy that we could even spare a little time for other people and took a long walk down towards Bray to visit my aunts. Of course we went down to Shankill for Mass on Sundays. I used a beautiful Missale Romanum, all Latin, printed in black and red on interesting paper and bound in vellum, the whole having cost half a crown, that's one eighth of a pound. Seán possibly had better value; a plain black binding, but he had paid only sixpence for it. Five sixpences in half-a-crown. And my mantilla — women still had to have their heads covered — cost less and lasted longer than a hat.

We were too far from the church to consider daily, or more or less daily, Mass. In part at least influenced by Eric Gill and Fr McNabb we had become members of the Third Order of St Dominic, together we would recite the psalms of matins and lauds in what is called The Little Office, one that does not have the complicated permutations of the Office recited in monasteries. We rarely bought a newspaper; the only magazines we subscribed to were *The Listener*, which was remarkable value at sixpence a time, the monthly *Blackfriars*, a far-sighted Dominican publication and, before long, a pocket-sized monthly called *Housewife*. It seems hardly credible now that while I was managing two babies and expecting another we don't seem to have been aware of the great public and political row about Dr Noel Browne's Mother and Child Bill.

I have moved ahead a little. The house itself faced east, so we could from our bedroom see the sun rising out of the sea. There were four rooms in a block, divided by a hall, with another small room tacked on in front, leaving a corresponding room-sized square behind, sheltered from every side and getting full sun for most of the day. A space cut off from the kitchen was wide enough for a sink. Into a narrow little room beside the back door we put an Elsan (chemical toilet, as on planes) and a shelf to hold a hand basin. (In good weather we could manage a shower by each throwing a bucket of water over the other.) One room at the back was our sittingroom; Seán had already lined the available wall-space with bookshelves, but the north wall in the other room was in such bad condition that we used it for storing turf.

Drinking water we brought from a spring at the top of the neighbouring field, a field full of corn marigolds and tiny pansies. Washing water was caught in rain barrels. Light came from candles, plus a couple of oil lamps; cooking was done with a pressure cooker on the primus stove or in the pot-oven on the turf fire. A pot-oven is a round cast-iron lidded pot with a flat base and three legs; it sits or stands on a turf fire, and the cook covers the lid with bits of burning turf. It is an excellent way of baking soda bread, brown or white, and I found I could even make a lemon meringue pie in it as well as ordinary cakes; when I tried to roast meat it turned into a stew.

All this was satisfactory. The walk up the hill was good for us. After several years we decided that only on about six days a year was the weather bad enough to make it really disagreeable, though we did feel that it was too much for our elderly 'temporary' postman. He had been 'temporary' all his life so couldn't claim a pension. We made some arrangement to collect letters further down the road.

There were just two drawbacks. The kitchen floor was made of worn concrete which we painted but which must have been poured straight onto the ground, because when I washed it it would take a couple of days to dry properly, this in spite of the gales that blew through if back and front doors were open. The other drawback was the paraffin. We needed it for the primus and the lamps. One lamp was designed so that it had to be pumped, like the primus, to release the paraffin vapour under pressure, and the two of them were only waiting for an excuse to choke if a speck of dirt got in. Now and again we were able to buy clean paraffin but most often our filter would catch enough flakes of rusty metal to send to a scrapyard. In hospital I learnt to loathe the polishing of copper and brass; during these first years I learnt to loathe paraffin.

The civilised reader will probably expect me to add the Elsan to the list of drawbacks. Not so. It would be the rare day that Seán didn't bring home one or two second-hand books under his arm. Quite early on he brought Sir Albert Howard's *Farming and Gardening for Health or Disease*. I cannot refrain from mentioning that after looking at the screen of my word-processor for a long time, trying to remember not only the name of the book but even Sir Albert's surname, I went just now to look among gardening books and couldn't find it. I knew I had lent it to one of our sons and had retrieved it a couple of years ago. I have just now fished out a faded, raggy Faber & Faber dustjacket from a higgledy-piggledy shelf and find that Seán paid two shillings in 1947 for this seminal book, which had been published in Mcmxlv, which is surely only two years earlier. A few sentences from the Preface:

> The purpose of this book is to emphasise the importance of solar energy and the vegetable kingdom in human affairs...to establish the thesis that most of this disease can be traced to an impoverished soil.... During the course of the campaign for the reform of agriculture, now in active progress all over the world, I have not hesitated to question the soundness of present-day agricultural teaching and research — due to failure to recognise that the problems of farm and garden are biological rather than chemical. It follows, therefore, that the foundations on which the artificial manure and poison spray industries are based are unsound.

Further on in the book, in a chapter headed 'Industrialism and the profit motive', I find this:

> The remedy is simple. We must look at our present civilization as a whole and realize once and for all the great principle that the activities of homo sapiens, which have created the machine age in which we are now living, are based on a very insecure basis — the surplus food made available by the plunder of the stores of soil fertility which are not ours but are the property of generations yet to come.

At present, every document that comes from The Green Party/Comhaontas Glas has at the foot of the page, 'We do not inherit the earth from our parents, we borrow it from our children.'

Meanwhile, the practical lesson we learnt from Sir Albert was to use the Indore method of composting. We divided the vegetable garden into three sections. In one, when the Elsan needed to be emptied, we would dig a fairly deep pit and fill it with armloads of green stuff cut from the ditches around, then pour in the remains of what we had eaten during the last couple of weeks and fill it up with soil. On this third we would sow only things that came far out of the earth — peas and beans. What peas! Never before or since have I had more sweet, fresh peas than I could eat. Next year, cabbages and things would go on that section, and in the third year, root vegetables. And in that third year we had a demonstration. We — well, mainly me — put in the potatoes in the usual ridges across the plot, the section that had been first manured as described. The plants developed in a pattern along each row; three or four very tall and strong, the next few shorter, then another group of tall ones, showing where we had dug those pits. A better way of dealing with the matter than throwing it into the

Atlantic, as we had done in Kilkerran, and as so many towns are doing still.

The strawberry bed did not share in this system. I made ordinary compost into which one poured a subtle mixture of herbs, the 'Quick Return' package. Perhaps that suited them or perhaps that patch had been fallow for a long time. I had provided myself with the largest size in cream-coloured pottery cooking bowls and the berries would be piled up and spilling out of it. Once or twice in the season people who had climbed to the top of the hill came to the gate and asked if there were tea rooms anywhere around. It was a pleasure to bring them in for tea with fresh brown bread and dishes of strawberries and cream, then send them back down delighted with Irish hospitality. The drawback to the strawberry bed was, of course, the weeding; my poor mother used to say that that was what I gave her to do every time she offered to help in the garden.

During the first year, or at least the first seven or eight months, I used to go into town on the train with Seán a couple of mornings a week to look after the patients who continued to come to my mother's flat. Every bit of extra money was useful. Seán's salary was twenty pounds a month but his mother needed five for the rent of her flat. A delightful surprise arrived when we had been only a few weeks married: an aunt of my father's left some money to be divided between her great-nieces and nephews; my share was seventeen pounds — more than a whole months regular income. We had the often recommended box with envelopes for mortgage and train fares and food; there wasn't any gas or electricity bill, only paraffin, which, however smelly, is at any rate cheap. We felt ourselves to be quite comfortable and Seán somehow managed to keep enough by to get me a private room in Holles Street Hospital when Barbara was born.

I have said that I am incapable of social dancing but we danced together when we decided that a baby was almost certainly part of our future. At the same time I mean to put it on record that, as far as I can tell, if years had gone by without increase, neither of us would have been upset. We would not have gone for tests, much less taken drugs that might encourage triplets. I was never what Margaret Mead calls a 'pram peeper', a woman who is charmed by every passing baby. Never the less, like most future parents, we were delighted. Future parents, that is, expecting a first or second child; later it's not quite the same, but time enough to think about that problem.

It must have been quite good weather for February when I packed a small case and walked down the hill, bought some Mars Bars in the shop at the bottom, and caught a bus in to Holles Street. From a call box on the street I telephoned Seán at his office and told him that contractions were coming at such regular intervals that it seemed best to go in to the maternity hospital. I had not done midwifery but I had found a useful book by a physiotherapist which told about the positions Indian women use when giving birth, explained how to curve one's spine so as to place the birth canal at the best angle. This was another example of my habit of betting on the horse which is going to win the race next week, or next year. Birthing chairs, not to speak of Dr Clifford Odent and birth under water, did not appear in glossy magazines until after my eleven babies had made their way as best they could. Two or three memories stand out. When I was offered pethidine I said 'No thanks'. The gynaecologist wanted to know why. I replied that I wanted to be as good as my grandmother. He asked whether I had been reading Dr Grantley Dick-Reade; I hadn't. By this time I was in a delivery room with two high beds in it; the baby in the other bed was born and I could see it through the screen being held up by its miniature ankles and thought it quite wonderful.

A little later it dawned on me that something was happening that was going to go on whether I wanted it to or not. I had read about it, but that's not the same. The uterus takes on a life of its own. At least I could try squatting to help it manage. The Sister was dismissive. 'Lie down if you don't want the baby to be a pancake.' Not a phrase one easily forgets. But even while I was lying down the energetic creature inside me was insisting that I push. At the same time the Sister was insisting that I hold on, wait until the Master comes. The Master being the Master of Holles Street, the National Maternity Hospital, a time-honoured title. I really didn't have the option of waiting. A wonderful cork-out-of-bottle explosion, pain-stopping, and in a few minutes they showed me a tiny wrapped-up person with glossy black hair like a Chinese, who looked at me out of one eye and whose fragile fingers grasped mine definitively.

Then I was wheeled back to the bed I had left, bringing the book I had been using for distraction — Johnson's *Rasselas, Prince of Abyssinia* — and I felt under the pillow until I found the Mars Bar I had providently tucked away. For weeks past I had had such heartburn that eating almost anything had been disagreeable. Two o'clock in the morning was a nice time for a snack and a comfortable, curled-up sleep.

114

Not so good when I woke. There were five other mothers in the ward and they all had babies. I hadn't. What had happened? Then I was in a single room with a small bedside cot. Did I try to have her in bed with me? I can't be sure. Seán came in and my mother and his mother, probably one at a time, because the hospital did not want new mothers to be tired out. In spite of their care, on the second or third day I found tears pouring down my face and I couldn't stop them. I told the doctor that I never cried; he mentioned, too late, 'baby blues'. By this time baby was crying a great deal. I thought I was feeding her but she didn't seem satisfied. She cried all night, her two little blue eyes open, and I felt so sorry for her. Hospital rules didn't allow a feed from a bottle. Another visitor was a doctor, friend of a friend. She was certain that one of the commonest problems with breast-fed babies was overfeeding.

Underfeeding I did not take into my calculations, nor did anyone else. The book on which I relied at this stage was by Dr Truby-King, something like a twentieth edition of his book on breast-feeding, of which the basic premise was that every mother could breast-feed successfully, even adoptive mothers.

Barbara Mary was baptised, as was customary, in Westland Row Church, where a delegation from the National Maternity Hospital could be expected every few days. Copies of the Baptismal Service were not to be had, so Seán wrote it out by hand, copies for all the family friends.

Then the new family went back to its mountain home. Not really a mountain, but starting from sea level the road was steep enough. My mother, newly a grandmother, made her way up after a couple of days. The weather had changed; there was a threat of snow. She found Barbara outside in her little bed with a hot-water bottle (properly wrapped) beside her, myself hardly able to walk, left leg almost refusing to function, and Seán in bed in a state of shock. We had been sure we could manage on our own but we couldn't. An energetic grandmother was very welcome indeed.

Seán recovered. It seemed that my lameness was probably related to shortage of vitamin B12, a deficiency found more often during pregnancy. I too recovered and got used to washing nappies and boiling them in a bucket on the primus stove. The person who didn't get better was the baby. I did everything Dr Truby-King advised, fed her strictly to timetable, splashed my breast with hot and cold water alternately, drank a great deal. By the time she was six weeks old I had given up the timetable and had been feeding her non-stop all day and most of the night. I got a bottle and gave her albumin-water (white of egg), the only milk-substitute the wise doctor permitted. We brought her down to the hospital, to a post-natal clinic, and found that she was still at her birth weight. Test-feeding showed that she was getting about two ounces of milk in a whole day.

From then on, for the next eight babies, it was complementary feeds; breast first, for a few minutes, while the bottle was warming up or cooling down. I always seemed to have some milk, but it cannot have been a significant amount because when baby number ten arrived the midwife, who had come to know me quite well, said, why bother. I didn't bother, and didn't have any bother either stopping the hypothetical flow.

I do not know why I was inadequate in this when my mother and my four daughters who have had babies were well provisioned. I think now that I went to a great deal of needless trouble because numbers ten and eleven, who had milk from a bottle whenever they wanted it, turned out to be healthy, affectionate, energetic chaps who would have been a match for any of the children in Dr Truby-King's photographs if they could have come face-to-face.

But once Barbara had some nourishment she was full of energy. She could really get around, creeping or crawling, by the time she was five months old. I made her a tough little outfit of trousers and tunic and it wasn't long before she crawled out the front door, round the house and in the back door. We had another adviser besides the discredited Truby-King: *Commonsense in the Nursery* by Mrs Frankenberg, published by Penguin. The Commonsense was rather diluted by the assumption that the reader employed a nanny, but we took seriously the insistence on providing children with as much fresh air as possible. It's laughable now to think how much trouble we took, when our windswept house had as much fresh air inside as out. The baby slept in the largest size Moses' basket. Whenever she was sleeping we would insert it into a well-made packing case of sufficient size, arranged with its back to the wind, so that the basket and its contents were sheltered on three sides and from above.

When she was awake the basket was carried from room to room, wherever I was. She would be propped up enough to see what was going on and to handle all the variety I could find: egg cup, wooden spoon, leather glove, furry toy, stone from the sea shore, boxes that fitted into each other. Once she could sit up unsupported, out of her basket, I sometimes gave her a paint brush and some paint to dab on the enamel top of a small table, turned on its side, making a sort of easel. This was before she was a year old. And at eleven months she could feed herself with a spoon. She was so eager to grab the spoon with which I was feeding her that I used to have three spoons in action; she would have one in each hand while I was loading the third, then she would drop one and reach for the one I had replenished. When she was eleven months old we got a low chair with attached tray and I could arrange her in that with food of suitable texture and let her scoop it up herself.

Day time was fine; she would usually sleep for a while in the afternoon and so would I. The siesta was a habit I cherished. Night was not so good. I remember evenings when Seán and I sat in the kitchen whispering as we read together (Tacitus or St Thomas, in Latin, on alternate evenings), moving only on tiptoe, but no matter how careful we were the rocking of the cot next door would commence and get more and more violent, until we felt we must go in and persuade the little person standing up so defiantly in her white nightie that the night was made for sleeping and the day returns too soon.

What success we had would be only temporary; for the next twenty years unbroken nights were rare delights.

CHAPTER 12

The Golden Age.
A learning child is a happy child

We have just reached the bottom of Quarry Road. We are, for some forgotten reason, in the car of a friend or acquaintance. I am in the back. Seán, in front, makes some reference to the weekly paper, *Hibernia*, and its editor, Basil Clancy. 'Ah, yes,' said the driver. 'They have nine children, haven't they?'

I heard and was thunder struck. People couldn't. I knew, of course, that my mother was one of ten, but everything had been different then. When she and Geg had been working in London and stayed in a hostel full of Irish girls theirs had been the smallest family. I was happy with Barbara and little Alasdar, I supposed I might eventually welcome one or two more, but nine would be nonsense.

It could be that Dr Halliday Sutherland's book about the Rhythm Method was nonsense; he did write years later that he would not apologise for some specific miscalculation which might have led to an extra baby here and there. We had no reason to blame that miscalculation; it was the Method itself that we were mistaken in adopting. Mind you, at the time, in Ireland, even to have the book was to be rather avant-garde. As I said earlier, we were in the habit of reading *Blackfriars* and the *Catholic Herald*, a very lively paper then, and Seán knew what to ask for. Halliday Sutherland was 'under the counter' in Catholic bookshops. If one were to mention in confession that one, or rather self and spouse, were using Rhythm, one would be told that it was permissible only in special circumstances.

Neither of us asked. It was apparent to us that it was logically nonsense to see anything wrong in refraining from intercourse at one time or another. Outside marriage one had to refrain; inside, it must be the couple's decision. We had no notion then of the special logic of 'tradition', in effect, of the thought of St Augustine. Since we did not know, I do not intend to discuss this literally vital question until the stage in my story when such discussion was filling double pages of Letters to the Editor day after day.

One central point I must make clear. We understood perfectly well that refraining from eating meat on Friday was a Church law, from which one might dispense oneself for all sorts of reasons. Mass on Sunday was a specific ruling related to the Commandment to keep holy the Sabbath Day, but again there might be dozens of valid reasons for non-observation. The prohibition of contraception was, we were constantly told, part of the Natural Law, available to all human beings without benefit of church or revelation. Humans were provided with Organs of Generation for the purpose of Generation. Full stop. It has become clear that the early Christian Church took this view over from the most influential Greek philosophers; it was, in theory at least, the standard of the best Roman families of the time.

This same standard had prevailed in Europe for at least fifteen hundred years. It cannot be surprising that we acknowledged it and acknowledged it as human beings, not as obedient Catholics. Oddly enough, nobody compared it with the Natural Law prohibition of incest, but such was the implication of the term, Natural Law.

So I must ask any readers who are frightened by the present population explosion to make an effort of imagination. After all, it seems that at that time the Pope understood warnings of explosion to be a Communist plot, while Chairman Mao dismissed them as a fabrication by capitalists.

And we did not recognise any warnings of a domestic explosion when Alasdar arrived fifteen months after Barbara, and the two of them were so enjoyable that really the arrival of Tinu fifteen months later was welcome. I had found Holles Street horribly hot and noisy when I went there for Barbara and Alasdar so I decided to stay at home for Tinu. Electricity had arrived only a week or so beforehand, not without urgent requests to St Philomena, making home more suitable than it had been. There were two grandmothers willing to take on one child each, Barbara to Granny Ad, Alasdar to Granny Martina (after whom Tinu was to be called, if she turned out to be a girl).

Oddly enough what's imprinted on my memory, as on the memories of Konrad Lorenz' ducks, is the duck I embroidered on the pocket of Alasdar's linen trousers during the last hours of waiting. When he was brought back home and introduced to the new sister he was wearing the duck and walked over looking lovely and so much older than I remembered — this at fifteen months. But I've noticed this every time; once you have a very small new baby the one who seemed small before, the poor knee baby, seems surprisingly grown up.

And new sister had looked lovely as well, crinkled and purple, but lovely. This was the first time I had a proper chance to see what was emerging. The midwife was of the traditional sort; her mother had been a midwife too; I was startled to find she had never trained as a nurse. I was by now devoted to Grantly Dick-Reade and relaxation so the midwife and I were not on the same wavelength. She could offer a couple of aspirin; they really did not meet my needs. I wanted to read for distraction, she wanted to tell me about new mothers who had 'just stood up out of the bed and dropped dead on the floor'.

To assemble the first half of the family, the hill dwellers, it should be enough to mention that Janet, the fourth, was born in a nursing home in Dún Laoghaire. By that time we had a telephone so it was possible to ring for a taxi, and walk halfway down the hill to meet it at three in the morning. A young nurse who was looking after me this time was much impressed by the technique of relaxing 'into' a contraction. I told her, there's a contraction now; she checked and said that if she ever had a baby she would like to have it like me. My control of affairs was interrupted by a command to come down to the labour ward — walk down three flights of stairs. After that experience I decided to stay at home again. This baby, the fifth, Máire Claire, was delivered to a mother who was considerably amused. Having had experience of how well pethidine suited me I arranged with the midwife — a properly trained nurse this time — to have an ampoule of the stuff at hand, to give myself when I was sure labour had started. When Seán rang for her she couldn't be found. It happened to be the fifteenth of August, the feast of the Assumption, and she was at Mass. I was sufficiently removed from the pressure of events by the pethidine, so I was sitting up in bed while Seán hurried backwards and forwards to see how I was getting on and then to look desperately down the lane. She arrived at exactly the right moment to catch the baby's head and all was well.

So, during our seven years on Carraig Olligan I learnt a number of things: vegetable growing, relaxation, spinning wool and weaving, sewing. I had made those trousers of Alasdar's from a pattern in *Housewife* and I had devised a way of making them so that they were completed, with lining, elastic across the back, buttons on shoulder straps, within an hour. I would just cut out and stitch two the same, one to be the outside, the other the lining, fit one inside the other with the straps in place, stitch them together all around the top, turn the result outside out and they were almost complete. It is agreeable when you find a better way and it works. Spinning was not labour-saving but it was remarkably enjoyable; I found it as agreeable as reading. Seán had seen a demonstration, encouraged me to go for a few lessons while I was still free, and gave me a spinning wheel as a first anniversary present. His mother used to knit enduring socks for him out of the wool I spun; when holes appeared I could knit in a repair. I made a little jersey for Alasdar using some wool I had dyed with onion skins and cochineal as well as the natural white. I have it still. Unfortunately I sometimes sat out in the sun to spin and the wheel warped and came apart. Some of the wool went for weaving on a proper six-heddle loom, but life had become too crowded for me to progress with this.

Seán built on a very satisfactory three-level lean-to all along the damp north wall of the house. One space, near the rain-barrels, was for laundry and held an electric boiler and a non-electric wringer. In the middle was a well-lighted platform for the loom, and next to that, at a lower level, Seán's work bench that he had made himself at a carpentry class. The whole kept the north wall dry and enabled us to put children instead of turf into the fourth room.

We made new friends, especially Colm and Nora O'Laoghaire who bought a house half way up the hill and called it 'At Swim Two Birds'. We still invite each other to meals and Nora is the friend every woman needs — the confidante, the one with whom you chat about anything that's happening, whether in the news or in the home. At that time they were friends in need — or was it the other way round? It was certainly Seán and I who were in need of a real bath with hot water coming out of a tap and this they had and invited us to use. Their first children were born while we were still neighbours.

Round the far side of the hill was another house, no larger than ours but with a charm quite lacking to our little box, and having in the garden something I still covet, a Daphne odora, a shrub of modest size and far-reaching scent. Yvonne and Thurloe Connolly lived there for a couple of years with their two little boys, he painting, she doing so many things in just her own way that I believe she influenced me a great deal. For example, Yvonne would hardly knit a plain jersey; mysterious unrepeated designs grew from her knitting needles, so I added colours also, but mine were never mysterious. After all, they were the only people we knew who had children. Though by no means in thrall to print as Seán and I were, Yvonne found it as natural to help her boys to read as to show them how to play the bamboo flutes she made.

This seemed quite natural to us also, but helping the children to learn had become a more organised activity since Seán had brought home a book published in 1912, *The Montessori Method,* by Professor Culverwell, then Professor of Education in Trinity College Dublin. This introduced us to ways of thinking and doing which became more and more significant and which, I believe, compensated both myself and the children for the hardships that are scarcely avoidable in the life of a large family.

Professor Culverwell had visited Montessori's Casa degli bambini in Rome about 1906, when she had observed the essentials of her Method. She had seen that young children love to learn, that they do best if they are given things with which they can do some specific activity, are shown how to do it properly, and then left to their own decision as to whether to do this or something else, to just watch the other children or to go elsewhere to play. She saw that most often they chose to 'work' and got highly visible satisfaction from completing a plan, such as putting one or more sets of wooden cylinders into their correct holes in a wooden block. Each cylinder was designed, short or tall, wide or narrow, to fit into only one hole. The satisfaction comes from 'Getting It Right'.

A set of cylinders would be a fine thing to have but was out of reach at the beginning. Fortunately, toy manufacturers had learnt that children like to fit one thing into another and had produced various sets of plastic containers graded in size. The first set of four, square in section, in heavy plastic, was very good for a baby sitting up in her basket. While she experimented with one of these in each hand her father cut geometric shapes, square, circle, triangles, ellipse, out of squares of plywood and varnished them to make the 'insets' which Montessori found so beneficial. We bought a set of multi-coloured plastic pyramid rings, designed to be assembled around a wooden pole.

We wanted to be ready in case Barbara should be interested. We had noted that Montessori had started with children of two and a half but we realised that if the child is to have even a modest choice we would need to assemble a few things in good time. And what would be good time? It had seemed natural once she was able to sit up to give her a pencil and a sheet of paper to make marks on. I have mentioned in the last chapter the paintbrush and the perpendicular table-top. This had been prompted by some reference to Japanese babies being shown how to paint. Someone who at eleven months is able to hold a paintbrush and to feed herself with a spoon will use a pencil properly without further instruction. Now, we had noted that Montessori stressed the importance of showing her children how to hold the knobs on top of the cylinders so that they would later hold pencils correctly, this for children already more than two and a half. One had to take into account cultural and economic background. A poor Roman family at the turn of the century didn't have reams of roneoed office paper on the back of which to draw, pencils would not have been lying around, crayons were not cheap. They would, on the other hand, have had abundant charcoal. I'm inclined to pat myself on the back for providing this for our children; it makes a much stronger line than pencil or crayon.

It was evident that Montessori's materials are in two senses self-correcting. Those cylinders will each fit only into the hole that is right for it. We could do no harm by showing a baby such things; if they were right for her she would want to use what was on offer, if she only wanted to throw things around we could take them away and give her a soft ball. (As well as her animals, Granny Ad made baby-right felt balls stuffed with kapok.)

I can best explain how influential this recognition turned out to be by a quotation within a quotation. In 1983 a book I had written about the family experience, *Anything School Can Do, You Can Do Better*, was published. In the introduction I said:

> I have just written, in the opening paragraph, that attitudes both to school and to early learning have changed radically since the forties and fifties. There is no reason why readers should have to take this on faith. I can produce most telling evidence from Professor J. McVicar Hunt of the University of Illinois. He was speaking to assembled psychologists when he said, in 1963:
>
> > Even as late as 15 years ago, a symposium on the stimulation of early cognitive learning would have been taken as a sign that the participants and members of the audience were too softheaded to be taken seriously.
>
> > Now, if you go back fifteen years from 1963 you find yourself in 1948 — the very year in which we had begun to busy ourselves with showing an eight-month-old baby how to fit squares and triangles into matching spaces.

In that book my purpose was to describe what opportunities we offered to the children and what use they made of them in later life, incidentally informing parents that the Irish Constitution regarded them as primary educators and did not compel them to send their children to school. In this one I am writing about me. But if the observer is part of the experiment, the experiment is part of the observer. When I said 'triangle' and 'circle' to my first daughter and took the wooden shapes out and in and she tried to do the same and showed she was satisfied when they fitted, I shared her satisfaction, remembering that when I was small I had liked to get things right. I was also pleased that in 'trying them out' with her I had got something right again.

If I can reconstruct an ordinary day when Barbara was three and a half, Alasdar two and a quarter and Tinu a year old, then perhaps I can show that involvement in early learning was a good investment for myself as well as for the children. Since this was after Tinu's arrival we had the electric cooker to make breakfast. For breakfast Tinu would sit in the chair with a tray, the other two at a low table that Seán had made. Ten minutes after Seán had left the house we would go to the door and wave when he reached the stretch of road that we could see and he would wave back. We might look out again to see his train. Then we would wash up the breakfast things in a dish on the table with water boiled in the electric kettle. The children would help dry and replace knives with knives, spoons with spoons. Then a question: would you like to do insets first, or tracing? It might be numbers or sewing. I, rightly, saw geometric insets as the backbone of the system, so I'll suppose Alasdar chose insets, Barbara tracing. We had, of course, washed hands for breakfast. Now we must wash hands again before using insets or needles or whatever. Washing hands Montessori style is a ritual; the child pours water into a child-high basin (Seán had fixed one in our 'bathroom'), washes attentively, dries each finger individually. I used to say, 'One little finger, two little fingers, three little fingers, four. And a THUMB.'

Barbara's tracing was from *Writing and Writing Patterns* by Marion Richardson; we had learnt about them from the author Herbert Reed. The children who used them grew up to have fine handwriting, basically italic, and in the meantime made pocket money from prizes in newspaper competitions. The insets chosen by Alasdar were the same wooden shapes which we had offered to Barbara when she was eight months old and which he had been introduced to at the same age. At first they give the simple satisfaction of fitting in and at the same time focus the child's attention on abstract shapes, shapes that are significant in themselves but which also seem likely to help later identification of letters. At two and a quarter Alasdar was familiar with letters and would be 'doing' an inset.

'Doing' an inset meant choosing one shape, say the ellipse or the pentagon, placing the plywood square from which it had been cut carefully on a sheet of paper and using it to guide a pencil to draw the chosen shape. The fact that it has been chosen is important. I would have to hold the square in position; at first each child needed a fair amount of guidance to help draw straight lines — hand movements are naturally curved — to make them begin at one edge and end at the other, and keep the lines closer and closer together. Some people think that such activity is unsuitable for children. It seemed to me that they appreciated a task which they could understand and at which they could see for themselves that they were getting better and better, that they had got it right. My guidance included words and phrases like 'inside' and 'outside', 'over the edge', 'a bit longer', 'could you fit a line between those two?' and 'Good, that's a lovely straight line', all parts of a useful store for people beginning to talk. And, of course, they had chosen to do insets in preference to some other learning activity or to going off to play with the toy town or with the dish of water that usually waited out in the sun.

Each child in turn mastered this skill, but Alasdar's insets were outstanding; one could forecast a career as a forger of banknotes. In fact when he was studying engineering he entered for the apprentice competition in technical drawing. The other competitors were working full-time as draughtsmen, he was doing a few hours a week; he took first place in freehand technical drawing, second place overall. The rest of the family also profited from early hand and eye co-ordination, but I was not looking so far ahead at the time. I thought the human hand was a wonderful gift and that it was right to develop its capacity, so long as the owner of the hand was contented. Years later I met Professor Jerome Bruner's judgement, that the best kind of child-care was that which enabled the child to master its own attention. That is what Montessori's method does, if it is given a fair chance.

On the morning I have chosen Barbara was tracing patterns and proverbs with the competence she had gained from 'doing' insets. Alasdar could not only match capital letters with sounds but had found out that they had further possibilities. In a recent book, *Early Reading*, I recount how exciting it was when Alasdar, knowing the sounds represented by some letters, realised that they could combine into meaning. That D beside A would 'say' DA, so DADA would say Dada. This explosion happened some months before the time I am recalling, around his second birthday. From then on it was more letters, new words, and certainly we would have done something of that sort when he had finished his insets. We might, for example, have had a look at OO, in BOOK, COOK, MOON (draw picture of moon), ZOO and possibly POOH.

Not long after this I read an article in *Housewife*. The writer had helped a child to read by making sets of cards, each pair of cards having the same picture and the same word, but with the word cut off one of the pair. We tried this, showed Alasdar how to set out five complete cards, suggested he put the matching pictures underneath, then gave him one of the separate words (written in CAPITAL letters) to see whether he would put it under the appropriate picture. He did. I let him know this was very satisfactory, then showed him how to check his results by matching letter by letter with the complete card. These cards turned out to be exceptionally useful. Alasdar soon needed several sets to take away at a time and lay out to show me. He read his first Reading Book non-stop one day when he was three and could read independently anything he wished when he was four — formerly not unusual but thought to be so now.

I have left Barbara tracing patterns or letters, Alasdar filling an ellipse; what was Tinu doing? She had possibly crawled out to the garden to root out any blue lobelias she might find in my modest flowerbed. Granny Ad planted them; Tinu wouldn't have them, forecasting her career in landscape.

In my first book I described some of the things we made for the children: button frames, number rods, picture cards with holes punched in the pictures they drew themselves so they could learn to use a blunt needle and thread to follow the outlines. Just as small Barbara had been entirely responsible for showing me that she could feed herself, a lesson I passed on to the others, six-year-old Barbara was entirely responsible for teaching herself how to read musical notation from a strip that fitted across the keys of a piano. I'm sure Seán helped her once she had taken it up, but by then Dublin Port was demanding much more of his time as an accountant than it had in our early days. When she had real lessons her teacher was delighted with her. Alasdar astonished me by being able to play tunes on his mouth organ as soon as he got it, this while we were living up the hill, which we left when he was five.

Montessori spoke of training the senses, how if they are not given anything to work on during their 'sensitive period' they are unlikely to catch up. I had boxes of fabrics of varying textures and I let the children smell spices as well as oranges, onions, herbs. We matched jars of hot, warm, cool and cold water. I made 'rattley boxes' for attentive listening, following Montessori's instructions as best I could. Later I learnt that the systematic matching of sounds was also a way of teaching logical thinking. The 'rattley boxes' were matched containers, in two different colours — tubes that had held Vitamin C tablets were ideal. Each pair held something that would make a sound; one pair would have lentils, another small stones and so on. The user would set all of one colour in a row, pick up one of the other colour, shake it beside her ear and then work through the other set to find the similar sound. I could not count on matching them myself unless I made some secret marks, but the children could.

Somebody did something on the lines I have described almost every day. We never attempted to do everything. The chosen work might occupy twenty minutes, it might occupy one student or another for most of the morning. We might play the 'silent game' all together. That consists in children sitting very, very quietly, listening for anything audible — birds, insects, leaves blowing — then for a whisper that calls one of them out of the room, the one called trying to tip-toe out without making a sound. In a real Montessori set-up, 'exercises of practical life', cleaning and dusting, would come first. I made sure that 'lesson things' were always tidy and in place but I was inclined to time housekeeping so that things looked well when Seán arrived home.

Meantime there was gardening to be done, sewing, washing, cooking. As the children grew older they involved themselves in whatever was going on, but at the time I have elected the best anyone could do in the way of gardening would be to lay beans in a row or to shell peas (and count them) once they were ready for eating. In the matter of food the children did quite well and I shared with them. There were three so to speak standard meals: potatoes and milk; porridge made with milk and some raisins added; rice with every vegetable in the garden added and cheese grated on top. My favourite vegetable was purple sprouting broccoli, Barbara's too. She was a pretty sight standing beside a plant taller than herself and nibbling the buds with her hands behind her back.

I had early found that, like most mothers, I could do a great deal in the way of sweeping or stirring with one hand while the other arm held a baby on my hip. While I was digging Tinu could sit in her basket beside me. I could take it for granted that the two older ones would be busy about their own affairs. Twenty years later I heard Professor Bruner say that when children were encouraged to do something that really stretched their minds they tended to go off on their own to do something of the same order. And that's what I mean when I say that early learning was a good investment for me as well as for the children.

Not only could they occupy themselves when I was busy, they understood that after lunch was rest time for everyone. Baby in her basket out in the sheltering box, the other two in their own beds, Mama in hers. My nights were so broken that I often had to get myself up in the morning by a reminder that siesta time would come and I would be able to close my eyes again.

As years went by this encouragement became more and more necessary, an afternoon's rest more indispensable. Dr John Collee writes regularly on the last page of the *Observer Magazine*. One Sunday he commented on some problems of sleep and concluded:

> If, in spite of all this sleep hygiene, you still can't get into tune with the rest of the population's sleep patterns it may be some consolation to know that the rest of the population has got it wrong. Studies of circadian body temperature rhythms suggest that our internal sleep-clock is designed not for one but for two sleeps per day, a sleep at night and a siesta in the afternoon. Northern European culture has resisted the siesta despite the fact that most people would probably be more productive as a result of it.

It has given me much satisfaction to copy that paragraph. 'The rest of the population has got it wrong.' It was by chance that I grew up in southern Europe and accepted this good custom. Again, it was by a kind of chance that Seán brought home the Culverwell book about Montessori when we lived so far from any school that we thought we should try to make sure the children would not be backward when they were old enough to go. Experience later showed me that 'the rest of the population had got it wrong' when they took it for granted, as most Irish parents did, that they should put their four-year-old children into large classes in school. That is why I wrote *Anything School Can Do....*

Further experience has brought some other convictions, including the conviction that mothers are mistaken if they want another job while their children are small. Experience has also shown that they need money, but that's a different matter. This is one of my reasons for writing this present book. It is too early in the story yet to explain why I believe, in company with many responsible people, that the way to deal with the problems of structural unemployment in our community is not to give a conditional sum to people for whom there are no jobs, conditional, that is, on their doing no paid work, and pile increasing taxes on the rest, but to give a similar amount unconditionally to every citizen, a Basic Income, which could then be recouped from those in employment. Under such a system a very great deal of useful work would be done that now remains undone and every mother and child would have income sufficient to live in a simple way or to make satisfactory arrangements with someone else who liked children and who would be free to earn something extra without loss of his or her untaxable Citizen's Income.

It appears now that we'd got it right in adapting Montessori's observations to earlier introduction at home; that I'd been especially lucky being able to combine the capital letters that Montessori had wanted to use, but couldn't afford, with the word-and-picture cards I had found in *Housewife*. The paint brushes for babies, the long ones called school fitches that we showed them how to use gently — 'don't squash the brush' — were good also.

Meantime, we have reached an ordinary afternoon. We used to spend a good deal of time in the sheltered sunny corner at the back of the house, myself spinning or reading and feeding a baby, but available. There was, as I said, usually a large dish of water sitting there, warming itself in the sun. They could pour the water, or float things in it, or get right in and sit in it. We might climb up the hill to pick fraochans (a type of blueberry) in August, or walk round the hill on a visit to Yvonne and her boys. Before Dada was due home we would straighten things up.

We had solved the tiresome problem of the kitchen floor that would never dry by putting in a floor of plastic tiles with a pattern designed to frame the pleasing table Seán had made. As soon as the new smooth floor was laid the two small people rolled around on it in delight. Not long afterwards, just before Tinu's birth, Seán persuaded the ESB to put up another transformer and let us have electricity. For a time it had seemed that power lines would end half way up the hill and leave us to perpetual paraffin.

One familiar problem recurred: chilblains in winter. Questions and answers in magazines would advise rubbing a cut onion on the spot. I kept the children fairly safe by bathing their feet alternately in hot and cold water a couple of times during the day. When I felt my own feet beginning to freeze I would try to go out and do some digging. If there were any boots lined with sheepskin or a substitute for sheepskin we didn't know about them. Seán had a pair of knee-high, lace-up lumberjack affairs for getting up and down in rough weather, something of a joke in the office. Ordinary shoe shops had never thought of boots for women or children, apart from wellies. Warm tights had not been invented either. We had an all-season game which helped; one child would come and ask me for jumps, I would hold their hands and help them to jump higher and higher, one, two, three, four, up to ten. Stop at ten. Give the next waiting child a turn, because they always queued up and wanted several turns; this gave them a bit of bounce in their muscles, tended to restore my waistline, fixed the decimal system and warmed us all up. And winter didn't last for ever.

We became aware that the Irish Montessori Society held monthly meetings in town. When we could manage, either Seán or I would go, and share our findings with each other on our return. We discovered, for example, that the sandpaper capital letters I had made for Alasdar were not the standard type. They were too small, and anyway the current practice was to use lower case letters. We had found that plastic capitals were best for earlier reading and so made a full-size set of boards with letters based on Marian Richardson's *Writing and Writing Patterns*, capitals on one side, cursive on the other. We saw the materials used for teaching mathematics and we copied as much as we could. The most valuable experience was to meet Nancy Jordan who was responsible for introducing such experiences to children in hospital. Miss Jordan herself studied with Dr Montessori and she radiated the authentic spirit of respect for the child.

We acquired new neighbours, who became our friends. Pat and Luan Cuffe built themselves a house in the woods on the side of Carraig Olligan that gave a view of the Sugarloaf. They had two children at the time and, unlike ourselves, two cars. At first it was a matter of giving us a lift down to Mass, then we found shared interests in books as well as children. One day it was arranged that they should come to one of these Montessori meetings. The short-term result was that they decided to send their children to a Children's House, admirably run by Veronica Ryan, and offered to transport any of ours we wanted to send. The long-term result was that Luan and Pat in turn became presidents of the society and livened it up considerably.

For the first term we sent Alasdar and Tinu; she was three, he about four and a half. The trouble with Alasdar was that since he was already reading easily and had a pretty good grasp of number and could work on his own for hours he did not seem to have so much to gain. His filling of insets was considered outstanding. Next term we let him stay at home to do geometry with his father before breakfast, other options during the day, and sent Janet instead; she must have been just old enough to start. The great benefit was that the children learnt to take it for granted that in the morning one normally chose some work and did it. The snag was that they had to be ready and dressed with their plaits plaited and their mid-morning snack packed punctually. It was our introduction to the morning rush.

Well, one summer's day a tinker woman came on her usual call — tinkers were part of society then, itinerants and travellers had not arrived. She proposed that I cross her palm — my palm? — with silver. She told me I'd be leaving this place soon, and I'd be glad to go. We were in the garden, near the strawberries. I looked down over the sunny fields, the Green Lane, a train puffing on the railway line below, Dalkey Island floating on a glistening sea. I laughed at her. How could I possibly be glad to leave this?

CHAPTER 13

Inside the black gate:
the blessings of technology

Even while the tinker fortune-teller was trying to convince me that I would be glad to leave, a train beneath us was on its way from Bray to Harcourt Street. Not long afterwards news broke that the Harcourt Street line was uneconomic and would be closed. This was the line that brought Seán to Dublin every day. We began to wonder whether we would have to find somewhere nearer Seán's place of work, the Ballast Office beside O'Connell Bridge.

That same summer Alex prevailed on us to join him for a 'holiday' in Pontevedra, a town in Galicia, in north-western Spain, where he was living at the time. We had to get over to London, then down to Southampton to take ship for Vigo, the port on the north-west coast of Spain most convenient to Pontevedra. I went first with the children, Seán was to follow two months later. I don't believe there was any contribution towards our fare and certainly I was to pay for our food. Seán had had a fortunate promotion at work but it took a lot of calculation to decide we could manage the expense. I wanted, if possible, to make up to my father for not having joined him in Argentina, but I think what decided us was the chance to introduce the older children, Barbara, then six, Alasdar five, Tinu going to be four, to another language.

That was a fine idea, best summarised in the picture of the helpful nun at school holding an apple over Tinu's head and saying 'Manzana, manzana' while Tinu jumped up to reach it, insisting instead 'Naughty nun, naughty nun!' Only Barbara could have told me this; neither Tinu nor the nun knew what the other one was saying. The four who could talk, Barbara, Alasdar, Tinu and Jenny, spent some of their time playing with the apprentice carpenters on the ground floor — teaching them English.

I now think it rather remarkable that I was able to bring them all home alive. Four small climbing or crawling children on board ship are at risk. But for the help of some Scottish fellow-passengers I do not know how I would have got them up and down the almost perpendicular companionways. I say four, because the fifth, poor Barbara, was confined to her bunk by seasickness, just as her grandmother used to be. The journey to school was also perilous. Barbara would escort Alasdar and Tinu down a long road without footpaths and full of thundering lorries. A little later in the morning I would bring a very lively Janet — known to all the neighbourhood by her family name of Coggi — and the curly-haired baby in the pushchair down the same road and over the bridge to the market. No more porridge with raisins; we had to have two meals of real food every day. I distinctly remember my father saying, 'Thank God I have always been able to eat meat twice a day.' I was thanking God that I had Columpia, who came to clean the flat and do the laundry, to advise me on marketing and cooking to suit el Señor. The two older children picked up enough Spanish to buy rolls from the baker across the road and sometimes churros for a treat.

The holiday element was to be found by walking down a couple of quiet lanes at the back of the house to an expanse of fine grass beside a small river. Twice a day, as the tide came in, the water in the river rose to cover a wide stretch of grass, providing a safe and pleasant place for children to bathe. Here they played with local children without apparently swopping language, but I could not withdraw my attention. One day when the tide was out, when the river ran between its green banks, someone shouted and I saw baby Máire Claire, not a year old, swimming just like an assured pink frog underneath the water. She seemed so much at home, so like a water baby, that I think I left her swimming for a dozen seconds. Perhaps it was only two; there wasn't a bother on her when I lifted her out. Barbara became a very good swimmer when she was a bit older but her experiments in Pontevedra were ended when a girl from the flat above let a heavy length of timber fall on her foot and she had to have plaster up to her knee and be carried up and down stairs. Since she could not walk she could not escort the other two to school; it was no great loss, though Barbara had been taught by the nuns to embroider surprisingly well.

Those stairs. They were the most frightful part of a mistaken enterprise. The journey over had been bad enough; now the money was a gnawing anxiety, since I couldn't do my own kind of cooking and had to pay for our share of the other kind. I missed Seán, and it seemed that he might not be able to come at all — the original plan was to sail round to Vigo in somebody's yacht. He managed to send me a letter nearly every day, telling me how well Pat and Luan were looking after him but how much he missed me. My neighbours would call out to me when the postman was coming up the street, but it was a struggle to find a solitary moment to reply and a further challenge to get to the post office in the town to post a letter out of the country. (I realised I was lucky to get letters; a great many husbands from this part of the world had gone off to find work in South America and might never return.)

To keep the children happy in the company of a grandfather who believed in obedience was not outstandingly easy. One day when Tinu was sweeping the floor I told him that she liked sweeping and he said that if that was so, then there was no merit in her doing it. He smacked her once and she never forgot it.

But the stairs were the worst. Alex — now Grandfather — had told us about his lovely flat, five large rooms, the floors not merely parquet but each inlaid in different patterns of coloured woods. The owner and builder of the house was a cabinet maker; those apprentices to whom our children taught English were carving swags of fruit on the doors of mahogany sideboards. They worked at ground level. Of the two floors above, which the owner occupied himself, one had marquetry so intricate that the family walked on it only in felt slippers; Grandfather had the other one. Unfortunately the cabinet-maker had been so preoccupied with inlaid floors that he hadn't got around to making any banisters. From our level you could look down six or seven flights of unprotected stairwell. True, there was a door to the flat, but anyone who has ever had a crawling baby will understand why this did not seem to be enough.

During those long three months I lost two and half stone and learnt that flats are not for families. I know that normal flats have protected stairs, or even a lift, but I don't care. Children should be able to go in and out easily, as they have been doing for tens of thousands of years.

Seán did manage to get to Pontevedra by rail, bringing the supply of Bewley's tea that Grandfather expected to sell, but couldn't. We managed to spend one day together, a visit to Santiago de Compostella, while Columpia minded the children. 'Los niños son horribles!' was a pronouncement of hers that stays with me; she didn't mean my children, just the whole race.

Máire Claire did not remember her father; she had attached herself to Grandfather, which was quite a good thing, since at the time of her first birthday she had attention-winning fair curls and the passing Spanish public habitually expressed admiration. For her birthday, the feast of the Assumption of Our Lady, she had a whole week of fiesta and firecrackers, since it is also the feast of Nuestra Señora de Pontevedra, La Peregrina, whose statue wears a pilgrim hat and a cockle shell, emblems of the ancient pilgrimage to Santiago de Compostella.

> How shall I my true love know
> From another one?
> By his cockle hat and staff
> And his sandal shoon.

Tinu had a birthday too, her fourth. Language or no language, her peers had made it clear to her that if she hadn't earrings it would be hard to believe she was a girl. They are popped into the tender ears of girl babies during the first week. So, on the birthday I brought her to a shop where we bought a pair of gold sleepers. The shopkeeper grasped an ear and plunged in the sharpish end of the sleeper. Blood spouted. The birthday girl yelled. And turned the other ear. This gift came full circle when she gave me a pair of pretty earrings for my sixtieth birthday. I had to get my ears pierced and now feel incomplete if I am not wearing anything in them.

We were all delighted to return home, to be in our own space with our own front door. The next event to plan for was Alasdar's First Communion. One of the books for bedtime reading was *St Patrick's Summer* by Marigold Hunt, published of course by Sheed & Ward. The story tells of how St Patrick, wearing a warm tweed cloak, meets on a hillside a brother and sister who are expecting to make their First Communion and introduces them to all they should know, not just by talking but by bringing them on excursions into the past, including a meeting with Abraham. I was reading this to the children in Spain when we had a visit from a very well informed Vincentian priest whom we had known in Gib. He travelled a good deal, giving retreats. He recognised the book and told me he had bought three copies, one for his sister, a nun, one for a friend and one for himself.

St Patrick explained to the children that he had never said that the Holy Trinity was a shamrock, then brought them to the Hill of Tara to hear what he did say. Reading this book often prompted interested speculative discussion. One day Seán, passing a church, brought Alasdar in for a visit. On leaving, he said something like, 'Ask God to remember you and help you to remember him.' Alasdar's reply was, 'If God didn't remember me, I wouldn't be.'

Fr Liam Breen, the priest in charge of our district, had found his way up to our fringe dwelling and kindly arranged for Barbara to join once a week the First Communion class in a small school near Bray. He came back to visit us and sat down on a low stool beside Alasdar and the two had a lengthy conversation. Fr Breen said that this five-year-old was well prepared for receiving Communion. This implied that the bother of bringing Barbara up and down to meet strangers had been superfluous, but if we had adapted to convention then, at least Fr Breen should have credit for an unconventional conversation.

The day we picked for Alasdar's First Communion turned out to have been picked by Heaven for the heaviest rain of the year, washing away our road, stopping buses between Dublin and Bray, imposing much hardship on visiting grandmothers and cutting off our electricity supply, so that myself and the smaller ones up the hill huddled around the cooling storage heater. I remember the floods; I remember Alasdar unperturbed. I don't remember how the rest of the day went but I am pretty sure it added urgency to our decision to move. It wasn't just a question of weather; we had realised that in spite of our calculations a sixth baby was on the way and we had to choose between moving or doing some serious building and water-pumping.

It was on a cold sixth of January, feast of the Epiphany, that Seán telephoned and told me to put on two pairs of his trousers and be ready for a journey on the pillion of his motorbike. We had almost decided on a new house near Monkstown, a standard semi-detached, with a tiny garden. But one sheet from the estate agent listed an old house in Rathfarnham with a ground-rent of one peppercorn. Seán had gone out to view it and had found the black gate in the wall with the brass plate saying THE MILL HOUSE, knocked on the Medusa knocker and said to the gentleman who opened the door, 'This was Bulmer Hobson's house, was it not?' The reply was either, 'It is' or 'I am'. [Irish readers will recognise Bulmer Hobson as a friend of Pádraig Pearse, who agreed that Ireland should be free from English rule but who thought that the rising in 1916 was ill-judged. He was also a great man for trees and had sound ideas about economics.]

Seán could not wait for me to see the house. I put on gloves and headscarf and warmest coat and we took the shortest way, down by

Puck's Castle, past Pearse's school, St Enda's, (I did not know that then) and to the door in the wall. Inside, we went up an unusual stairs running up the left-hand wall of the wide hall, to stand on the step of the almost square drawingroom, fire in the distant fireplace, bookshelves lining the nearer walls, and feel that, however we might manage it, we must live here.

It was indeed a matter of management. Selling one house and buying another is not often easy. It is more difficult when building societies do not want to give a mortgage on anything not newly built and, when that has been dealt with (two friends nobly gave guarantees as well), you find that the solicitor of the building society who gave the mortgage on the first house has decamped with funds, so there is an almost insoluble problem with the title. At least the couple who wanted to buy Carraig House were as keen on their side as we were to get into the Mill House. They arrived up early on Saturday morning, in snow, the day we put the advertisement in *The Irish Times*. They had been looking at the cottage before and were delighted to find it was for sale.

Bulmer Hobson, for his part, was even more co-operative. His 'country Georgian' house had been on the market for three months, at the same price as a modern semi-detached, but people did not want it because there was no garage and no way of building one because the only entrance was through that door in the wall. He saw how much we loved the house, he was a Quaker, he allowed us a year's grace to pay the last hundred and fifty pounds.

On the day the sale was arranged, as I stood with one hand on the white marble mantelpiece and turned to see my father coming down the step into the drawingroom, I recognised suddenly that I was grown up. I was thirty-three, had five children, had been a responsible nurse. Now, in our new home, I found I was not afraid of my father. Not that I had been consciously afraid of him for years. He had headed off a week before we were married but used to turn up in Ireland from time to time and visit us. I always greeted him, but never invited him. So perhaps 'afraid' is not the precise word, though it is what came to mind. It was more a matter of recognising that he was not to be taken seriously. It was pleasant to feel grown up.

We had, in fact, been another couple of hundred pounds short and I had asked him, by letter, for a loan. He agreed, but once he had seen the house he added a simple condition, that he should live in that drawingroom, that my mother should leave her flat and come and live in the remaining part of the first floor, and that the house should be in his name, though Seán would be paying off the mortgage. Quite apart from the space question, the mortgage nonsense, and the fact that my mother had no wish to move, any agreement would have been risky; since his retirement he had bought and sold either three or four houses, losing on the deal every time. When he came into the room he must have thought that he was going to get his own way, but Seán had just told me that he had got the money we needed from another source. Hence the moment of sudden illumination; that man is unreasonable, but it doesn't matter. As it happened, the priest who had visited us in Spain, who had known Alex for years, had taken the opportunity to give me a bit of advice: don't ever let him live under your roof.

The deeds of the house date back to 1810. Two architect friends told us that it was 'country Georgian' and unusual for its time in being built facing south. One of them, Luan Cuffe, brought Fr Donal O'Sullivan, then chairman of the Arts Council, to see it. He told us that Evie Hone, the eminent artist in stained-glass, had known it and referred to it as a 'little gem'. I suppose it seemed little by comparison with her family home, Marley House, but in modern terms it is spacious. It's the word 'gem' that matters.

There were only two real rooms on the ground floor, the diningroom and the long tiled kitchen; the door you could see through the archway when you came in the front door was at first a pantry, now it holds the washing machine. Upstairs, two rooms again, the drawingroom twenty by twenty-seven feet, taking up the whole width of the house and large enough to contain all four rooms of our former home, though perhaps not the passage between them, and what Mr Hobson called the study, which had two windows facing south, as had each of the other rooms, and a third facing west, filling it with warm evening sun. Above, three large bedrooms, one small bedroom and a box room. Outside there was a long triangular garden, narrowing towards the south, sheltered by trees on a bank to the east, by a wall to the west. On the other side of the bank ran the mill stream, from which our deeds gave us the right to take water. Towards the further end were two copper beeches, which I now know to be marked on the county maps as having protected status. The first time I saw the house in daylight, when living in it was still a matter for prayer, I stuck a couple of slips of rosemary into the ground beside a path. They grew far and wide and I now use them to spread sheets and pillowcases to dry with fragrance. We brought down with us a Daphne mezereum (fragrant pinkish winter flowers) and most of our raspberries. For the first few years I thought the latter were not thriving, until Janet and Claire went away for a holiday in early summer and those who stayed at home were smothered in raspberries.

For years the garden was principally a play space. Indoors the exciting thing was to have not only water coming out of a tap, but HOT water — provided the boiler in the kitchen was kept alight. Off the middle landing was a bathroom with, Mr Hobson told us, the largest bath he had been able to buy. We were able to put all five children in at once, a great time-saver, while for my part I was able to indulge comfortably in reading in the bath; I always feel it is a waste of warm water just to pop in and out.

The kitchen floor was tiled with a draught-board pattern of yellow and terracotta quarry tiles; the walls, window-sills and all, were tiled in cream. The walls of the house were so thick that the window-sills offered generous surfaces, and by raising the sash window the children could slide out directly to the garden; I could myself when I wasn't pregnant. Running down the middle of the kitchen was the massive table made by Bulmer Hobson himself; it is at least three yards long with a central sheet of marble and aluminium sheets at each end. We were perhaps mistaken to buy it during the auction; it was indeed a bargain at two pounds ten shillings, but since it had been built in the kitchen I don't see how anyone else could have taken it away. That marble sheet was ideal for making Edinburgh Rock as well as for drawing and writing on.

Upstairs beside the bathroom there was a water closet, a WC, a loo, call it what you like; now everything we ate went out eventually to sea instead of back into the land. Too bad, but we had no space to grow vegetables anyway and life was becoming more complicated, so I shall say no more on that topic. Well, very little; the cellulose lining from babies' nappies used to go on the compost heap, to encourage bacterial activity.

With five, and eventually eleven, children, washing was part of living. At first I was pleased to have the washing trough beside the sink in the kitchen, just like the ones in the laundry in Gibraltar. I even had a sophisticated glass washboard — a corrugated surface on which one rubbed the difficult bits, like shirt cuffs. Didn't make them last any longer. At that time, though we had so little money, it was normal to send tablecloths and pillowcases to the laundry down the road, from which they would come back starched and smooth, with sometimes a bit of a hole marked with red thread.

The next technical advance was the spin-drier, designed to do the work of the mangle, and do it better. I never expect anyone to believe this bit, but it's true. Quite early in their history spin-driers were given a safety device; the inner drum could not spin until the lid was closed down. The object that was brought to me must have been designed before anyone thought of that. It was a cylinder about two and a half feet high with a short length of rubber hose coming out the side at the level of the top of a bucket, a round hinged lid and an electrical connection. The man who brought it plugged it in and showed me, with the lid open, how rapidly the inside went round. All you had to do, he told me, was to have a bucket in position under the hose, switch on, lift the lid and drop in the wet washing which would be spun tidily against the sides while the water would pour out. It must have been his first demonstration. I hadn't any washing handy so he did not witness what happened when I followed his instructions. The moment I dropped in the first garment the new, shiny white gadget danced and plunged and rattled all around the kitchen floor, spitting water, shaking itself apart. There was no chance to switch off, I couldn't catch the brute, but it did slowly calm down once I pulled the plug out of the socket. I was thankful there hadn't been a small child within reach of the berserk robot. If there had been a consumers' association in existence I suppose I would have got a replacement. Instead I carried on for years with a drier that would spin the washing almost dry — better than most automatic washing machines — but which while doing so leaked half the water all around.

The next step up was a Thor washing machine which had a very large tub with paddles inside to move the clothes to and fro. One filled it by means of a hose attached to a tap, either hot or cold; it had its own heater. Once washed, things had to be taken out with a large wooden tongs and put into the spin-drier, rinsed and spun, rinsed and spun. It might sound like a daunting programme, especially when you include batches of nappies to be washed separately, but it was a much-appreciated improvement on the woman-powered wringer (I was afraid of electric wringers, having heard some literally hair-raising stories) and it was probably better than wringing things out by hand. Probably, because if there was time to spare I didn't bother with much wringing; I could hang things on the clothes line or spread them on the bushes and just wait until they were dry. Patience was my problem.

The Thor would behave perfectly if you kept your eye on it, but too often I fixed the hose to fill it and just went out for a moment to see how the children were getting on at lessons, lost track of time and came back to find the kitchen floor deep in water. Well, this washed the floor thoroughly.

Overflows apart, myself or the older children had to wash that floor quite frequently, not only because of the ordinary spillage from cooking but because twice a day the boiler had to be filled with coke and have the ashes raked out, and this left crunchy black traces all the way through from the back door. I always got down on my knees to wash it; that was how I had seen it done. When I found a rubber kneeler with a front raised for protection I was pleased. Then sponges at the end of a handle that could squeeze them appeared in the shops. This was probably an advance but it was still hard work and the sponge left marks where it was lifted.

The Aga was the first thing I bought when my other Uncle Francis, my father's eldest brother, died in San Diego and left me five thousand pounds in shares. Since the Aga cost only £190 (they cost at least £2,000 now), that legacy made many differences, like new shoes for everyone at the same time, and at last an automatic washing machine. This did not arrive in time to wash nappies — the youngest baby was over two — but it never overflowed like the old one and it helped to give me many hours of useful freedom.

To return to the house itself, as it was in our first days here, with only five and a half children, it was immediately evident that if the kitchen floor was one of the good features the hall floor was not. The shape of the wide hall, with stairs on one side, a single door on the other and a deep arch at the further end, was pleasing. But the curling brown linoleum on the floor, like something long discarded from a government office, I disliked very much. I knew there was no money to replace it — remember, we still had to save one hundred and fifty pounds to repay Mr Hobson — but I had to get rid of it somehow. Perhaps we could paint whatever lay underneath?

I pulled up one corner. What was underneath was a floor of once-glazed brick in alternate large squares of black and red, as old as the house. The squares at the edges were still faintly glossy, the middle ones more worn, there was a red one that should have been black; they were blotched with whitish mould because of having been covered, but all they needed was a coat of cardinal red polish or black shoe polish to turn them into a floor I couldn't have bought and wouldn't have parted with for any money. We had to polish again at intervals, but even the babies could help, sliding around on a bit of blanket. I painted the inside of the arch dark red to match.

I cannot quite say that those two floors were the beginning and end of my housekeeping, but over the years I find that certain standards have emerged; if one or two visible surfaces are shiny and there are fresh flowers I feel that the house looks as if it is being looked after. I have noticed that I am as likely to paint a door as to wash it. We had to persist with painting whenever we could afford paint because so much of the woodwork was black. One room was a pleasing apricot colour, the room to the right of the front door, with one window in the same wall as the front door, facing west, looking out towards the garden wall with its black gate, overhung with red-berried contoneaster carried on sturdy dark twisted trunk. The other two windows look south on to the garden, each window-sill forming a window seat inside, one window opening onto an old wide stone seat outside, sunny from breakfast time until evening. In this room, or spilling out into the garden, we had lessons.

CHAPTER 14

Painting on the kitchen wall.
Montessori's 'Three steps'

The first year in the Mill House, when everyone was at home, set the pattern for the years to come. Barbara and Alasdar had been working in their own time up the hill. Alasdar could of course read anything he wanted to; when we were on our way to Spain and he was a month past his fifth birthday a priest sitting in the same railway carriage had asked me, after some observation, 'Is he really reading that?' I was surprised at the question but asked him to read aloud. The priest told me he was the headmaster of a junior school. Many years later I sought and found a book written by Thorsten Husen, Professor of Education at the University of Stockholm. It was called The *School in Question*. This railway-carriage conversation perhaps first prompted me to wonder about the value of schooling.

Barbara, as I have mentioned, had begun to teach herself the piano. Both had been using our imitation Montessori mathematical material. Now they were joined by Tinu and Janet who had been in the real Montessori environment for two or three terms. I have a sort of mental snapshot of Tinu coming to me when we had not been very long in the new house — she must have been four and three quarters. She has a Beacon Reader in her hand and is asking, 'Listen to me reading'. We sit down side by side on the bright, bare upper stairs and she reads about Lambkin in the drumkin, and goes on until she finishes the story. Little Máire Claire naturally saw lessons — insets and so on — as normal, what everyone else was doing.

A convenient way to show how things were is to move on a couple of years with an extract from my eye-witness report of a day in the life of a five-and-a-half year-old, Janet. Hardly an average day, as my comments suggest, but still an intensification of her normal activity.

The narrative is embedded in five pages of handwritten foolscap in which I am already explaining to parents the advantages of using Montessori's method in the home. The whole is much too long for a 'Letter to the Editor' so I do not know why I was writing it, but I used Janet as an example:

> Today — the day I'm writing this — is Sunday. After Mass Jenny, aged five and a half, turned up with her workbook in her hand and asked to have her pencil sharpened. Each page of the workbook presents a different sort of problem, with everything needed for solution on the same page (e.g. Bottles are made of...., and a list of words to choose from). By lunchtime she had done three pages. This was especially difficult because I suggested that this book was advanced enough to demand 'grown up' cursive writing. She had galloped through two other books using capital letters. Well, the suggestion was enough. She knew the forms of cursive letters but she had never before used them while thinking things out for herself. As soon as lunch was over she was back on the job. By the time she had done seven pages the writing was coming quite easily but I felt the questions were becoming rather difficult. I persuaded her to do some easier word-building for a rest. Then Seán offered to take the six elders for a walk, leaving me at home with the baby. Janet was quite willing to go. 'Yes', she said, 'and I'll come back happy and ready to do some more work.'
>
> It was while she was out that I took her pencil and noted down what I have just written. When she came back she did two more pages while I was getting dinner ready, making a total of nine pages between eleven in the morning and half-past-six. Several times I asked, 'Don't you think you've done enough, Jenny?' The answer would be 'I like it'.
>
> That was fine, but the other half is just as important. After dinner she volunteered to do the washing-up along with the older children and then insisted on doing a clean-up of the gas cooker, which meant taking off and washing the bars on top, the tray underneath. When I came down she was washing the kitchen floor.

Bursts of energy like this did not happen every day; though she did spend the whole of Monday filling in more of her workbook I have not recorded any more housework.

Since I wrote that record in order to show the advantage that home can have over school it suggests that I was already actively dissatisfied with what was happening in the schools which Barbara and Alasdar, aged nine and eight, had begun to attend. The point I wanted to make was that, when in the mood, a child at home can work away without the regular interruptions of change of class. Of course, school-going children can work at home if they want to. To my mind, the key advantage of basing learning at home is that when they are working they are working, when they are not working they can move freely out. They don't have to sit in their desks passing the time by day-dreaming or writing notes to each other, learning how to cope with boredom.

I do not know how often I have been told that that is all very well but that I am forgetting about socialisation, about the need to be able to mix easily with others. Well, even when children are unfortunate enough to live in high-rise flats, I cannot see why they should wish to mix with twenty or even forty others of the same age at the same time. From my own experience, both as child and parent, I am inclined to believe that children spontaneously link up into pairs or small groups with other children wherever they are, rather as drops of mercury coalesce. I remember looking out into the garden here and counting a dozen children swinging on the unfortunate laburnum tree and the rope hanging beside it; only two or three were Mullarneys; none of the family went to school with the visitors. The difference between that and socialisation at school is that nobody had to spend time with someone whose company they did not care for, while the age range was quite wide.

I leave aside the problem of bullying, which enquiry shows to occur to some extent in all schools. To my mind conformity, the need younger children feel to have and do whatever their age group do, whether it's having new school-bags or Barbie dolls or tanks with flashing lights or plastic turtles mis-named Donatello and Michelangelo, may be just as undesirable. I am not convinced that a few years further on the same young people will not smoke or take drugs or steal cars or bring about teenage pregnancies because these are the things everyone else is doing. I produced this argument once when I was on a panel with two psychologists and was not contradicted. The opposite result does not please me either; while waiting to go on the air in an environmental programme I asked two schoolgirl participants what they would do if they didn't get a place in college. They had never thought of anything else besides going to college.

Máire Claire, who was next to Janet, first went to school when she was eight. She happened to tell me, one day when she had come home from school, that she had heard three or four girls teasing another who had a hare-lip. They were telling the victim that she had no friends.

Claire had interrupted, 'Of course she has friends. I'm her friend.' I gathered that she had never noticed the girl before. The question is, who was socialised?

Now that this discussion has surfaced I had better explain how I think the problems of schooling could be resolved. It must be evident that I would prefer to see children beginning school already fairly competent in reading and able to work by themselves. I would like to think that most would have some other abilities, whether in music or art or acquaintance with wildlife. Once they were enrolled, I believe their time and their teacher's would be used to much greater advantage if the children were to attend at various times in small groups so that they could explore some subject with their teacher and follow it up independently, using some of the almost unlimited sources of information we have at our fingertips nowadays. Teachers are constantly, and understandably, demanding a reduction in class sizes; this would be a means of reduction that would cost nothing extra.

Janet, who somehow led to this diversion, had found her way to reading and writing following the steps that had suited Alasdar and Tinu: first those geometrical insets to help recognition of abstract shapes; next came plastic capital letters, two at a time, each a distinct object with a sound belonging to it. When I showed her the letter J I did not say 'Jay' but a short 'juh' as it sounds at the beginning of JUG. Similarly, U was 'uh', not 'you', and G was simply G, not 'Gee'. 'Two at a time' means that she, like her siblings, learnt to identify the letters according to Montessori's 'Three steps'. The adult first names clearly two objects, which may be a sock and a shoe, an onion and an apple, a triangle and a circle, or eventually, the letters S and T. For the second step one asks the child to point to one of the pair. If the right one is picked, the other is asked for. If the guess is wrong, the game is quickly abandoned. The third step is to ask 'What is this?', 'And that?' This is a multi-purpose routine. If babies meet it as a game with shoes and socks, when they can only make a shot at saying 'shoe', it has become matter of course by the time they meet letters, which is likely to be something around age two. Really this only means formalising slightly something everyone does anyway; it is part of natural adult behaviour to name things for younger humans.

With us, the next move was to bring a few known letters together to make a word, as Alasdar had 'blended' D A to make DA and then DADA when he was just two. After words came paired picture cards, then a few pages of a home-made book, then real reading. This whole

146

sequence I later called Early 3-D Phonic Capitals; it turned out to be unexpectedly important in my own career.

From the cards and homemade book each beginner, Barbara, Alasdar, Tinu and Janet, had moved on to Beacon Readers. These Readers had real stories, matched with graduated phonic word-lists at the back. The students, aged three or four, were happy to go through some lists before reading their story; because of the list, they never met a word they could not read quite easily. We never read a story twice unless we specially liked it, so we moved through the series quite fast, on demand, as with Tinu sitting on the stairs. Shortly after that she was reading on her own, and did not need to ask me to listen.

Since we had found the Beacon series so well planned and helpful it is not surprising that when we discovered that a Beacon Teacher's Manual existed we bought and read it. We found that we had been doing the wrong thing. We should have had two books before the First Reader. The children should have begun by recognising whole phrases — 'Kitty sees the ball' — and by that means learnt to recognise thirty 'sight words' before moving on to the Readers.

Máire Claire had been about one and a half when we moved house. She had her insets and sewing cards and things to smell and feel and count and unlimited drawing and painting and climbing and plenty of being read to, but for her introduction to reading she had Kitty seeing the ball. In comparison with the way her sisters and brother had glided through the more advanced Readers this was a slow and frustrating exercise. I made a set of flash cards, I believed that I was doing the right thing, but it was tiresome for both of us when, so often, she would meet a word or phrase that had occurred three or four pages earlier and would not be able to 'read' it until I turned back and showed it to her. This was disappointing, so when it was the turn of Aidan (whose unplanned arrival had instigated our move) I gave him 'phonic' letters like the others, but lower case letters because that's how the books were written. These were confusing: b, d, p and q are the same 'object' turned around or reversed, m and n and h not nearly so individual as M and N and H, and so on. They were designed to be parts of words, not to have a life of their own.

Neither Claire nor Aidan were in the way of following me around asking me to listen to them reading. They would do it readily enough if I asked them, for example, whether they wanted to read or do tracing, but they did not have either the energy or the excitement of the others. All this I have discussed in my book about reading. The result of this experiment — which I had not recognised as an experiment — was that I went back to early three-dimensional phonic CAPITALS, and Pierce, Killian and Alison learnt to read effortlessly, to say the least. I made a few notes at the time: Alison, age five, bringing me two pages of verses she had found, mostly not seen before, and reading each of them with the right rhythm. And once when Pierce was five I remarked that we hadn't read the 'back of the book' for ages; in fact, he had not been reading aloud. I turned to the final page of the word lists and said I would help him with the difficult ones. 'What difficult ones? Symphony? Determination?'

The fourth variation in reading instruction astonished me. When each of the last few babies was born a friend of mine, Ronnie Dooge, brought me accumulated copies of the big thick *Ladies' Home Journal* from the US. I used to save up books as well and go in to the nursing home with an enjoyable prospect. One of these journals had an article about how Glenn Doman taught young brain-damaged babies to read by showing them single words written in very large CAPITALS. I emphasise this because when he later published his book *Teach Your Baby to Read*, he used lower case letters. I would not have tried this simply as an experiment; our own 3-D method was doing all I could wish, but it did depend on the baby beginning to talk at the usual time. This Eoin did not do. Then, one morning when he was two years and four months old (by chance I have just found a diary entry), I heard him in the garden reciting night prayers — God bless Mama an' Dada an' Barbara an' Alasdar n' Tinu n' Janet n' Claire n' Aidan n' Pierce n' Killain n' Ali n' Eoin n' Oliver. I remembered the Doman article, went in, cut four large pieces of white cardboard, wrote a name on each with a thick felt marker: ALI, KILLY, MAMA, TINU. When he came in I showed him the first two (using the Three Steps). He got them right, noticed that I had two more, had me demonstrate, got those right as well, then, to quote the diary, 'read MAMA, K. ALI, Tinu almost at once ! ! !' Next day the diary says he read his own name, sorted through the cards and found MAMA, made a mistake about ALI, but corrected himself. The diary exclaims, 'This is wonderful.' Wonderful because he corrected himself, but delightful also because he was talking at last. Later we found he was slightly, remediably, deaf. The same diary entry adds, '*Daily Mirror* took photographs. Said "relaxed family". No wonder.' The photograph was of six of the children who had from time to time won prizes for painting.

Lessons were on offer every morning. At almost any time someone was likely to be drawing or painting. The wide white marble middle section of the kitchen table has a surface that is pleasant for a pencil and as often as not was covered in drawings, some of which I thought too good to wash off at once. The tiled walls gave excellent scope to children who until then had had only a square yard of enamel or small sheets of paper. I used the Children's Allowance to lay in a good stock of poster paints and powder colour, so there was never any scarcity. The children could paint at a higher level while the current baby used the space near the floor.

One day when Tinu was about seven or eight she painted on the wall a quick sketch of me kneeling down pulling up carrots in the garden. (By that time we had cleared a small vegetable garden.) I hadn't the heart to wash it off and lose it for ever, so I asked her could she paint something like it on a sheet of paper. Then I saw the announcement of a children's art competition run by Texaco. I sent in her painting; Tinu, wearing a dress we had both embroidered, was presented with a tennis racquet and we had lunch at the Gresham Hotel.

From then on for about twelve years some of the family won something at every session, once at least four in the same year. An Irish company, Glen Abbey textiles, ran a similar competition. One or other used to announce thirty thousand entries. The standard of entries got better and better and I should think these competitions raised awareness of children's abilities and gave painting a higher position in schools.

For my part, this meant a spreading out of paintings every spring, a taking down of those pinned to the diningroom wall, a discussion about which we didn't want to part with (if you won a major prize you might get your picture back, you might not; minor prizewinners vanished with the rest) and which to send to which contest. We lost a couple that I still regret.

When Barbara was sixteen she sent a painting of Tinu holding a very new baby Oliver to Glen Abbey; that took first prize. I happened to overhear a woman, looking into the hall and seeing this picture in a central place, turning away, saying, 'I thought this was child art.' Within a few days we found that Barbara had also won first place in Texaco with a picture of Alison standing beside a red table. These were both dashed off quite rapidly in coloured Indian inks. At the same time one of Alison's own paintings had made her the youngest prizewinner, which was very neat, while Janet and Killian had also been among the top of their respective age groups. These attainments brought about radio interviews, press photographs (after all, the events are planned with an eye to publicity for the donor), and account for the diary mention of the *Daily Mirror* above.

While the family's involvement in art competitions caused a few days of activity every year when it was time to send, or bring, the entries in, it also resulted in a couple of days of festivity — Texaco prize-giving was always on Ascension Thursday when schools had a free day. There were also annual handwriting competitions in which the children's years of using Marion Richardson's writing patterns enabled them to collect welcome pocket money — even allowed Alasdar to acquire a large silver cup for his school and ample ice-cream for all his class. During the rest of the year I found myself caught up in other preoccupations.

Soon after we arrived in Rathfarnham I had taken the opportunity to consult the Principal of the local Boys' National School, who was in the habit of standing on the footpath outside, leaning against the wall and smoking his pipe while his pupils raced around in the very small concrete playground. I explained that we had not lived near a school, that we had a boy of six, that he liked maths, could read, and was asking me for Latin lessons because we had an amusing book called *Latin With Laughter* at home. The Principal was most aimiable, and said, 'There wouldn't be any point in sending him here, and for God's sake don't send him to the nuns. When he's a bit older you could try the de la Salle school.'

We found that the National School recommended for Barbara had eighty children in the class. We read the Report of the Commission on Primary Education, more than twenty years old but still the most recent, and saw that, in everything except Irish, very low attainment for age was expected of the children, and that many of the most practical and attractive subjects, like art and gardening, had been discarded to make more time for Irish. We could not but recognise that, largely by accident, we had given the children a more favourable start and greater independence than if we had sent them to national school, or probably any school, at the customary age of four. But sometime they would have to learn Irish. You could not get the Leaving Certificate without at least a Pass in Irish. If we had known how things were in the schools — the constant change of teachers in one, the unreal standard in another, where every child in the class was on the list for grinds, worst of all, the brutal leather in the boys' school

— I am sure Seán would have taken charge of Irish for a year or so. He would have been well able to. Instead, when Barbara was eight we sent her to a convent in Templeogue. The nuns were grand women and they used the same handwriting series. We took the schoolmaster's advice and sent Alasdar to the de la Salle, their private school. We chose that because the class was half the size of the corresponding class in their National School. Not such a good bet; in his second year they amalgamated two classes, so there were as many as in the non-fee-paying school.

The first thing that upset me was the leather. For years I had been in the middle of a group of children who learnt quite industriously, by choice. I could not grasp how punishment could be associated with learning. It appeared that on most days every boy in the Irish class was lined up for the leather. Religion suffered also; a small boy was beaten for saying 'welt' instead of 'dwelt' when reciting the Angelus. However, Alasdar himself found the schoolwork so easy that, apart from the routine in Irish class, he suffered much more from boredom than from punishment. After a term or so I ventured to suggest that he might bring a book to school to read during the time in class when he had done whatever was required (I suppose I was looking back to my own fruitful experience with Euclid). This seemed to be a rather shocking notion, but the headmaster said that it might be a good idea to have him assessed by a psychologist to see whether he were bored because he was below par or otherwise.

Since a glance at any records, if he kept them, would have shown that in every report Alasdar had the top marks in the class in every subject, except Irish, quite often 100%, it wouldn't seem that the head was much interested, but he did refer us to Fr Dermot Casey, SJ, a qualified child psychologist who had set up a small school of his own. Fr Casey said he was the most intelligent child he had ever tested, but I should think the children sent to him usually had different problems. Fr Casey came to see us quite often and adopted for his school some of the material we used, the *Writing Patterns* series and Colour Factor maths.

[I do not intend to go into detail about Colour Factor. I had seen an advertisement for it in *The Listener* when Aidan was six, and ordered and received a box containing a quantity of light wooden rods of increasing lengths, from the one cubic centimetre unit to twelve centimetres, coloured significantly and harmoniously. The unit was white, the two-unit pink, the four a stronger red, the three light blue, twelve, of which two and three and four and six are factors, a harmonious deep purple, and so on with yellow and orange for five and ten units. They were so attractive that from then onwards they were the first choice in the morning; the books that came with them were so brilliantly well worded that the children could work by themselves and move ahead on foundations they understood completely. Neither books nor blocks are available any more.]

Fr Casey had taken up child psychology because he had so often found when dealing with the psychological problems of adults that they had their roots in childhood. Now he was depressingly aware that adults were actively planting problems among the current generation of children. One thing he could do; save a certain number of children who were being swamped in large school classes, give them a term or two to find themselves in classes of not more than ten. By some magic of his own he had his school, St Declan's, recognised as a National School. He would have been happy to take Alasdar but he was either too old by then or too well informed. Fr Casey recommended Gonzaga (an elite Jesuit college), but there was no space there and anyway Alasdar was by no means miserable at school; he had an excellent, civilised teacher of Latin, Brother Patrick, geography was rewarding, he brought home new jokes every day and his practice of conjuring, learnt from Uncle Frank's book, was good enough to allow him to join the real, grown-up, Magic Circle when he was twelve.

Meanwhile I had my first shot at promoting change. Looking back, I see that I was seeking change on an absurdly large scale. By the time three children had gone to school I began to be caught up in the fringes of homework. Each child, in one evening, might have three or four different subjects with no relation between them, then a couple of further odd elements the next evening. It seemed to me that we could do better without any expense.

I worked out a scheme according to which children under twelve would, in language, geography, history, art, and even to some extent in mathematics, focus on pre-history and move up towards the year from which we count backwards and forwards, the year AD 1. I know Jesus was probably born about BC 6, but that is not the point. Part of the idea was indeed to emphasise the significance of the Incarnation — I was thinking of Christian schools — but a contributory motive was my feeling that before the age of twelve one is better able to absorb epic awareness, whether the Old Testament, the *Iliad* and *Odyssey*, the Irish Mythological Cycle or the classic folk tales. I was perhaps a little ahead of my time in wanting to have young children know that there were other ways of counting besides the decimal system, that for example the Babylonians used base six.

In second level schools I wanted geography and history to overlap or converge and literature to be selected to fit in. I collected many examples and sent the whole lot off to the monthly journal *Studies*. In return I got a most encouraging and enthusiastic letter from the editor, Fr Burke-Savage, SJ. How fortunate my children were; such an interesting scheme; could I manage to work it out in further detail and send it to him again? I spent most of one summer on the job, and sent it off. And waited. And waited. And could still be waiting. Years later I mentioned this to Professor Jim Dooge, then chairman of the Senate; he told me that I was not the only one who found Fr Burke-Savage a will-o'-the-wisp; he had the same experience himself.

While I was waiting, and of course before and after, I was reading. In spite of growing numbers I contrived to have my rest almost every afternoon and a book was part of the rest; I always read in the bath and in bed and at meals and perhaps too often while I thought I was doing something else, like tidying. I got great value out of Trollope, read almost everything he wrote except his travel journals. I found that some of the lesser known novels were down in the basement of Rathmines Library. Phineas Finn is my favourite character in literature; I believe that he was Anthony Trollope's day-dream self. I bought *Phineas Redux*, the sequel to *Phineas Finn*, and saved it up for the peace of the nursing home when one of the babies was due.

On a different plane, the most significant book that I read in that decade was Teilhard de Chardin's *Phenomenon of Man*. It opened up a new universe. Until I read it I looked on evolution as probably the way things had come about but not specially interesting. Teilhard was a Jesuit and a palaeontologist. He cared about the emergence of the human from the anthropoid family tree, but his enquiry reached much further back. He proposed that a 'within', which might be called the rudiments of spirit, developed gradually throughout creation according as the 'without', the purely material elements, became more complex. I did not find his survey easy to follow, but more than worth the effort when I met the passage where he compares the transformation by reflection, self-awareness, of our first ape-born ancestor to the change in heated iron from black metal, growing warmer, to glowing red. I do not know whether the term biosphere to describe the layer of life around the earth was in common use, but the term noosphere for the increasingly dense network of knowledge and information that envelopes us was Teilhard's.

With the children we used to read only books that we found agreeable ourselves: *Winnie the Pooh*, C. S. Lewis's *Narnia* books, E. Nesbit, selected Grimm but no Hans Anderson, *Robinson Crusoe*, *Gulliver* (some), James Stephens' *Celtic Fairy Tales*, *Rasselas*, Helen Waddell's lovely bible stories, *St Patrick's Summer* that I mentioned earlier. During a three-day relay when Alasdar was eleven he and I shared C. S. Lewis's *Perelandra* trilogy; he would leave his book outside his bedroom door before he went to sleep, he might have time to read a bit before school, I'd read while he was out. I enjoyed it as much as I had when I was eleven. This reminds me of another shared reading. One morning when Oliver was four we were in the kitchen together and he had asked me to read the story of Pooh and the Heffalump. Alasdar happened to come in for something; he stood at the door listening until Christopher Robin came to the rescue in the end.

I kept my thoughts to myself for some time after my educational effort for *Studies*. Then I began to write letters to *The Irish Times*. Either through that, or through correspondence with Dr Paddy Randles, in Navan, I found myself a member of the Language Freedom Movement, whose aim was to have success in each subject in the Leaving Certificate recognised separately, so that students who had failed Irish could still get that essential Certificate. We would have been pleased if Irish were no longer required for entry to the National University, but that was too much to ask. Christopher Morris, who started the LFM, used to insist that if the threat were removed more students would like Irish. It seems that this happened; the number of all-Irish primary schools is increasing, in response to the demands of parents.

With another doctor, Jim Loughran, some of the same people set up Reform, to campaign against corporal punishment in school. It is notable that even then it was not used in the Vocational School system. Jim made a protest about events in the National School in his own parish and the parish priest reprimanded him from the pulpit. I wrote a strong letter about this to *The Furrow* (a moderately radical Catholic monthly published in Maynooth) and we sent copies to every bishop in Ireland. The editor of *The Furrow*, Canon McGarry, had a generous custom of sending several copies of their own contribution to anyone whose letters or articles he published. (I once looked through my shelf of Furrows and found that, over a period of twelve years, my name appeared at least once in every yearly index.)

In this chapter I have been writing about the time between coming to Rathfarnham and the birth of the baby who turned out to be, after all, the youngest. I had been sure that several before him were going to be the last. This unfounded certainty gave us a great deal of worry about which I decided not to expand until I could say something about the solution and its consequences. In Ireland at least the argument is not yet over.

CHAPTER 15

Light breaks on family planning and I spread the news

So far this narrative has been without complication. Infancy, youth, study, marriage, children, what could be more straightforward? But after eighteen years of uneventful child-care the pattern changes. Language learning in youth, study of theology and of the Bible, consideration of the economics of marriage, observation of children learning, concern about the size of the family, each strand developed into a distinct activity, but sometimes several became interwoven.

The shift begins, naturally enough, with the birth of the youngest; any family that still has a baby around functions differently from a family of children or young people. We had all at the same time. Eoin was one and a half when Oliver was born; Barbara was sixteen; a couple of months later she painted that picture of Tinu holding him which won the first prize in one of the art competitions and thereby encouraged her to make art her career and on that account to leave home at seventeen. Alasdar was studying in a College of Technology, Tinu, Janet and Claire were at school, Aidan, Pierce, Killian and Alison at home.

The reason that Oliver's arrival marks a peculiarly significant change is that he did not simply happen to be the last; we found it possible to decide that he should be the last. The next step was to assist other parents to make similar decisions, and that endeavour took up so much of my energy during several years, and the arguments in which I became involved are still so relevant, that I intend to follow this strand first. It was mere coincidence that an article I wrote about Oliver beginning to read when he was fifteen months old should have introduced me to journalism, but almost at once those two strands became entwined. Consider some of the further complications: when

Dr Dermot Ryan, future Archbishop of Dublin, invited me to join the board of Veritas, a publishing company that took over the Catholic Truth Society, he knew that I was already on the executive committee of the Fertility Guidance Company — it had not yet changed its name to Irish Family Planning Association. When we were first organising Fertility Guidance Dr Ryan had asked me whether we might not postpone it for a year or so, until the difficulties in the Church had blown over. It would have been a long wait.

Dr Ryan knew me because Pat Cuffe had sent me to his extra-mural lectures on biblical themes, which I enjoyed for ten years or more, and had sometimes asked us to dinner when Dr Ryan was coming. His lectures ended when he was made archbishop, but before that he had recommended his regular listeners to enroll for the lectures he organised in New Testament Greek. While taking these, I did a short intensive course in German and wrote a piece for *The Irish Times* contrasting the Greek and German methods and results. I was writing for the *Times* because, when Oliver was fifteen months old, I had offered him a couple of words in large capitals on cards, like Eoin, and he took to them so well that I wrote an article about early reading and sent it to the paper. The next day the features editor rang to say he was using the piece at once and could I write anything else on any topic.

I never had to search around for something to write about. From this time on, that is, from Oliver's second year, I have so many newspaper cuttings of articles based on immediate concerns that my difficulty now is to decide what might deserve a place in this book. There is one about the Botanic Gardens, written when Tinu was a student there, studying in the mornings, working in the afternoons. (She cycled nine miles each way every day; she was awarded a gold medal at the end of the course.) There's another about the well-known riding school in Burton Hall where Claire was teaching, where she had such rich experience of equine and of human nature. (Uncle Francis' legacy enabled me to buy a pony which would otherwise, apparently, have been condemned to death. From then on, when she was about twelve, Claire was only vaguely aware of school and started to teach riding when she was fourteen.) There is another article that reminds me of the long-drawn-out struggle to get all the tradesmen together at the same time to install the Aga, a welcome product of the same legacy, and there is one about feeding a family which is so lacking in reticence as to say that the payment for the article will be used to buy an electric potato-peeler. There is a series on the education at home in which the younger children were still engaged and many other reports and interviews concerned with children and learning.

I suppose any reader may wonder how I found time to write and to fit in meetings. Once I could get a night's sleep I found I was quite bright early in the morning and there were no distractions. Both running the house and getting out of it for the odd meeting were not so difficult when there were a number of competent young adults around and also, post-legacy, a competent washing machine and dishwasher. If I were out Seán would read to the younger ones at bedtime; in more crowded years we used both be on duty, he reading in one room, I in another.

Some of the articles I consider most important were concerned with that question which I have just said took up so much of my attention over at least the following four years, the question of controlling fertility, more generally known as family planning, to which I must give quite an amount of space both because I was so much concerned and because the question is still with us — Pope John Paul II and the official Catholic Church still steadily condemn contraception, while a generation has grown up which cannot understand what they are talking about. Unfortunately, at the time I am writing about, Catholic apologists persisted in condemning 'contraception and abortion' as if the two were much the same thing. One result, it seems to me, is that people who know that the majority of Catholic couples find contraception justified assume there is no need to worry very much about abortion. I do not know whether it is still the case that young women seek abortion because they had been told it was wrong to use contraception.

Looking backward has prompted me to spend time reading one or two of the books that most influenced us then. I have also looked again through a more recent book, *The Encyclical That Never Was*, the story of the Pontifical Commission on Population, Family and Birth, 1964-66, by Robert Blair Kaiser, published by Sheed & Ward in the UK in 1987. Kaiser was *Time Magazine* correspondent at the Vatican; he knew plenty of people who were closely in touch with what was going on or were even close enough to modify decisions. It is satisfactory to find that Seán and I were quick off the mark. In the spring of 1964 the Papal Commission met for the second time. They numbered thirteen. They had been warned to keep the existence of the Commission highly confidential. They had started out to prepare the Church's customary arguments against birth control so that organisations then promoting population planning around the world could appreciate the Holy See's point of view. Kaiser reports how it first dawned on them that they might need to ask fundamental questions.

As recently as 1944 the Holy Office had re-affirmed that the primary end of marriage was the procreation and education of children. Now this new Commission included lay, married members. They exchanged information. A report on this meeting stated, 'The group unanimously affirms that love is the heart of marriage and a majority of the members agree that the love of husband and wife should not, in any way, be ranked among the secondary ends of marriage.' This does not sound revolutionary; royal dynasties or business empires may look for heirs, but the average couple are thinking of each other when they decide to marry, unless, of course, they are marrying because the heir is already in the making. Even so, positions are reversed; procreation requiring marriage, not marriage requiring procreation. The point is that the edifice of wisdom and authority constructed by the Holy Office had seemed immovable; human experience was not expected to challenge it. This affirmation was a challenge that led further.

At this time, the end of 1964, Seán and I knew nothing of any Papal Commission but knew some discussion was going on. We read a report that Fr Bernard Häring had proposed that it might be permissible for a mother who was not able to breast-feed to take the Pill to prevent conception, on the grounds that this would have been prevented by lactation. I had a baby five months old; I wasn't breast-feeding; I asked our doctor for the Pill right away.

I did not consult anyone with a Roman collar. I might not have picked one who read the more adventurous journals. Ten years earlier, when I was expecting Máire Claire, we read in the *Catholic Herald* that a new decree allowed pregnant women and people who had to travel a distance, to receive Holy Communion without having to fast from midnight. Very welcome; I had to walk at least two miles down hill, then up again. During Mass on the following Sunday the priest announced that some concessions had been made, said that they would not affect anyone present, did not mention pregnancy. He was an uncommonly shy man; should have been in a monastery, a remote monastery, not a parish. After Mass I told him that I, at least, qualified and that I found it hard to believe I was unique.

I am writing in 1992. It occurs to me that many readers may be wondering, if I could make up my own mind on that, why hadn't I made it up long before to use effective contraception. The difference between the two rules is immeasurable. Everyone knew that fasting from midnight was a ruling imposed by the Church authorities which they could modify if they saw fit, for example in case of illness. After the Vatican Council it was reduced to one hour for everyone, nothing for the sick, and a drink of water any time. Avoiding contraception was a different matter altogether. We were told that it was not a ruling by the Church, it was part of the nature of things, the Natural Law. Generative organs were designed by their Creator for generation; to have intercourse while frustrating that design was against Nature.

This certainly looked reasonable; when we learnt more about Tradition, it did not look quite the same, but I must emphasise that we did not keep within this framework simply in order to obey Church rules. The rule was philosophically consistent; as we learnt later, it was borrowed from Stoic philosophy. And as I have said, by the time we were married Rhythm was available to moderate family size, or so we supposed. (In 1941 the Irish Censorship Board banned a book about the infertile period because spreading knowledge about it could lead to indecent conduct and public immorality.)

I have mentioned Rhythm several times, without explanation. There can be no one of my age or a good few years younger who does not know that sometime in the twenties or thirties scientists had ascertained that a woman could conceive only during a few days each month when an ovum had been released from one of her ovaries. Fertility control using this 'rhythm' was based on the hypothesis that one could predict these days, the potentially fertile days, by noting the number of days that usually elapsed between one menstrual period and the next. The remaining time was the 'safe period'.

All very well for women whose periods are regular; all very well for couples whose fertility is low. Quite otherwise for the rest of us. Other methods of prediction were later proposed and one is even now funded by the Irish Department of Health, but as will appear they are not relevant to the main dispute. In those days a bitter joke did the rounds: Q. What are those Catholics called who use the safe period? A. Parents.

It took the Papal Commission, with the help of married testimony, years to recognise that whether or not Rhythm regulated numbers, it did not harmonise at all with what they had come to recognise as 'the heart of marriage', love between husband and wife. In 1964 a book was published in the US, *Experience of Marriage*, by thirteen Catholic couples: 'the presentation for the first time in nineteen centuries of the opinions and comments of a group of articulate Catholic wives on marital sexuality'.

So much in it we could recognise; I could remember a chat a few years earlier with two other well-informed wives with several children each. We agreed that with this blessed Rhythm, by the time the 'safe period' arrived we wished sex had never been invented. You see, if you were well-informed, as we were, you knew that, not only must the husband not ejaculate, but the wife must not allow herself to experience orgasm. This while sharing the same bed.

So different with the magic Pill; I could say, 'Well, not tonight, if you don't mind, but tomorrow will be fine.' And it would be. Formerly there used to be the waiting and wondering, would a period ever happen? And a husband depressed for months when, after all our care, I was pregnant again.

Another book appeared, Professor John T. Noonan's *Contraception. How the Catholic Church has viewed birth control — from the earliest times to the present day*. In the earliest times it hadn't paid special attention; there was general disapproval of taking potions which might be magic, might be for abortion, might be to avoid conception. Then Augustine appears, around AD 400. As a Manichee, he believes material things are evil, it is wrong to bring unwanted babies into the world. He uses (non-scientific) knowledge of the 'safe period' to avoid them — though he had one child, Adeodatus. Once converted to Christianity, he went into reverse. 'Procreation is not an imprisonment of divine light, nor is sexuality, when directed to procreation, morally distinct from eating to nourish the body. But intercourse performed for pleasure is sinful, though as a rule not mortally sinful.... Physical procreation is now less important than spiritual, and couples advanced in perfection will abstain from sex altogether.' I am quoting here from Egner (*Birth Regulation and Catholic Belief*, Sheed & Ward, London 1966) who points out the most extraordinary thing of all in what Augustine says. 'There is not a word said about love or affection as motives for intercourse; the spouses are supposed either to want to procreate, or to appease desire.... God made man and wished him to multiply; to the procreative act he attached pleasure; man was to perform the act as the need for procreation demanded.... Given that Augustine believes all this — and thinks that this is all there is to believe — he is not likely to think that intercourse can serve to deepen love and intimacy between spouses. The very opposite is true. If sexual pleasure is now only a spiritually disturbing phenomenon incidental to the generative act, then it is bound to be just as impervious to integration into the personal life of the spouses as, say, the pleasure incidental to scratching one's back.'

This matters, because by chance of history, and by the fact that Augustine was by profession a master of rhetoric, that is, persuasion, his teaching had a near monopoly on Christian instruction for more than a thousand years. This is the Tradition that the Papal Commission was wrestling with. And then, on top of that, Noonan's history made it clear that, while a Manichee, Augustine would have used a version of the 'safe period'; when he changed sides he specifically ruled out intercourse at a time when the woman might be expected to be infertile. To quote Noonan, 'In the history of the thought of theologians on contraception, it is, no doubt, piquant that the first pronouncement on contraception by the most influential theologian teaching on such matters should be such a vigorous attack on the one method of avoiding procreation accepted by twentieth century Catholics.'

These researches fascinated Seán and myself. We found that during most of our married life we had been putting a great proportion of our energy into planning, calculation and self-restraint, that was trebly misguided. In the first place, the Natural Law tradition was largely a creation of Augustine's; secondly, this tradition outlawed the 'safe period', though those who pontificated about Natural Law by now talked about Rhythm as if it were peculiarly meritorious; finally, in spite of using a thermometer every morning, of feeling safe in making love only three or four days a month, and pretty anxiously then, we had had eleven children in sixteen years, which would seem to be rather more than would be likely if we had made no attempt to control production.

Debates filled newspaper columns. *The Irish Times* sometimes gave over a second page to letters, so did *The Times* in London, but it was evident that many correspondents had not studied Egner or Noonan. Indeed, I somehow found myself an associate member of the Irish Theological Association. During its AGM I sat down to dinner with a priest and a nun. A younger priest joined us and began to complain about dangerous new-fangled opinions. We asked whether he had read Noonan; when he said no, we just suggested he stop worrying until he had acquainted himself with that book.

I think I may permit myself a small boast. During that conference I took part in a discussion about original sin. I think I was able to refer to the Council of Trent, I know I had some of the ideas of Teilhard de Chardin in the background. A priest I knew slightly told me later that he had overheard two colleagues saying, 'That woman knows her stuff.'

I happened to have a piece in *The Irish Times* about St Augustine and how he treated the mother of Adeodatus and I got a fine innings that evening on the *Late Late Show*. Augustine's mother, St Monica, persuaded him to put away his socially unacceptable partner of eleven years in order to marry a good match. Meanwhile (having taken another mistress) he had his famous experience of hearing a voice telling him to read the book beside him, which contained the Gospels. He became a Christian, an enormously influential bishop, and had the nerve to write of a woman who lived with a man to whom she was not married, but who, when he put her away, 'remains faithful to him and, after he has taken a wife, does not plan to marry and is prepared to refrain absolutely from such an act...she is a sinner but I could not easily bring myself to call her an adulteress'. At that time the *Late Late Show*, a chat-show hosted by Gay Byrne, occupied 'peak time' on Saturday night television and had an unprecedented influence on Irish society.

With so much public debate going on it is not surprising that the group who had been trying to curb corporal punishment should discuss this also. Dr Jim Loughran often saw children who began bed-wetting when they started school; they were afraid; he noted that they were in huge classes in school and often came from families so large that the mother was anxious to get them to school out of the way. He arranged some lectures from a psychologist, a theologian and others. Someone met an official of IPPF — International Planned Parenthood Federation — who offered some advice and help. I had a chance to visit a FP clinic in Lisbon, organised by a priest, which was furnished like a comfortable family home. (I was on my way to fly home after escorting sixteen-year-old Tinu out to Spain to spend a holiday with her grandfather; she and I had so much fun on the boat together....)

Six of us became an action committee, Michael Solomons, Joan Wilson, Jim Loughran, Robert Towers, Dermot Hourihane, all doctors, and myself. It happened that Michael had been house-surgeon in Baggot Street while I was a student nurse there; he was now an esteemed gynaecologist. Joan came from Scotland, was married to a professor at Trinity, and worked as a GP. Dr Hourihane was an academic, Robert Towers a pathologist, neither intended to work in the proposed centre, but they were very concerned to set it up. My own motive, and Robert's also, was to help people to control their fertility and to know they could do so with a clear conscience. We got on very well together, never needed to take a vote on a decision; Michael said that if he found two meetings booked for the same evening he would always come to ours.

We co-opted a wise moral theologian and sought legal advice (importation or distribution of contraceptives was illegal; giving advice should not be; neither should information about addresses from which required articles could be ordered). Not by any means all doctors would prescribe the contraceptive pill — our doctors would prescribe it and they kept up with developments. The Pill did not suit everyone; a range of options was needed.

We set up a limited company and looked for a place for a clinic. We were refused several suitable places when the owners had to be informed about our subversive purpose. On one interview with a solicitor I look back with amusement; he was Mr C. C. O'Mahoney. I explained to him just how good and helpful family planning advice would be; I did not know that he would soon enough have his own highly conservative radio station. At last Jim found respectable consulting rooms in 10 Merrion Square, we furnished them in a welcoming manner and opened our doors two evenings a week, with a brass plate saying Fertility Guidance Association.

It was necessary to have a lay-worker to meet newcomers and re-assure them while noting their names and addresses and family size. Reassurance was my forte; since there were three doctors able to take sessions and only one of me I met all our early clients and could see how numbers were growing, especially after some radio interviews. We rather expected to be picketed by 'Maria Duce', to have bricks thrown through the window, even to go to jail. Nothing of the sort happened. Instead, Ladies' Clubs began to ask us to send a lecturer.

Michael was our star lecturer, an engaging speaker, able to answer any technical question and happening to be distinctly good looking as well. He would explain delicately all the methods of contraception — and he would be asked only about the 'safe period'. One evening I had accompanied him. Someone recognised me, asked had they not seen me on television. I said, possibly yes. But wasn't it a religious programme? Yes. In fact Fr Romuald Dodd, religious adviser to RTE, had got me on his list around that time. But if I was a Catholic, how could I be mixed up in this family planning business? We had to start the whole discussion all over again.

I would never be as polished a speaker as Michael, not to mention my appearance, but a practising Catholic mother of eleven, who could clarify questions of moral theology, was what women wanted then. A two-day seminar on public speaking organised by the British FPA was very helpful. When I debated at school people had found me difficult to understand. Now, at some panel discussion, a listener at the back of the hall called out that they couldn't hear anyone except that woman wearing whatever I was wearing. I have no doubt that years and years of reading aloud to children had cured my deficiency.

These evenings of discussion were very satisfactory. Often a club would be having its routine meeting, women would have come not knowing whether the talk would be about foreign travel or flower arranging, but their questions about family planning would be keen. I especially remember one large club in Dún Laoghaire where a questioner suggested that, if contraception made intercourse available during most of the month, might not men come to take their wives for granted? This floored me for a moment. Then I asked the whole club to help. When they went home, how many husbands were going to ask them what had happened this evening? What had been the topic? Who was the speaker? Was it interesting? Had they made a contribution? The whole roomful roared with laughter. When I went on to hint that wives were expected to have an interest in what their husbands were doing the meeting began to verge on consciousness raising, which was not, I believe, due to reach Ireland for some years.

I do not intend to write about the international debate on birth control or about the Irish solution. Each needs a book; for anyone curious Kaiser's should be easy to find and he gives references. Egner I prize because of the detailed scholarship with which he disclosed the lack of logic or system in the 'Roman Position', while sharpening the whole with witty footnotes. As for me, I am writing about me, about my experience of involvement in Irish family planning and what I learnt from it. After all, I suppose it to be the most influential activity I have found open to me. I answered invitations to talk over about four years. In Belmullet, where the weather comes from, the discussion went on until two in the morning. In Stillorgan, when one woman sighed that she wished the Pope would change his mind, the whole club turned on her and told her it wasn't a question of the Pope's mind, it was a question of something being right or wrong in itself. In Tallaght, where Dominicans have had the parish for hundreds of years, I showed the audience two booklets, one summing up the moral question, the other giving practical methods and failure rates. They chose the latter because the parish priest had already told them there was no need to worry. After this I told IFPA that I wasn't needed as a speaker any more.

Meanwhile our clinic opened for longer hours and more doctors and lay workers worked in it. The Papal Commission had given its report to the Pope, or rather its reports; four theologians produced a minority report. These reports were not published officially but were leaked to the National *Catholic Reporter* in the US and to *The Tablet* in Britain. Very reassuring, especially a few sentences in the minority report, to the effect that if uncle and niece can live together without carnal contact, why can husband and wife not do so.

Then, at the end of July 1968 news broke that the Pope had issued an Encyclical on the problem but that it didn't follow the advice of his own Commission. Mary Maher, who was then editor of 'Women First' in *The Irish Times*, a page that everyone read, asked me to come in and write about it while the complete English text was arriving by telex. I feel that the article deserves to be included here. Never before or since as a journalist have I handled such 'hot' news and I think my immediate reaction has a historical value, the more so since *Humanae Vitae* still lives. It was published under the title 'Marital Celibacy', with the following introduction:

> Máire Mullarney, mother of eleven children, is a WOMAN FIRST contributor specialising in pre-school education. In an article in *The Irish Times* of June 1967, she wrote of her own unsuccessful experiments with the Rhythm Method and investigation of the various theological works on the questioning of traditional Catholic attitudes towards birth control. She wrote then, 'If a formula is still being sought, would it be forward to suggest something on these lines: At one time authority supposed that money could not breed, while those dealing with it knew that it could. It was long held that sexual intercourse could, properly, only breed; those concerned are aware that it can do much more. In neither case does the second standpoint condone excess, whether usurious or uxorious'. Here Máire Mullarney discusses her own reaction to the papal pronouncement.

Then the article:

166

There remain only the religious and political questions, and the latter is likely to prove the most difficult, since the religious problem is virtually solved by the decision of the Pope to leave to each family the right to control or not to control the number of their children.'

That's what they thought in Brazil last December. There was a national conference of gynaecologists and obstetricians in Rio de Janeiro then, and 97% of them approved contraception under medical supervision.

In Germany, about the same time, the 'Family Planning' Study Commission of the German Catholic Physicians Association decided that 'practical experience proved that none of the known methods of contraception, in principle, destroy the complete personality factor in sexual intercourse. The defects of each method are reduced to the minimum in each individual case by the possibility of making the right choice from a great number of available methods. On these grounds also, it can no longer reasonably be put to the modern Christian that any of the known methods is in itself morally bad.'

What is going to be their reaction now that it is put to them that the whole lot are morally bad? It is particularly worth noting that the new Encyclical says that even Rhythm is only permissible 'when there is sufficient reason'. This seems to suggest a situation where the ordinary couple should make their minds blank with regard to the likelihood of fertility. It has always passed my understanding how the question of permission could arise in this matter. Either you know you have a fertile period or you don't. Once you know, how can you possibly ignore it?

Life must be very simple for women who are as regular as the moon. I cannot believe that any couple who could expect to keep their families within normal limits simply by staying apart four or five nights every month would think of burdening themselves with pills, much less any other complications. Sometimes when you read the more doctrinaire theologians you'd think that was all there was to it; that people who are not satisfied with rhythmic marriage are obsessed with sex.

In fact, of course, it's the other way round. Leaving aside the 10% who can't work Rhythm at all — and they are quite a lot of people — the majority have to think so much about times and thermometers that they begin to feel a little unbalanced. And then every so often there is a little mistake with the thermometer and the problem becomes that much more urgent.

The majority of the Pope's own Commission on Birth Regulation was quite definite in its recommendations. He has chosen to ignore them;

were they perhaps a bit too general, too abstract? If they had pointed out to him that the difficulties of clerical celibacy look pretty slight when compared to the marital celibacy that he now imposes on the very, very numerous couples who already have two more children than they have room or means to bring up, would they have had any weight?

I am not thinking of the kind of slums he is so soon to see in Bolivia; the sort of thing the President of Colombia meant when he spoke of moral wickedness having its incontrovertible origin in the crowding of people who are victims of the demographic explosion: promiscuity, frequent incest, child slavery, casual abortion. It is not for me to talk about something I have never seen; it is also unlikely that any papal pronouncement is going to have much weight with those who are able to do anything to relieve this sort of misery.

No, I'm thinking only of the dutiful Dublin homes — and who can know how many there are — where the mother sleeps with the girls and the father with the boys. It seems really incredible that the rulings which bring about this arrangement are being upheld on the grounds that the use of contraception can open up a wide and easy road towards conjugal infidelity and the general weakening of moral discipline. How is conjugal fidelity encouraged by a state of affairs in which a man dare not touch his wife?

A little further on, the Encyclical says that even if periodic abstinence demands continual effort: 'it brings to family life rich fruits of serenity and peace, and helps in solving other problems.' One must ask, did the writer consult even one ordinary couple who had tried, say, fifteen years of Rhythm, and then a few with the Pill, to learn which were more serene?

We are asked, too, to consider carefully what a dangerous power would be given to those public authorities who pay no heed to the precepts of the moral law. A very relevant question, if what was being debated were whether contraceptives should be invented or not. They now exist; the public authorities referred to will presumably go on their way regardless. Yet this argument is expected to influence married couples who want nothing more than to be faithful friends, each free to show the other how dear they are, especially when everything outside is impossibly tough.

I would like to have space to wonder about the fate of the Lisbon family planning centre where advice is given by priests as well as doctors and married couples; I was told it was under the protection of the Cardinal Patriarch.

There are interesting possibilities opened up by the French priests who hold that Catholics are free to obey the directives of the Council rather than the Pope's personal opinion.

But the question I would really like to put to our teachers is, what would the position be if Rhythm (for what it's worth) had not happened to be discovered? If there were not this plausible looking escape hatch, would the theologians be warning young couples that they must be prepared to rule out love-making for most of their married lives?

As a footnote to this article I would like to mention that the previous article containing a comparison with usury appeared first in *The Furrow* and was reprinted by *The Irish Times*, which was gratifying. And soon after this one appeared, Nuala Fennell (later Minister of State for Women's Affairs) told me how much she liked it and asked why I had not joined the NUJ (National Union of Journalists).

And to bring it up to date I shall add a paragraph from another newspaper, *The Observer*, of 7 June 1992, at the opening of the Earth Summit in Rio de Janeiro, where street children are being shot.

> Many Catholic developing countries, which recognise the economic and social sense of increasing availability of contraception, are reluctant to act because of Vatican opposition. The Holy See was a powerful participant in the final round of talks before Rio, held in April in New York, when population was finally discussed. With the support of Argentina and the Philippines, it forced the removal of the words 'contraception' and 'family planning' from the summit's green action programme, agenda 21.

After reading this, some people may wonder why I am still a Catholic. Essentially, because I believe in what the Catechism used to call 'the great mysteries of religion', the Unity and Trinity of God, the Incarnation, Death and Resurrection of Our Saviour. If God wanted us to know that we were loved, wanted to pass on a message from generation to generation, S/he had no other messengers except people. Now, even the apostles who lived with Jesus were constantly falling short in understanding what he told them; in two thousand years there were bound to be shortcomings, to say the least. In the nature of things, people who get to the top of any organisation are likely to be those with a taste for the top. When Jesus washed the apostles' feet before that Last Supper he told them that he was among them 'as one who serves'. (All right, I'm conflating two different gospels.) The point is, we have the gospels for comparison; we would not have them if there had not been some kind of organisation; at any time, a great many people live better because of them.

One could try to guess why Pope John Paul II is so hung up on contraception; I am more puzzled by the support of Argentina and the Philippines. And, come to that, family planning is not the key question; if one thing stands out, it is the crushing debt imposed by the 'First World' banks on the 'Third World'. But for that, millions of families might be growing their own food on reasonably fertile soil instead of using the best soil for cash crops while turning poor hillsides into desert by their efforts at cultivation. I have often wondered whether, if the Christian Churches had continued to oppose usury, would what we call 'development' have come about more slowly and quite differently? Might smaller industry have emerged using electric power instead of steam?

The 1992 Summit hasn't done anything worthwhile to deal with international debt, or energy, or saving species. And I am forgetting that I have only come as far as 1968.

CHAPTER 16

Getting it right in Helsinki and at home

To see the Fertility Guidance Company being accepted, battling through the courts and winning, to be one of an efficient Executive Committee doing something valuable, to be making more friends, to be welcomed by quite varied assemblies of women, was satisfaction enough, but an extra benefit came my way.

Once the company was set up it was appropriate that we should apply for association with the European Region of the International Planned Parenthood Federation. Two delegates were needed, one a doctor, one not. So Dr David Nowlan, of *The Irish Times*, who had joined the FGC, and I went to a conference in a very fine hotel in Stresa, on Lake Maggiore. Lunches were luxury and in the evenings we went out to eat real pizza. During the meeting I was especially impressed by a Polish philosopher whose thought spread wide, for example on the need for early education of children on the responsibilities of parenthood, but whose command of English did not allow him to bring out these ideas to the best advantage. I noted that the 'rapporteur' for each working group happened to be a native English speaker. I was a rapporteur myself, even though I was not long in the organisation, and during the group discussion I interpreted, by means of Spanish, for the priest from Lisbon.

I took advantage of a free day to hurry down to Florence to visit daughter Janet, who was established in a small garden-house of her own in Fiesole, where she was working as macrobiotic cook for the daughter of the ethologist Konrad Lorenz, and had enough free time to attend the Academy of Fine Arts. A delightful visit, the more delightful to see that she was recovering from her anorexia, which had been our greatest worry for several years.

Well, our hotel in Stresa had a wide, pillared terrace in front, looking out on the lake. Around each pillar grew a rose with red-tinged leaves and delicate single flowers which changed colour from elegant pointed scarlet bud, opened to apricot and gradually darkened to a cloud of rich dark ruby. I had that rose in my garden, a cutting given us by Nancy and Billy O'Sullivan. By now every family member who has a garden has that rose. Then, I did not know its name. I happened to borrow a library book by an Australian woman who collected roses everywhere she went. She had the pleasure of staying in Stresa in a hotel which had been George Bernard Shaw's favourite; it had a pillared terrace looking onto the lake, and the rose that grew around the pillars was Rosa mutabilis.

The following year, when Ireland's application was accepted and welcomed, IPPF Europe Region met in Helsinki. Not so comfortable; the Finnish summer sun shines all night and the curtains in our student residence did not even try to keep it out — the students wouldn't be there in summer. Smörgåsbord breakfasts were marvellous. I was given enough information about the child-care system to write two articles for *The Irish Times*. The Finns made excellent provision for the handicapped, right up into the Arctic circle. They had teams of well-trained child-carers who would go into the home and look after a sick child so the mother would not miss work. Even so, they were worried because the birth rate did not reach replacement levels. My own view was that there is not much point in having a child unless you can live with it, ill and well, at least when it is young. At the end of this book you will find that some Finnish mothers think much the same.

On the way back from Finland I was able to break my journey at Copenhagen and meet Seán for our first real holiday abroad — Spain had hardly been a holiday. Using an ordinary camera but with much care in composition, he took photographs that bring back a happy time, wandering through rose-red fortifications, admiring swans, enchanted by the waterfalls of fireworks in Tivoli. A pleasant surprise on Sunday was a beautifully sung Latin Mass in the Marmorkirche — English had taken over at home but I had found Latin still in use in Finland also. A further pleasure was to feel well dressed in clothes made from the airy hand-printed tweeds that Barbara was then designing and printing for McNutt's of Carrigart.

The meeting in Stresa was in 1972. A diary shows that I had a busy year, every week notes an article or a review or a speaking engagement somewhere, but the note hardly ever records the title of the book. The annual report of Fertility Guidance says I spoke to more than twenty groups, while the much enlarged team of doctors spoke to doctors and medical students. By that time even Oliver was attending school in the mornings — he started to go to the German school three mornings a week when he was six.

So many of the articles reflect fragments of everyday life at the time, fragments I might otherwise have forgotten, that they must find a place here. One, for example, about having a Seder, a paschal meal, on Holy Thursday, was published first in one religious magazine, then copied in another in 1968, the very year during which we were preparing to set up family planning. It starts by recalling 'a real Lent'; the black tea and dry bread my mother had told me about. I suggest that 'that tradition was very Irish: Rome could hardly have laid down rules about black tea, since they don't really know there what tea is. As for butterless bread, that's what they normally have, but they wash it down with wine.' I explain that I do not remember when we first tried this meal, certainly it was before the eldest was twelve but that now the children think it the best meal of the year. It was a simple version: lamb, wine, salad, matzos, grated apple and nuts, eventually an almond cake, included on the advice of Fine's of Terenure, a Jewish shop quite near us.

> I can assure anyone interested that a lamb chop tastes much better with those accompaniments than it does with potatoes and vegetables. That's presumably one reason the children enjoyed the meal; with eleven children altogether, wine and the better sorts of meat were not plentiful. The real excitement, though, came from eating it standing up around the table. We had taken the instructions in Exodus literally, at least to that extent.

We had a special prayer for the celebration, but the essential part was the question from the youngest present, 'Why are we having this different kind of bread?'

> In a Jewish family the father replies, 'We eat unleavened bread because when our fathers were leaving the land of Egypt, *on this night*, there was no time for the bread to rise' and the Christian parent will add, 'and this is the bread that Jesus gave to his friends *on this night* when he was eating this meal with them.'

How much more you say depends on the children you are talking to. It seems to me a reasonable guess that when Jesus was a boy it must sometimes have been his role to ask the questions, with perhaps Joseph answering, perhaps some older relative. More important is the folding up, the telescoping of time, so that our 'now' is also that 'now'.

For myself I like to reach back further and remember that the meal commanded in Exodus and the sprinkling of the blood around the door seems to have been a traditional ceremony before Moses was ordered to make use of it. This links the Mass of today with innumerable holy meals before history began.

It is not easy for technological humans to understand that in earlier biblical times every animal that was killed for food was also a sacrifice, that Greek and Roman literature, our European foundations, are littered with sacrifices, wine and oil as well as animals. It seems the least we can do for our children is to make available to them some links with their ancestors.

I am glad to have this record, not only because if I hadn't got it I would not remember (at least until next Holy Thursday) what we used to do, but because the magazine in which it appeared, *Reality*, sent a photographer round and there's an affection-prompting picture of Eoin, just past being a baby, holding a matzo and looking up with enquiry and trust while Seán stoops down to explain. There's me and Killian and a bottle of wine and a favourite Spanish dish in the picture too.

It seems to come naturally to me to feel that Time is ephemeral; it amazes me when I ask Seán about anything, he can place it right away. I asked him when did he think we'd been in Copenhagen and he said, off the cuff, 1973, which places Stresa in 1972. I find a piece commissioned about then. I was to write some reflections on the fact that one can be one's true self at home. I compared two fathers arriving home rather late to the same meal.

The soup in both kitchens has been kept warm for quite a while, has been quietly evaporating and is now on the salty side.

At one table are a couple of children, eight and nine years of age, doing their homework. They could have done it earlier but they find it useful to have a father available.

'Yes, if there is one puppy you put an apostrophe — the little comma on top — after puppy and then put s; if there are several puppies you write p-u-p-p-i-e-s and put the apostrophe *after* the s.... I wonder could I have a drink of milk with this, darling, the soup was a little bit salty.'

Apologies and milk.

'Not at all, it's my fault I'm late. The potatoes are perfectly alright.... No, for men's you put the apostrophe before the s. Men is plural just as it is.... Is this our own rhubarb....

The next paragraphs picture a husband who grumbles about being poisoned with salt and thinks with the whole day to do it she could manage a bit of gravy 'and it does not go without saying that rhubarb is not food for human beings at all'.

I had had models for both approaches to meals. I reflected, of the first, that at the end of a working day his interest in the use of the apostrophe was minimal. I find a few other examples, like my own conversation with a travelling woman at the door.

Her story seems inconsistent in several respects, but it would be impolite to question it. I listen and make sympathetic responses while my real self is thinking, 'We both know that what I'll give you will be just the same anyway; I'd give a lot to see you housed and educated, but these chats don't really advance the matter.' But perhaps they do; anyway, actual self plays its part.

However, I'm writing on a day of gale force winds; there are trees down here and there and we have been without electricity since morning. A twelve-year-old comes stamping in from school, furious. They're silly, useless; if we pay for electricity we should have it. I give a short meditation on the trials of linesmen. Do him good to be up there with the cables being blown out of his hands; then he wouldn't be squawking because he couldn't make toast. Half an hour later I find him in the kitchen and he says, 'You know, Mama, I was wrong to make such a fuss.' I'm charmed with the acknowledgement, and say so.

I'm coming to the rather cheerful conclusion, in spite of what St Paul says about not doing the good we would do, that in ordinary society most of us, most of the time, are doing quite a lot more good, or at least avoiding a great deal more selfishness, than our natural selves would feel inclined to, and we don't give ourselves any credit. Home or abroad, real selves are kept in order most of the time, and just as well they are.

There is some more: an apt quotation from Dostoevsky, which I had spotted just then in *The Tablet* (it has a column of such excerpts every week): 'You pass by a little child, you pass by, spiteful, with ugly words, with wrathful heart; you may not have noticed the child, but he has seen you, and your image, unseemly and ignoble, may remain in his defenceless heart....' Then, my final paragraph:

> It's comforting to turn the last corner on the way home, to see that your arrival has been watched for by a skinny six-year-old, that he's running full pelt to be picked up and hugged and given your basket to carry; to know that some at least of the feelings of your real self can be demonstrated without misgivings.

I do in fact remember quite vividly Oliver running down to meet me on one particular day, but the apology in respect of electricity linesmen would have vanished totally, along with thousands of other exchanges, if I hadn't happened to be asked to write it down in time.

I should think it obvious that the model for the helpful father was Seán at his most patient. The model for the father who does not muzzle his real self was partly based on my own father, but I find I must add that though he would bluster about food he would have helped with homework if help had been needed. He tried in many ways to be good and I should think he would have been glad to know that when he died it was going to be quickly, after a heart attack, in a hospital dedicated to Our Lady of Fatima. I got a telegram summoning me to come to Alicante, where Alex had been living for a few years. By the time I arrived he was already buried, and arrangements had been made by the British Consul, who had at least one burial of a retired citizen every week. I visited his grave, found orange trees in fruit around it — it was early in January — and arranged for a headstone. The feast of Los Reyes, the Three Kings, the Epiphany, happened while I was there and I thought I would love to bring the younger children some time to share the celebrations, but they are no longer children and it never happened.

The most memorable thing about that journey was not the orange trees or a feeling of loss — I'm afraid I had no such feeling — but the gain from having hours of train journey in both directions to read Karl Popper's *The Open Society and its Enemies*. It is the sort of book that requires more time without distraction than I could manage at home. It is immensely valuable for anyone who wants to think about politics, as opposed to simply happening to get involved. He said it was his contribution to the war against Hitler. For me it seemed to be a compressed education; it also vindicated the distaste I had felt for Plato ever since I read *The Republic*.

Popper argued that Plato had at first given a fair report of Socrates' conversation but in later dialogues had foisted on Socrates his own increasingly authoritarian leanings. Popper further traced Plato's penetrating influence on European education through the centuries. This book is similarly challenging in respect of Hegel and Marx. He held that all sweeping political change was problematical; that remedies should be tried out on a small scale; that scientists should always have the humility to recognise that their discoveries are only approximations to the truth; that only a hypothesis which is capable of being disproved can claim to be scientific. Indeed, I am not sure that these later arguments are found in *The Open Society* but once I mention Popper I find his best-known conclusions follow on. I read with satisfaction his sceptical views on schooling.

Ivan Illich published *Deschooling Society* in 1971. I find that it was in 1970 that I began to write the book that thirteen years later was published as *Anything School Can Do, You Can Do Better*. I had been writing for some time about early learning, about maths or reading or language or art, suggesting that children would profit much more from a short time in small groups than from long days in enormous classes. I had reported talks given by visiting lecturers to the Pre-School Playgroups Association or similar societies.

I had written about Montessori from several aspects. People running two different Montessori associations (which used to be rivals but which now get on well) have told me that my articles were influential in putting it on the educational map for parents, even if nothing could convince the Department of Education. By now it is not just on the map but all over it. Irish establishments send teachers (properly titled directresses) to Sweden, to the USA, even to Rome itself, where the movement started. The current L.1,000 note in Italy carries a benevolent portrait of Montessori on one side, a picture of her talking with children on the other.

However, nothing that I could write in a thousand or fifteen hundred words gave a balanced picture. If I mentioned children doing work around the house there wasn't space to say that they were enjoying multiplication of fractions as well, and vice versa. The end products were beginning to appear. I have already said something about the art competitions in which Barbara and Janet took top places and mentioned that Alasdar had been notably good at technical drawing. With four A-Levels in one year he had won a scholarship to Bolton Street College of Technology to study mechanical engineering, and while there a university scholarship which he preferred not to take up. Tinu had been awarded the gold medal of the Botanical Gardens, plus a university scholarship. She had done her Leaving Certificate at the age of sixteen, got the honours which, in the following year, would have given her a scholarship, but the scheme was still only a promise, so she went to work instead. Barbara and Janet had also got results that would allow them to go to university if they wanted to — or could afford to. Go to university — I realise that if I am writing about 1971 she was already at the Royal College of Art in London, on her way to a Master's degree, M. Des. RCA.

In short, they were doing rather well, in various ways, having had four or five fewer years of schooling than was customary — starting at age eight instead of the more usual four, most of them finishing at sixteen. Furthermore, when we had three children at the German School — Pierce, Killian, Alison — we were very pleased with it, but had doubts about sending Eoin, the chap who didn't talk until he was two and a quarter, but latched onto whole-word reading. Two doctors, in hospital and in the local clinics, had said he wasn't deaf, but he didn't seem to pick up everything that was going on. The Professor of Psychology at UCD had said, in an influential paper, that children with an average IQ should not be required to learn a second language. I think, indeed, that he said 'an IQ less than 120' but I have no reference; his point was that all Irish children going to National Schools were being faced with a numbing input of Irish at an early age; teachers were supposed to pretend that they did not understand English. Well, I had doubts about asking Eoin, at six, to do half his schoolwork through German.

I arranged to have the two, Eoin and Oliver, tested at the St John of God Centre quite near us. Oliver went off happily with his mentor; Eoin was fussed, so the psychologist testing him allowed me to be present, if silent. I was very interested. So was Eoin. The two faced each other across a table. Eoin was eager to do everything he was asked, understood everything, perhaps because of being so close to his questioner. When both had been assessed Dr John Stack came out to me and said that, while at that age (Oliver was four) measurements could only be general, the two had qualified as 'superior', and he added that he wished more mothers did as I had been doing. I explained that I had brought them because I was not sure Eoin would be able for the challenge of another language, and I mentioned that we had been told he was not deaf. Dr Stack's answer was that, while he was reading uncommonly well for his age, the mistakes he made were of the sort associated with deafness; he told me where to go for accurate testing.

It turned out that he was missing a range of sounds; this could be remedied by the insertion of a small tube in each ear. He now has an honours degree in human nutrition and speaks German with ease. If he had been let go to school at four and slide to the back of the class because of not hearing everything, this might not be so. Just as, if Oliver had not being doing maths with Colour Factor for a couple of years at home he might not have found a degree in mathematics so manageable. He said himself that it was not until he was in college that he realised how good CF was. At the time I was curious, saw a possible subject for an article, checked with my editor, and arranged to have the five school-age offspring tested at the Department of Psychology, UCD. The report said something nice about what a pleasure they were to deal with; figures for full-scale WISC were 117, 122, 122, 125, 137. I have Verbal and Performance figures too; no need to bring them in — though I see one of the 122s had a Verbal IQ of 134.

It is interesting that the three lower figures were the three who were latest to read. One of them, the 117, didn't much bother with lessons because he had been birdwatching since he was three or four; if there had been anything ornithological in the WISC battery of questions he would have shot up. The other two were the unlucky ones who were taught in the sequence planned by the Teacher's Book that accompanied Beacon Readers; the ones who had to check up on tedious Kitty and Rover.

I was able to compare these results with a very large-scale assessment which was begun in England, taking in all 8,000 children born during one week of March 1946; they had been assessed at intervals ever since. A report of this study said that, though clever children are of course found in large families as well as in small, the average level of mental ability declines with each increase in family size. Children from really large families (of six or more) are at as much of a disadvantage if their fathers are in the professions as if they follow some middle-class occupation.

I must be thankful that the survey found some 'really large families of six or more' with fathers in the professions. It might no longer be so easy. Our children's father is an accountant; whether he is middle-class or professional, the younger children are not apparently intellectually disadvantaged. Come to think of it, it was the seventh who was awarded the highest IQ of those measured. I certainly do not believe that a WISC figure is a measure of a person's worth but it was the type of measure used in the large-scale assessment. I cannot believe that in all those families there were not many parents as attentive as we were. The difference was that we unwittingly experimented with provision for 'early cognitive development', including reading. It looked as if we might have got it right; as if there might be material for a book.

On the morning that Oliver set out to school with his brothers and sister I sat down blissfully at my typewriter; I was going to have three empty mornings every week to write my book. I began. That afternoon they arrived home with temperatures which could soon be seen to signal mumps. Well, it is a good thing for boys to catch mumps young. It is also an eye-opener for a mother who has for twenty years thoroughly enjoyed having active children about the place to find that she experienced painful deprivation on being cut off so early from her book.

Eventually some mornings were my own again and I had the pleasure of writing without counting the words. I still had the other pleasure of lessons with Oliver on the other mornings, and I could get on with journalism in his company. In the next term he went every morning, I got on with the book, but I was very pleased when, on the last day of term, he said, 'On Monday, Mama, we'll have lessons. I'll do Colour Factor, and we'll read *American Indian Mythologies* and then I'll do some writing.' That, after all, was why I was writing the book; because children like learning under their own steam. *American Indian Mythologies* was a present from a visiting member of IPPF who had stayed with us; Oliver loved Indians but the book was hard to read, so he arranged that we should read paragraph by paragraph turn about.

My book had its own adventures. I sent some chapters and an outline to a major publisher who had other books about children learning. I was encouraged, and finished it — my title was *Dinosaur on a Watershed*, because I thought there would be few large families in the future. It was returned in the post — on Christmas Eve. But the editor said he had liked it well enough to give it to five readers, who liked it also; two voted for publication, three said that mothers do not want to stay at home. So I tried again, had a London agent for a while, re-wrote for another publisher, then gave up.

Meanwhile my mother came to live with us, not because she was not contented on her own but because the house in which she had her flat was sold and she had to move. She also had to be compensated; some of the money was spent on setting up a wooden — well, we call it 'the hut', it is a large room of the garden-shed family, well placed, higher than the rest of the garden, with windows carefully arranged. Each of the older children in turn, Alasdar first, was eager to live in it. This extra space allowed us to give Granny Ad a large room upstairs, from which she could look down on our own garden and also on the pastoral fields across the road, where there was still a stream bordered by willow trees and a few ornamental cows. Those fields are filled with houses now; at least the trees and hedges in the gardens have grown up.

Just when she came I do not remember, but it was not before May 1969. The twelfth of May was Granny's birthday. An old-fashioned creamy rose growing on the wall near the stone seat was and is always in bloom in time for that date. She used to come over to us from Donnybrook and a birthday cake would always be waiting. When Eoin was six years old he asked whether he might make Granny's birthday cake. I thought this a good idea and said he could begin while I was out shopping in the village. He could buy what he needed from the little shop next door, Miss Crimmins's. I went off on my bicycle, for half an hour or more, allowing for conversation. When I returned I asked whether he had got everything he needed. He said he had. 'The cake's in the oven and it will be done when the pinger goes.' Good work, but not too surprising when I say that I almost always made the same Victoria Sponge mixture and used the same proportions — five ounces of flour, three ounces of sugar and three ounces of butter or margarine to each beaten egg, with a little extra liquid — and one or two children often multiplied, measured and mixed.

During the first years she was with us Granny had continued almost as she had when in her flat. She told stories to the little ones, helped the others with sewing, disapproved of my engagement in family planning — though she had also disapproved of increasing numbers in the family. A friend of hers had locked her bedroom door. This would not, of course, have any connection with the bad humour of that friend's husband, which had alienated his sons. I would not have dreamt of suggesting such a connection to an elderly Catholic lady. I really sympathised with her distress when she found that the older children were not going to Mass; I was sorry about it too. She used the word 'apostates' and implied that that was what I could expect when they heard so much criticism of the Church.

It was not as simple as that. Indeed I asked Janet later on why she dropped out. She thought about it and said that our celebrations at home — Ash Wednesday, Holy Thursday, Good Friday, Easter, and some lesser festivities — were so much more effective than what happened in Church that she couldn't be bothered going. Parents can't win.

Granny and I on the whole avoided confrontation. She went to ten o'clock Mass every morning as a matter of course and in good weather got value out of her free travel pass even though her walking aid would have to be handed up to her. [In Ireland, people over 65 can go anywhere free by bus and train, with a few restrictions around peak hours in the cities.] She also used to read *The Furrow* so she must have been well aware that I had well-informed company in my by-passing of Rome.

Of course the journalism carried on. It is a pleasure to read again my review of Elaine Morgan's *The Descent of Woman*. My editor, Mary Maher, was so impressed with this book, published on 5 October 1972, that she gave it two reviews, one she wrote herself, one she gave to me. She ended her own by saying, 'As for females, I don't think any of us should go through another day of the future without examining this revolutionary viewpoint of our past. *The Descent of Woman* costs 50 bob, and get it out of the housekeeping, no matter who goes without what.' I wrote,

> Elaine Morgan's thesis is that our primate ancestors went into the sea when Africa got too hot for them and stayed there, or thereabouts, slowly adapting for some ten million years until the climate made land attractive again. If this is so, it would account for the shortage of remains between Proconsul and Australopithecus (people used to talk about the 'missing link').... It would do much to account for our shape, both inside and outside, our noses, our frowns, our tears — the only weeping primate of any kind and the only one that frowns. It gives really good reasons for the development of speech and standing upright; it tells us why we need marriage counsellors and major-generals and offers some suggestions about why there aren't many women in politics.

I suggested that if to Irish readers evolution doesn't seem very exciting, it's because we have been looking over our shoulders at Adam and Eve. British children are saturated in cave-man lore from an early age. I knew this because, with the children at home, I had for years been making use of valuable BBC schools programmes on radio and getting their year-plan pamphlets.

And that is why an alternative hypothesis about human evolution must be of special interest to women. It's because the version that holds the floor is so centred on competition and aggression, assuming that women are the passive rewards rather than developers, while this new version explored the long-term worth of female values. Mary's review was illustrated by a photograph of confrontational rugby players, with the caption '...all our governance is based on male-bonding, and male-bonding on at least a low-powered rumbling of aggression.... We are constantly in danger of seeing our communities revert at intervals into the terrible agonic semblance of a troop of baboons.'

Elaine Morgan remarked that right through the animal kingdom, and especially among primates, females enjoy their babies. This holds too among less complicated humans. She recollected her own childhood in a Welsh valley; when a new baby was being shown off everyone would glow and someone would always say, 'Can I hold him for a bit?' The mother would graciously grant the favour but would take him back if he cried. Exactly the behaviour of baboons. My review continued:

> Other primates clearly enjoy carrying their babies around and watching what they do. How have we come to think of them so often as something someone else should mind? Well, we've become civilised, babies haven't. They make us feel rumpled, disorganised, housebound. Mrs Morgan suggests that efficient contraception should soon tend to confine motherhood to those who want to be motherly, who should in turn get the support and esteem they deserve. For her own part, she's sure that a child is happier and thrives better if it can establish a continuing relationship with one adult.

When I see that in the review I referred to 'Mrs' Morgan I realise that all of twenty years have passed since I wrote it. During those twenty years women have gained substantially in self-confidence. To some extent at least this self-confidence is based on demonstrations that they can do the things men do. Still, I have been heartened by evidence from here and there that women who have proved they can do the things men do are catching up on Morgan's view that if a mother got half the back-up for her work with a baby that a man (or woman) gets for work in an office she might even rediscover that this job is far more rewarding and creative than most, and that young children are even more fascinating to watch than otters.

Perhaps women's thinking is subject to the same pull of inertia as the thinking of theologians, bishops and scientists. Elaine Morgan is a professional researcher and writer for television. In her latest book, *The Scars of Evolution*, published by Souvenir Press in 1990, she explains how she came to write *The Descent of Woman*. She says that in 1930, when Alister Hardy as a young marine biologist conceived the idea of an aquatic phase in human evolution his friends warned him that publishing such a heresy would mean committing professional suicide. He admitted later, 'I wanted a good professorship; I wanted to be a member of the Royal Society.' So he kept quiet about it for the next thirty years. When he finally published his idea in 1960 the response from the scientific community was nil. Elaine Morgan was interested. She had no ambition to be a member of the Royal Society. She has pursued her research, putting together recent findings from different disciplines, seeing how they converge. *The Scars of Evolution* is enlightening not only about the peculiarities of humans but about the innocent way in which scientists can avoid dealing with anomalies that do not suit the prevailing theory. Several quite distinct discoveries in geology and molecular biology have emerged that can no longer be ignored.

> 'In 1987 an international conference was held in the Netherlands where the pros and cons of the aquatic ape theory were publicly debated, and that event represented some kind of a watershed.'

Where *The Descent of Woman* was about what women can do, *The Scars of Evolution* is a splendid example to all of us of what one woman has done, and it is sharply funny throughout.

I read an article about this book in *The Observer*, and told Tinu of it when she asked what she could give me for Christmas. Later I went to visit a friend to whom I had promised to lend the book. It's a longish bus journey, but not long enough to read a whole book. When I arrived I said, 'You'll have to finish this quickly; I can't wait to read it again.'

CHAPTER 17

A second language for everyone: Vienna leads to Budapest

One present recalls another. The book Tinu gave me reminds me of her most recent gift, a set of compact discs, and prompts me to write something about my fortunate discovery of the music that best satisfies me. I have said more than once in this book that I am musically deficient: I cannot sing, I cannot play any instrument, I do not seem to have the memory that other people have, people who can tell one Brandenberg concerto from another or know for certain what is going to come next in a piece of music they have heard only a few times.

Seán encouraged me to listen to music on the radio, to guess from what century and what country it came, possibly identify the composer. I recognised that Mozart could make me feel happier, that there was plenty of music that I enjoyed, that Wagner was much too noisy for me. Once I had my own tape-recorder I could have background music while writing. Other people do that, though I understand that truly musical people think it wrong. One evening I happened to go into the drawingroom when the television was on although the room was empty. Dame Janet Baker was singing the role of Penelope in Monteverdi's *Ritorno d'Ulisse*, broadcast live from Glyndebourne. It was for me a new experience of music. I sat on the floor, forgetting everything until the end of the act. Then I remembered that the tape-recorder might capture some of the remainder. So it did, though of course inadequately.

After that revelation Seán helped me to collect more music by Monteverdi on cassette, copied from the radio or from records borrowed from the record library. Some madrigals, of which I could not catch all the words, I might use as background for other activities, but where I had the text, as in the combat of Tancred and Clorinda, I would have to read and listen. For me at least Monteverdi is an alchemist who enables words to transform themselves into golden music. I am most grateful to the scholars and singers who have, it seems, only rather recently disclosed his quality. I bought a tape made up of recordings of Gigli singing arias from operas by Donizetti, Bizet, Mozart and Monteverdi. Marvellous voice — I remember records I heard when young. What will he make of Monteverdi? In effect, just what he made of Handel, a lovely sound, but not special. And that recording was made in 1947.

So how fortunate I am to have the whole of *Il Ritorno d'Ulisse in Patria*, the music played on original instruments by Concentus musicus of Vienna, on three CDs, accompanied by complete text, the whole a gift from Tinu when I told her that I had treated myself to a CD player. She knew that I had gone to London by boat and bus, in the winter, when a review said that the opera was being beautifully performed. So it was, but in English. This is deeply satisfying and I can listen to it whenever I wish.

It would be incorrect if I were to give the impression that Tinu alone gives presents. A few chapters ago I described the house when we first came here. Now on the walls there are Barbara's earlier paintings, pottery that satisfied her Japanese teacher in Washington, wall hangings made when she was a weaver, prints made by her own technique, rugs on the floor that she designed, woven by Tibetan refugees in India. The most lasting record of Alasdar's presence here are the garden paths which he took up and laid properly when he decided that my builders had done a sloppy job. He gives me cases of wine but somehow I do not manage to keep them. Janet's cherrywood lady, one of her earlier sculptures, reclines on the long Swedish settle in the drawingroom. Aidan made the saw-horse on which I enjoy sawing logs for my wood-burning stove — look back to the first chapter where I remember my mother sawing wood for the fire. The white roses blooming now were gifts from Claire. Killian has contributed drawings of birds and small animals; he has also asked an incredulous mother to give him one or two of her own amateur watercolours, painted so many years ago, so weak compared to his own exquisite observations. He has had them framed and says he likes them; that's another kind of present. To round out the list neatly I can say that the computer on which I am writing was a gift arranged by Oliver, Eoin and Pierce, with contributions from the others.

To return to the seventies, we had agreed that two flights of stairs was too much and my mother moved down to the room on the ground floor in which we used to have lessons. Sitting in her chair beside the further window, with window-sill on one side, small table salvaged from Gibraltar on the other, she could look out on the garden while reading, writing or chatting with her visitors. The wide stone seat was outside that window and she made sure it always had crumbs for the birds. Across the path was, or is, a rose bush, now taller than I am, which was there when we came to the house and which every year in early June becomes a glow of warm apricot. It appears to be a hybrid tea growing on its own roots, unbothered by aphis or blackspot. Now and again I try to raise cuttings but none have survived.

This rose, and a quantity of peonies and hydrangeas, are on this side of the two pear trees that I planted as year-olds when we came and tried to train as espaliers to make a division between house and garden. I wanted to imitate a row of pear trees I had seen in the gardens of St Columba's College; mine are not quite so orderly, but the division is just as I wanted it, with an Irish Juniper as an exclamation mark at the corner where the path up the garden begins. The edge of the path along the front of the house (laid by Alasdar) and a sort of rockery beside the wall are, in season, thick with cyclamen, coum and europaeus, roundy pink-backed leaves or marvellous marbled pointed shield-shaped ones, I can't remember which is which. Their trusting, folded-back little pink flowers bring, when the leaves are gone, half-inch spheres full of seeds, each on a stalk which has curled into a spring. I have been assiduous in directing ripe seeds where I want them to spread and by now have quite good cover also around the base of the copper beech.

The path up the garden winds in the way we used to walk up to the yew arch when there was nothing but grass and a peach tree. We marked our steps and laid flat blocks two or three yards out from the wall, planted our raspberries in a bed beside the wall, sheltered from the east wind. Now the grass has long been stacked to make humus and one is pushed off the path by the pink genista which flowers like a fountain, later by the white cistus with a purple blotch. There is a further narrow bed on the outer side of the path, a river of blue for weeks when the forget-me-nots are in flower, all descended from one packet my mother sowed even before she came to live here. And in every flower bed except one (I banish it from the grey circle) the butterfly flowers of aquilegia wave in their various purples and pinks; my aunt Geg is responsible for these, she gave me a few from her own garden when we came here.

What is happening here is very like what happens when I go into the tangible garden and am tempted to pull up just a few infant Robin-run-the-hedge. One weed leads to another, I forget that I came out for tansy for the rhubarb and by the time I remember the rhubarb has boiled over and there's toffee on the Aga.

I intended to say that my mother at ninety was still walking slowly down to daily Mass with her walking frame and making new friends, who would drop in to visit. We disagreed strongly about contraception but agreed about flowers. Gradually she found walking more difficult. After a slight stroke, she was sent home from hospital with a list of twelve drugs; I took her off all except three and she came back to her intelligent self. The parish priest then came up to drive her down, but eventually it seemed better for her to wait in bed in the mornings and he would bring Holy Communion three days a week.

From my selfish point of view this regime tied me to a timetable; it seems to have begun when Oliver was twelve or thirteen, when all the children were old enough to look after themselves in the morning, but I must still be on duty sharp at ten past seven. Well, it was her turn; I used to waken her in the morning many years before. She would not, however, willingly acknowledge that our roles were now reversed. The parents' meetings in the German School were convivial affairs. When we arrived home well after one o'clock in the morning I noticed a light on in Granny's room. She was sitting up in bed, waiting to scold me for staying out so late, neglecting the children.

How did Seán and I manage to get away to Austria for three whole weeks in 1979? There was a bargain flight, on a plane bringing scouts to a jamboree in Ireland. As far as I remember we persuaded Granny to go to a nursing home, the one where de Valera had been, Talbot Lodge. She met nice people there, corresponded with them afterwards, but once was enough.

We had an excellent time both in Vienna and up in the mountains. It is mean of me to mention chess, but I'm going to. We had now and then played chess at home, impromptu chess, not the serious game one studies in books. I loved it, though if I won more than one game in three or four I was surprised. But it was the case that at home in the evening my concentration was frequently interrupted. If there wasn't bread in the oven at risk of burning there was something I must remember for Granny or one of the children. We brought a pocket set on the holiday and had agreeable games on the plane and in parks in Vienna. Up in the woods on the mountains life was very peaceful and undistracted. We took out the chess set. I won the first game. And the second. And the third. And somehow, we have never played chess since then.

That did not interfere with our enjoyment of the rest of the holiday, a voyage on the Danube, the return to Vienna. When we were there I decided to visit the Botanic Gardens for a second time; Seán was off to one castle too many. When I had looked again at the plants that interested me I sat on a bench to read. A hand on my shoulder, 'Máire Mullarney, is that you?' We had told Janet, still living near Florence, about our plans. We had called frequently at the Poste Restante to get news from her. She had written, then hitched up to meet us; they hadn't given us her letter, though they found it all right when it was too late to be of any use. She had slept out in a park for a couple of nights, had decided that she had missed us and had better go home when she said to herself, 'Ma always goes to visit Botanic Gardens; I'll have one more try.' I don't know when I have had such a heart-warming surprise. The three of us had some good days together, Seán and I taking advantage of having a well-informed guide to the Belvedere, now a picture gallery, Janet having proper meals. As for me, I find it difficult enough to get used to the idea that our grown-up children really like us; to find that Janet would hitch so far, then risk sleeping out in a sleeping bag just for our company amazed and humbled me. Any reader who feels that it is a matter of course to seek out one's parents must remember that from the time I was twelve my inclination had been otherwise.

Seán and I had already engaged in exploration that had unforeseen results. When he was a boy scout he had been introduced to the international language, Esperanto, and had learnt enough to make some post-card pen-friends. He noticed that on the tourist list was the Esperanto-Museo in the Hofburg. We wandered through furlongs of corridors before we came upon a series of long, sunny rooms lined with laden shelves. The Director was pleasant, but Seán had quite forgotten the language and neither of us had enough German for complicated conversation. He gave us a few typed sheets of information which I put into my case and forgot.

Three summers later I had breakfast in a fine hotel in Budapest. Naturally I engaged in conversation with the gentleman who shared my table. After the usual discussion of the congress; 5,000 people perhaps too many, but the stadium very suitable; he asked me a not infrequent question. What country did I come from? What language

189

did I speak at home? Ireland; English. Favourable comment on not having an English accent. And how had I come to learn our language? Well, I had happened to visit the Esperanto Museo and the Director had given me some leaflets. 'But I am the director who gave them to you!'

Months had gone by before I needed to look into the suitcase I had brought back from Vienna. I glanced at the duplicated pages and found that I could almost understand them. To show what I mean by 'almost understand' I am going to copy the first paragraph of a printed letter that came to me yesterday from the office of the Universala Esperanto-Asocio in Rotterdam:

> Kara UEA-membro, De propra sperto mi scias, ke forgesi estas home. La komputilo de UEA tamen ne kapablas forgesi — ankaŭ tion ĝi ne forgesis, ke vi estas malnova membro de UEA, kiu eble pro simpla forgeso ankoraŭ ne pagis kotizon por la nuna jaro. Ankaŭ mi mem kelkfoje forgesis rekotizi kaj suspektis la poŝtiston pri nericevo de la revuo. Tiaj aferoj okazas. Ĉi-jare tio okazis 1628 fojojn en nia asocio!

It seems to me that almost anyone would be able to guess that the UEA computer is not able to forget and gather that here we have a gentle reminder to pay my subscription. These few lines contain several examples of the concision with which one can express oneself. *Kotizo* is 'subscription'; *rekotizi* is 'to renew one's subscription'. *Malnova: nova* is 'new', *malnova* the negation, so in English probably 'a long-standing member'. *Nericevo*, non-reception, failure to receive the review. [For readers who do not care for any sort of puzzle I shall translate: Dear member of the Universala Esperanto-Asocio, from my own experience I know that it is human to forget. However the UEA computer is not able to forget — this also it does not forget, that you are a long-standing member, who perhaps through simple forgetfulness has not paid a subscription for this year. I too have sometimes forgotten to pay and have blamed the postman for (my) non-reception of the review. These things happen. This year they happened 1628 times.]

One thing I half-understood from those duplicated pages given to me in Vienna was that a medical congress had taken place in Israel, another was that the Esperanto Group of the British TUC (Trade Union Congress) had distributed 100,000 informative leaflets. This gave me an address to write to, which replied with another address, which in turn directed me to St Columba's College, three miles further up the Dublin mountains than we are.

Christopher Fettes teaches French and Latin, with Esperanto as an optional extra, in St Columba's, one of Ireland's most esteemed boarding schools. He had to drive past our house anyway when he went in to the monthly meetings of the small Irish association. He brought me in to a room in Trinity College where four or five people gathered, two fluent in Esperanto, one Spanish and rather mixed, one a beginner like myself. He explained the supersignoj, the circumflex over the letters c, g, h, j and s which enable the written language to be phonetically consistent and told us about the verbs — ending in 'as' in the present tense, 'is' in the past and 'os' in the future. Look back to *okazas*, happens, *okazis*, happened, above. He gave us copies of a Chinese magazine in Esperanto, with colour photographs of improbable landscapes.

Well, when I opened the magazine I found that with those few explanations I could understand quite a lot. Indeed, I showed the Chinese photographs to my mother and when I returned she said she could understand a good deal of an article about new factories. I may as well say here that I have written a book to share the information I would have liked to have then and I have made a cassette tape which runs through the essential grammar and pronunciation in a mere eighteen minutes.

But there was another book to be re-written first.

I have mentioned that after publication of my comments on the birth control Encyclical Nuala Fennell had suggested I apply for membership of the NUJ. After the usual inquisition I was accepted and attended monthly meetings of the Dublin Freelance Branch. One evening, when attendance was small, the minutes secretary had to leave early; somebody asked me to take the rest of the minutes. Two months later I was hon. sec. of a trade union branch. Another step in my education. On the executive of IFPA I had learnt about the orderly conduct of meetings; I now learnt for myself how meetings can be steered towards remaining orderly if the secretary does not go into details of the heated discussions at the previous meeting which can too easily come to life again 'arising from the Minutes'. I also found myself processing applications for membership and, while Frank Delaney was a very busy chairman, I often enough chaired meetings. We had a freelancer's strike, which succeeded rather well, thanks to the support of indispensable freelancers in Brussels and regular columnists whom the public expect to see. After three years as secretary I resigned more than once; there was no competition for the job, interesting though it was. I simply had to pass it on because my mother needed to have me within reach.

But Nuala Fennell was on the same NUJ committee. Once again she did me a good turn; she told me about a publishing house set up by four women, Arlen House. I sent them my *Dinosaur;* Terry Prone read it. Catherine Rose, untypically, sent me a copy of this report, which began, 'This is one of the most enjoyable books I've read in years.' She sent it because the report indicated clearly the sorting-out that Terry thought essential. I was able to do this without going out of the house. Everyone liked one of the alternative titles I offered, *Anything School Can Do, You Can Do Better.*

I had to work quite hard to get it into shape according to instructions. I had been told not to argue too much. I collected the arguments for early reading into a single chapter at the end, a collection to which I had been able to add many more than I used in the *Dinosaur* manuscript. Since writing that I had engaged in correspondence with Professor J. McVicar Hunt and Professor Burton L. White, who sent me the full 1972 report of the Harvard Pre-School Research Project; in 1970 I subscribed to *Reading,* the journal of the United Kingdom Reading Association and, alerted by this, I had taken part in the first European Congress of the International Reading Association in Paris in 1977.

An article about this last occasion had contributed to expenses; I never managed to get any paper to send me anywhere. One thing that struck me there was that French children were being introduced to reading by a method quite different from any used here — syllables in handwriting instead of whole words in print — but special tuition for children who had difficulty consisted of more of the same. Just like home; a different method, but remedial reading here meant more of the same. A Swiss teacher and I agreed that the French remedial pupils we observed were manifestly bored. A French teacher, Dr Rachel Cohen, was pleased to find someone who agreed with her about early cognitive development. Her thesis on early reading had won her her doctorate, though she was 'only' teaching infants.

The observation I found most encouraging was in a book called *Children's Minds* by Margaret Donaldson, published in 1978 in a Fontana series edited by Professor Jerome Bruner. She suggested that 'those very features of the written word which encourage awareness of language may also encourage awareness of one's own thinking and be relevant to the development of intellectual self-control, with incalculable consequences for the development of the kinds of thinking which are characteristic of logic, mathematics and the sciences.'

All this, with additions I acquired during the next few years, is laid out neatly in *Early Reading*, for anyone who may be interested.

Once my book was finished other things cropped up that I could do within reach of the house. I volunteered to help with a group of Down's Syndrome children and their mothers who met once every couple of weeks for mutual support and advice from a physiotherapist. It was most interesting to see how well the children were developing, having had active training almost from birth. I saw how my little brother Frankie might have been if such advice had been around in his time. There were several volunteers. Some made tea, others stayed with the mothers and babies. I minded a few older children, too young to go to school. I found quite remarkable the number of things they couldn't do. They couldn't recognise a triangle and fit it into a triangular hole, had never walked on a low wall, and seemingly found it a novelty to fish around in a puddle with a twig. All carefully dressed, all with mothers who were ready to work for hours to develop intelligence in their handicapped baby, but who missed little things they could have done without effort to give more scope to their ordinary children. There is a widespread unaccountable assumption that learning begins with school.

I was also accepted on the rota for looking after flowers in my local church. Both the work and its companionship were enjoyable.

About this time I fortunately chanced to see a couple of paragraphs in *The Observer* about a system of relaxation called AT, initials of Autogenic Training. I wrote to the Maudsley Hospital, was sent some information, and was later told that someone in Dublin was teaching the system, eight lessons, each one hour a week. As I have said, I had the habit of taking a siesta and usually tried consciously to relax my muscles. This method, where one also thinks of one's heart beating slowly, one's solar plexus being warm, I found markedly more effective. After a couple of years I noticed that bronchitis, which had been an accustomed winter visitation, simply was not happening; my emergency supply of Penbritin was untouched. Various minor rheumatic aches had been forgotten; to 'do an AT' in the morning seemed as refreshing as the whole night's sleep. I wrote a short account in *The Irish Times* and I was happy to learn that it brought Liz, my teacher, so many new pupils that she was able to stay in Ireland.

The immediate benefit was more important. I was beginning this practice during the months when my mother was getting more and more feeble. I believe that the calm it conferred helped me to be a more patient daughter than I might have been. One afternoon I asked her would she like anything. She said, 'Would a cup of tea be too much trouble?' I replied that of course it wouldn't, and brought it in to her in a light glass cup that Janet had given her. I helped her to drink some. She said, 'That was *lovely.*' I put down the cup, looked at her, recognised the change, said, 'Shall I go for Fr Toohey?' In reply she nodded solemnly, three times. As so often happens on these occasions, the priest had left his house, but remembered that he must go back for something, and was no sooner inside the door than the phone rang. He was in good time to anoint her and give her Viaticum — such a lovely word for the Host, food for the journey — and I held her hand while he recited the farewell and welcoming prayers. When she had ceased to breathe I felt that those last words, 'That was lovely', had put right between us anything that had been imperfect.

That was on 22 March 1983. In the following June *Anything School Can Do, You Can Do Better* was published. Drawings by various children, mainly Alison, decorate the cover and the beginnings and ends of chapters. Of course I was very pleased when Fontana bought the paperback rights; that edition earned me a vote of confidence; I had asked the children did they mind if I used their real names: Killian and Alison appear in the first edition as Thomas and Rebecca, but decided to unmask for Fontana.

I noticed recently an observation by Seán Kelly, the racing cyclist, that when he had won the Tour de France he hadn't really appreciated it. Well, there's only one Tour each year, while many, many books are published, but I thoroughly appreciated having half-page reviews in all the national papers and seeing my book in the bestseller list week after week. When the paperback came out I had about twenty interviews around Britain; I mean Britain, not England, because one TV interview was in Glasgow. It wasn't just my book; it was my side of several debates and it must have been as useful as a good few Letters to the Editor.

For two or three years following I had a stream of requests for information about where to get the Colour Factor material and books; alas, not only were the books out of print because they had included pounds shillings and pence (I made many, many photocopies) but Evans gave up manufacture of the blocks. I can understand that they might have been difficult to keep in order in a large class, but they were ideal for children at home. I deplore the idea of introducing young children to number directly by computer.

Last year I met someone who told me that he was educating his children at home. The eldest was twelve and was now coping easily with a correspondence course. He just happened to know that twelve families in his neighbourhood were doing much the same. Because of my book; because I quoted the Constitution to show that in Ireland parents have that entitlement.

John Holt's 'Growing Without Schooling' bookshop in Boston stocked *Anything* as long as supplies lasted. One order I delivered in person, in Boston, and had the good fortune to meet John himself. When I read about Boston Common I know how it looks.

But back in 1983 I found myself for the first time in about thirty-five years fairly free from responsibility. Seán had just retired; Killian, Alison, Eoin and Oliver were still living at home, but I had never ironed a shirt or made a bed for them — they iron shirts slowly and exquisitely; I allow less than two minutes for one of Seán's or my own. I noticed an announcement of a three-day international seminar organised by IRAAL, the Irish Association for Applied Linguistics, and decided to go, as a journalist, to find out how Esperanto stood in academic esteem. Not well. But while I was having coffee out in the sun with a group of, presumably, linguists, I was urged to sign on for the graduate diploma in linguistics, a one-year course in Trinity.

It was perfectly timed for me. I had learnt Esperanto by reading the witty detective stories of Claude Piron, had got away for a week in 1980 to an ecumenical congress in the Netherlands where the Catholic organisation, IKUE, combined with the Christian one, KELI (E stands for Esperanto), and had found that, with 149 supportive teachers — there were 150 of us, from thirty countries — and a dictionary in my bag, there was no discussion in which I could not take part. It seemed a kind of natural miracle, as if I had found I could sing. So much so that when I arrived home after a varied journey by train and bus and ship, staying in London with Barbara and her family, meeting so many people to whom I could talk about it, I had to give up because I had lost my voice.

That breakfast in Budapest which I shared with the Director who had introduced me to the language, was eaten during the Universala Kongreso of 1983; I went there after the IRAAL conference, before beginning the year of study which convinced me in theory of the excellence of this language, of whose excellence in practice I had already been convinced.

While still active in journalism, and while I still knew only a little about Esperanto, I had had an article in each of the daily papers and others in one or two magazines, each of which brought some enquirers. By the time I knew rather more and had finished my diploma, editors responded to any suggestions I made about further articles by saying 'We've done that already'. There was nothing for it but to write a book explaining what Esperanto is and how much fun I was having since I encountered it. While explaining I inserted all the information that is found in a normal introductory textbook, together with increasing amounts of reading in the language itself. My year of study had a chapter to itself, a chapter written entirely in English. I reassured readers that if they didn't want to read about linguistics they could skip that chapter without missing any new material on Esperanto, but I said that, to compensate for its absence, I would first of all fill in some background in that language. If I translate this paragraph, it will fit in neatly here, and do double duty since it allows me to explain that I was able to write it at least as easily in Esperanto as I can write this translation.

> Most of the students were teachers, so we could only attend the university in the afternoon, from three to seven. As for me, it was nice to be out of the house at dinner time three days a week, but even though I was out, the others had to eat. There always had to be soup, made from fresh vegetables, not out of a tin or a packet; also something simmering, or that could be put into the oven; in winter cold meals don't go down well. Afterwards, usually fruit salad or cake or pudding. There were six of us living at home, Seán, my husband, and I, two children who were employed, two who were full-time students. One of these had already qualified as a chef after he finished school. Now he was a university student studying human nutrition. It was supposed that he would be inclined to help. In fact when he was young he had been very helpful, even when he was working hard as a chef, but once he became a 'student' the help disappeared. Perhaps he was afraid that when I was out the others would expect him to do everything; perhaps he too was just too busy. Anyway, he often made our wholemeal bread.

There the Esperanto ends and I revert to English and hope that some day Esperanto will be as fashionable as wholemeal bread has become. I add that it was difficult to fit in five or six hours for lectures and travel, with maybe twice as much time for study and writing, but it was exhilarating.

Perhaps, before I forget about the family, I may say that there is something peculiarly pleasant about becoming a student at the age of sixty — and quite often meeting and having coffee with one's youngest son who is a student of mathematics in the same building.

I had supposed that after one book that sold well I would not have too much trouble placing the next. Arlen House, unfortunately, was no longer publishing. The publishers I approached did not like the idea of Esperanto. At last one Irish publisher looked on it favourably. I sent in a manuscript, then another, with major changes as requested — a good deal of work before I had a word-processor. I had made it plain that I especially wanted it to be available in time for the 1989 Universala Kongreso because that was being held in English-speaking Brighton. Three months before the date I telephoned to ask what was happening. I was told that the publisher had changed his mind a couple of weeks earlier. I felt hopeless. Then I noticed that another publisher, Poolbeg, was re-issuing some Arlen House books. I got in touch. The publisher, Philip MacDermot, managed to fit my book into his schedule when I said I would arrange for the typesetting in Amsterdam. A postal-strike prevented proper proof-reading but the book was there, delivered to Brighton in the middle of the congress week, with the title *Esperanto for Hope*.

Then it had a very lively launch in Dublin. Gemma Hussey, recently Minister for Education, agreed to push it off. Our Irish association had undertaken to organise a post-congress holiday following the Universala Kongreso in Brighton. We brought our group of fifty, a dozen Japanese, two from Iceland, two from Israel, the rest I'm not sure about, around Dublin and Wicklow and Wexford for another week and invited them to the launch. It seems to me that if even one journalist had turned up in Buswell's Hotel he or she would have been impressed, if only by the noise level from such a mixed group being excited in an 'artificial' language.

No journalist came; an old hand at distributing information, I should have made sure that the press releases went to the papers, but I was distracted. The book sank without trace as far as Ireland was concerned; no advertisements, no reviews, though it does move slowly from bookshop shelves. Our holiday-makers, bless them, were eager for copies; the Japana-Esperanto Ligo has several times ordered ten or twenty copies; it goes to Brazil and the US and to the Libroservo in

Rotterdam, but I had hoped to raise awareness in Ireland. I will admit that I even hoped that it would be on sale at railway stations and airports. It teaches the language gently as well as trying to explain why it is so well worth learning, and a reader could pick up a respectable introduction over a couple of hours' journey, or so it seems to me.

Well, there's no harm in hoping, especially if the cause in respect of which you hope is called 'HOPING'. ['Espero' is hope, 'ant' is the present participle ending, the 'ing', while the final 'o' indicates that the word is a noun.]

There have been a few encouraging developments lately....

CHAPTER 18

A green thought in a green shade: through language to politics

It is now time to say that the years that I spent near home were not occupied only by church flowers, children and gardening. I also found time to help found a political party and stand for election to the Dáil.

I observed in chapter seven that *The Breakdown of Money* by Christopher Hollis long ago laid the foundation for my scepticism about the current economic system. Because of my lack of faith in the way things are run I was alert to notice in 1979 that the Economic and Social Research Institute had been asked to consider how to remedy the 'poverty trap' that results from the way unemployment is dealt with. I hope most readers know that the 'poverty trap' indicates that there are many circumstances in which unemployed people will find themselves at a loss if they take a job or go on a 'social employment scheme'. The ESRI report suggested two methods of linking income tax and benefits but concluded that by far the most promising scheme was a National Dividend which would give to every citizen the amount then given as unemployment benefit; those in employment would repay the amount with their income tax, so no loss to the revenue, while those not in formal employment would be free to work, paying tax on their earnings if they were high enough. At that time the Dividend could have been financed by the funds from income tax and social insurance. I had long felt that it was uneconomic as well as demoralising and probably immoral to tell people that, if they needed a little money to live on, they must not work. I interviewed the author of the report, Mr Brendan Dowling, for the women's page of *The Irish Independent;* one aspect I brought out was that women at home would clearly benefit. I said that every Women's Club in the country should be demanding information. The article did not provoke even one Letter to the Editor, as far as I know.

The government of the time (Fine Gael) attempted to take the first step. Unfortunately, instead of following up their original idea of giving this 'dividend' to all women at home, deducting it with the family income tax if appropriate, someone changed their mind. They produced an advertisement which proposed that women who thought that their husbands were in a low income bracket should apply for this payment. This advertisement banjaxed the scheme that might have eliminated the concept of unemployment. Predictably, the very women who most needed it did not dare ask for something that might affect their husband's tax; many would not know what he earned anyway.

I managed, after many alterations, to get a substantial article into *The Irish Times*. Christopher Fettes sent the article to someone he knew; I was invited to an introductory seminar in London organised by the National Council for Voluntary Organisations. At the end of the day even people who had never heard of the idea before agreed it would be the answer to many of the problems they met. They also agreed that Basic Income should be the term we would use to indicate this unconditional universal income. The Basic Income Research Group — BIRG — was set up in 1984.

But haven't I mentioned Christopher Fettes before, in a quite different context? Yes indeed; it was Esperanto that led me into the Green Party. Christopher and I had talked about economics as well as language and found much to agree upon. There really is a notable similarity between the language and the economics. Both are aimed at the worst-off: at people who haven't any capital to enable them to set up a business, who have to depend on a shrinking market for employment or on a reluctant husband or father for any money to spend; at people who were not born as part of the ten per cent of the world's population who speak English from childhood, who have therefore much more difficulty in getting access to science and technology, who haven't got the words or the power to talk back to the World Bank.

Believers in both a learnable language and an unconditional income meet the same obstacle, lack of means to share the information they have. It is true that both ask the 'haves' to share with the 'have nots', but both can show that benefit would flow in all directions. English-speaking travellers, business people, politicians, really would be better off if they could communicate with others who understood exactly what they were saying without the intervention of interpreters or the strain of listening to mangled English. People who now have regular salaries would be wise to note that the source on which they rely might fail as economic problems increase, while on the other hand if all were free to work without being penalised, crime could be expected to decrease and a great many things that contribute to a generally agreeable life increase. If someone with millions of dollars or yen to spare would pay for a large-scale advertising campaign, the climate of opinion might change.

Well, in December 1981 Christopher invited people he knew, Friends of the Earth, opposers of experiments on animals, vegetarians, Esperantists, to come together to discuss the possible need for a political party which would have in its programme matters ignored by the existing parties. He asked me to take the chair, so as to leave him free to speak. He asked people who disliked the idea of getting involved in politics to please not involve themselves; there would be quite enough to do finding common cause between varied motives.

This began a very enjoyable and creative succession of meetings, fortunately near my home, to work out our policies. Instead of a chairman, facilitators taking turn about; instead of 'points of order' and 'amendments to motions' we would reach consensus or bust. There is a methodical way of looking for consensus, but obviously it's best if a group does not have to look too hard. A visiting Green MP from the Netherlands was present while about forty people put together 'Seven Principles', word by word; he said he was full of admiration for the way we reached agreement.

Everyone now recognises that Green aspirations are respectable. When we began we could not use the word Green; it had only republican connotations, so we set up the Ecology Party. It must have been under that name that I figured on the ballot paper in the 1982 election. I could not go out canvassing because of looking after my mother so I monitored the telephone. I stood in Dublin South-East, a constituency that had several hospitals, including my own Baggot Street. I was confident that I could go along to the Nurses' Home and pick up a ward of votes. Surprise; there were no nurses in residence any more, all living out in flats.

Another thing I remember from that election is a newspaper interview in which I said that we were different from other political parties because we would be content to vanish, if only the other parties would take on board the whole range of our policies, not just a green tinge here and there. Of course we did not get a seat but we did much better than the television commentators expected.

Christopher and I were clear about Basic Income from the beginning. I emphasised that a great deal of the work people are paid to do is not worth doing or might be better left undone. It will not surprise any reader if I say that I was inclined to put bringing up children at the top of the list of worthwhile work that isn't paid. His other special interest was Site Value Taxation. When I see that even still the County Council dare not re-zone land that has once been given planning permission for building because the owners can claim notional compensation for profit they might have made, it seems very clear that any extra profit from change of use should be fully taxed, so that such claims would melt away. There has been a change in the law, but not enough of a change.

Policies like these required a great deal of productive discussion before they were agreed throughout the party. The first draft of the education policy started on its rounds through all the groups some eight years ago. The one accepted is considerably longer than the draft but it retains the points that I feel are essential. I am Education spokesperson. By the way, for years now we have been The Green Party/Comhaontas Glas, we have had candidates in two further elections, and in the last one, Roger Garland won a seat in the Dáil, which convinced the public that a Green Party really existed.

However, I was not able to give much attention to politics of any colour during that challenging year of college. Challenging is exactly the right word. I was accustomed to learning from books and from observation but, leaving aside pathology and the history of the British Empire, always by my own choice. Here I had to absorb rapidly some material that I would not have looked at otherwise. I would wake at five and sit up in bed and read, sometimes struggling with Chomsky, sometimes meeting something in plain English, saying that language is enormously complex: 'What the learner has ultimately to learn goes far beyond what the textbook contains, beyond what the teacher can explain, and even beyond what the linguist has described. The studies based on linguistic theories of universals and markedness are particularly helpful in illustrating the complexity of the learner's task and the inadequacy of the best pedagogical grammar to deal with it.'

We had the option at the end to write one 10,000-word dissertation, or two of 5,000 words. I have told in *Esperanto for Hope* how a paper entitled 'The Case for Case' gave me a foundation on which to write about the case system in Esperanto and I could easily have used up the ten thousand words with that, but I could not resist reacting to a minor component of our course, reading acquisition. This sent me to the library of the ITE (Institiúid Teangeolaíochta Éireann) where I found fascinating recent research. I did two shorter papers instead. Of course they were each too long, and reading research that had not been done in an academic context was not quite what was required, but I got my graduate diploma and the director of the department bought several copies of my book.

That summer found me in the Vreij Universitat in Brussels where I took part in 'AILA 84', the triennial conference of the International Association for Applied Linguistics. The students on our course had been encouraged to join. A call for papers arrived; I did not look at it until after the closing date; I could not resist dashing off an outline of why English is not a good choice for a world language. To my considerable surprise, my offer was accepted. No need for surprise; there were 1,500 participants and I should think very few who did not speak. But I had a delightful time; I met a nucleus of Esperanto scholars in a congenial atmosphere, I listened to a couple of papers on reading acquisition and found I was accepted as a colleague with something to contribute, people wanted copies of that section of my book, my abstract was in print in one of the four volumes of contributions, and I had been allotted a pleasant student flat all to myself.

Over the next few years I came to know Brussels rather better. For various reasons I was a suitable person to be Irish delegate to the European Green Co-ordination. We met three or four times a year, at first from only five countries, by the time I last attended officially there were twenty-one. I kept flying or sailing backwards and forwards for four years, got to know quite a few people, and noticed that being a native speaker of English gave one a relative advantage. When the expense of hiring a room equipped for simultaneous translation was discussed, I would remark that there was an alternative. This experience incidentally enabled me, in *Esperanto for Hope*, to contrast two styles of international meeting.

The last time I joined a Co-ordination delegate meeting I was an observer. I had handed over the role of delegate (with travel allowance) to a very competent successor. Then the Greens decided to hold the spring meeting for 1990 in Budapest. I could not resist the temptation to go back. In January of that year I had given a paper in Esperanto to a really high-powered conference on Transport and the Environment, for which I had signed on principally because it was jointly organised by engineering and Esperanto faculties of Budapest universities, with the Fondajo Talento, and the languages were Magyar, Esperanto and English, in that order. The Fondajo Talento had been set up to improve education in the early years.

I arrived a little early at the university, where something else was going on in the room where the conference was to take place. When I said 'Esperanto' someone went off and found Pasabi Janos, who within minutes had offered me a room in his flat. It was empty because he had sub-let it to a Romanian couple who had now been able to go back to visit their country. As I had already found in Warsaw, where Esperanto's centenary congress was held in 1987, those dreary-looking iron curtain flats may be more comfortable than they look from the outside; Janos had a good deal more space than another friend who put me up in Paris. He told me to let him know if I were coming to Budapest again.

The Transport conference was most satisfactory. Technical translation into Esperanto went smoothly; an Englishman, a transport economist, told me that the English did not stand up to the strain. My own contribution was rather low-level; a criticism of closing small local schools and bussing children long distances, wasting energy and wasting children's valuable time while ignoring the potential of information technology. There was a bonus for me in the conference. Professor So Gilsu, an economist from Korea who was a member of the *estraro* (standing committee) of UEA gave a paper. There were enough Esperanto-speaking economists there for him to arrange a seminar, in which, of course, I joined. He was extraordinarily interesting and genial and it was a lucky chance to get to know him better. I should not be surprised if he were elected president of UEA during the forthcoming election. The two of us were interviewed in Esperanto for Hungarian radio.

Well, with that recent experience and, I supposed, a valid visa, it is not surprising that I decided to go to the Green Co-ordination meeting two months later. It was quite in order to have two people from one country but I had to pay for myself. In fact it was most agreeable to have friendly company and no responsibility, especially gratifying to share the job of putting up Green posters outside our meeting place in the square beside the Hungarian Parliament.

As it happened, I was wrong about the visa; I had the experience, which I had missed so far, of being yanked off the train, bag and baggage, by three soldiers at the frontier and seeing the train move off.

A taxi-driver rooked a Romanian couple from the US, telling them, with very little English on either side, that for $200 he could get them to Budapest, where the train would wait for an hour. The poor things had never thought they would need a visa simply to pass through a neighbouring country. I paid up for a visa, refused the taxi, and waited for a local train. The 'hitch' was that I arrived at Janos's flat at midnight, nobody there, and when I got back to the Metro the last train was disappearing.

After a two-day meeting in French and English the Bulgarian delegate, hitherto silent, was asked to contribute. He very hesitantly said a few words, indicating that he could not really speak English. When the meeting was over I went up to him and said, 'Bonvolu, sinjoro, ĉu hazarde vi parolas Esperanton?' 'Kompreneble, jes. Multaj el ni parolas ĝin.' We were able to continue a useful conversation.

You may suppose I put that information on paper for the co-secretaries of the Euro Greens. When they/we had the annual convention in Zurich in June 1991 Esperanto was one of the four working languages, that is, one of the languages available in simultaneous translation. This may have been mainly due to French prompting, but I must have contributed. One of the old hands met me on arrival and asked was I satisfied. Of course not; the whole point is to get away from translation, but bringing in Esperanto is a step in a useful direction.

And when I returned from Zurich I found that I was Green Party/Comhaontas Glas candidate in the local elections for my own territory, Rathfarnham, with two and a half weeks to campaign, and not a leaflet printed. However, I did have some advantages: a number of voters knew one or other of my children; a number knew my views on education, from journalism or from my book, and approved of them; Roger Garland, TD, with whom I had been working since the early days of the party, canvassed for me and rounded up helpers. I had canvassed for him when he was elected to the Dáil.

I was elected to Dublin County Council and it was a significant victory because four of us were elected in the city, five in the county, and both city and county now had an opposition majority which included the Greens. One of the others elected was David Healy, about the age of my youngest son. He had come to Zurich because of Esperanto. I had the satisfaction of introducing him to Claude Piron, and we quite often use our second language when we meet in the Council. We both take every opportunity to mention that the Council would not be so short of workers for essential jobs if everyone had Basic Income.

How do I find the Council on the whole? It is a surprise to have a new job at this time in my life; not only the Council, but the VEC (Vocational Education Committee), through which I am on the interim board of the new Regional Technical College in Tallaght, which I feel convinced will be a very good place indeed in which to learn. I've been on some interview boards for the staff of the RTC and was much impressed by the ability of many candidates, pleased to find how often my judgement matched that of the varied board. I think it's worth remarking that whether on the Council, on the South Dublin committee, to which I belong, or the VEC, a woman would have to be paranoid to feel oppressed. We are in the majority on the VEC, eight out of twenty-six on the South Dublin committee. A highly responsible woman, Eithne Fitzgerald, holds the chair of the County Council for the coming year. I do not say we are all paragons of wisdom and brevity but we agree that the men are far, far more likely to say everything three times. County Councils should have more control over their own income, more responsibility, but what we have is on the ground, within reach, we can see what is happening or not happening. It is rather an enlargement of house-and-garden-and-family-keeping; if it were done well everywhere what a fine world we'd have.

Alas, a fine world we have not. Some of the programmes Greens propose might solve the problems of international debt, of global pollution, of unemployment. I have a reasonable answer to the Northern Ireland question — too reasonable. It is when we read about the ethnic massacres that have erupted in the former Yugoslavia as soon as tyranny ended, in the same pattern as we have seen elsewhere, that we wonder whether it is worth while trying to do anything.

Well, the best research into teaching Esperanto was done in the Zagreb Centre. At the beginning of this year, 1992, the co-ordinator, Zlatko Tišlar, left Zagreb with his family because he could not conceive of killing others. In his letter explaining his future plans he says, 'Why such barbarism in the minds of the East Balkan leaders? Must I hate my dear wife because she belongs to the ethnic group which is now the enemy of mine? Should I believe my President who does nothing to avoid the coming tempest and now requires that I offer my life for an independent Croatia, which will be meaningless in a few years if Europe accepts us?'

So it seems worth trying to do whatever little one can to support those who think as he does.

But now I have come to the end of this book. I have greatly enjoyed writing it, remembering so many things that were buried in the past. It has its own history. When I had finished *Anything* my publisher, Catherine Rose, told me that she was sure I had another book in me. On her recommendation I went to the Tyrone Guthrie centre in Annamacarraig for a week of undistracted writing and wrote what might have been the draft of a third of a book. It was going to be about the roles of women and men. I had half a shelf of books about this question and I wanted to argue with that which I still think is the best, *The Sceptical Feminist* by Janet Radcliffe Richards. A few paragraphs from that draft have found their way into these pages, but life took over from argument.

Through the last few pages of this book the linguistic and Green strands have been so intertwined that I could not find a space in which to insert the 1990 BIEN (Basic Income European Network) conference, significant though it was for me. I had taken part in two other BIEN conferences. Discussion was at a high intellectual level, more especially at the previous conference in the university of Louvain-la-Neuve, on philosophical arguments in respect of Basic Income. When I read a call for papers on 'Competing Justifications for Citizenship Income' for a conference to be held in the European University in Florence, I ventured to propose one on the rights of children — the right of children to the presence of their mothers.

There were far more contributions than the organisers expected, I think about sixty, including speakers from forty different universities. There was time only for each of us to give a ten-minute summary. Even so, the observer from the European Commission found my contribution particularly interesting. On two days he took lunch with myself and the editor of the BI research group bulletin and said he had long believed in the need for early education. Before we left the editor asked me to prepare a short version of my paper for publication. Summaries of a few others were published but mine was the only one to claim several pages. [I suppose I should say that many of the new arrivals gave papers going over ground familiar to the rest of us.]

I am more proud of this than of anything else I have done. Some of the best thinking I have met I found within the BIEN network; I feel it an honour to be published in the same space, so to speak, as James Robertson. In this paper I brought together most of the things that are important to me: children's ability, women's values, justice and freedom. I believe that a change to Basic Income would be a truly enabling revolution. The next meeting is to be in Geneva, with the support of the International Labour Office. I hope to be there, with a copy of this book.

The rights of children — a justification of Basic Income, hitherto unremarked

The following is a shortened version of a paper given at the conference organised by the Basic Income European Network (BIEN) in Florence in September 1990.

When — last June or July — Mr Nicholas Ridley (Britain's former Trade and Industry Secretary) expressed alarm concerning possible loss of national sovereignty, there was a good deal of talk on television. An interviewer asked an eminent banker whether he thought the issue significant, to which the banker replied: 'Oh, yes. This is a very important question. It is not like deciding whether to increase the Child Allowance. This is about the kind of people we are.'

Apparently, a kind that doesn't care tuppence about children. For this gentleman had not noticed that the kind of person a person is depends a great deal on the sort of care they were given when young.

Children are people

BIEN *pensants* would never say anything like that. Nevertheless, when listening to the papers given during a BIEN conference in 1989 (in Louvain-la-Neuve), I felt something was missing. Whether the references being made were to John Rawls' *Theory of Justice*, to Robert Nozick's views on entitlement, or to John Locke's principles regarding the private appropriation of natural resources, all were concerned with distribution among or appropriation by adults.

The gist of Locke's argument is that 'he who has gathered as much of the wild fruit, killed caught or tamed as many of the beasts as he could...by placing any of his labour on them, did thereby acquire a propriety in them....'[1] There *he* is, strong, active, not just picking fruit but capturing animals — and forming a traditional part of the discussions of philosophers. Not merely an adult, but an adult male.

Something is overlooked, as in the usual picture of the Ascent of Man. Our ancestors are pictured hunting together in groups, running across the savannah, having spare hands in front to throw stones, able rapidly to climb any trees that might occur. In her remarkable book, The *Descent of Woman*[2], Elaine Morgan points out that a significant proportion of those early 'Men' would have been pregnant, or carrying babies, and in no form for running or climbing. Instead, she showed how lakeside development would have suited both sexes and encouraged the invention of speech.

I wish to suggest quite simply that if we are concerned with 'a person's natural right', we should never forget that at some time that person was very small, quite unable to capture animals or cultivate the soil, and neither had, nor asked for, anything more than his or her mother's milk and attention. Warmth, clothing and so on depend on climate; the first concerns are love and nourishment.

Children need their mothers

The core of my argument lies in this concluding paragraph from *Love and Hate* by I. Eibl-Eibesfeldt, Director of the Human Ethology section of the Max Planck Institute, hence successor to Lorenz and Tinbergen:

The means of bonding have always remained fundamentally the same and they are in origin essentially derived from the behaviour patterns that bind mother and child. The mother-child relationship was historically — and still is in the development of the individual — the nucleus of crystallisation of all social life.... It is innate to us. From the personal mother-child relationship we evolve the 'basic trust' from which our fundamental attitude of sociability then evolves and hence a general commitment. For these reasons attempts to prevent the growth of such family ties are highly questionable. What has to be done is to strengthen our trust in our fellow men who are not known to us and this starts in the family. Only in this way do we evolve that social responsibility which is a prerequisite for a peaceful communal existence and indeed for our future existence as a species.[3]

'Our future existence as a species.' The penalty for error could not be clearer. Yet the market economy *as we know it*, and the partly-planned effects of the conditional support which is (in some systems) designed to fill the gaps, combine to prevent the development of that mother-child relationship judged essential by Eibl-Eibesfeldt.

By the way, I am frequently in trouble with my Green colleagues — male and female — for talking about mothers when they would prefer me to talk about parents. They say that fathers must — for their own sakes and for the sakes of their children — share equally the child-rearing and house-keeping roles. To which I reply that there would be a great advance in civilisation if this should become the general custom — and indeed BI may steer us in that direction — but there is a long way to go yet.

Child poverty

Meanwhile, is there any need to cite figures to show that the present market system tends to separate mothers from their children — or else relegate both to poverty? The nature of the market is to get work done for less money. In the US women who work full time earn only 66 cents to the man's dollar —

the higher they advance, the larger the wage gap. In one US survey, in reply to the question who suffers most when women combine marriage and a family with a successful career, 42% said it was the children. And if the marriage goes, women and their children were estimated to suffer a 72% drop in their living standards.

In Britain lone-parent families are reported to be the poorest group. In my own country, Ireland, where there is no divorce, only 13% of maintenance orders are fully paid up, and the sums awarded for maintenance are in general pitifully small. Moreover there is more to this than the mere feminisation of poverty.

My purpose is to underline the privation of children, who are penalised by the market whether their mothers are relative winners or losers. Those divorced women whose incomes drop by 72% may have more time to attend to their children, but that they are cheerful and relaxed seems unlikely. If the child is to develop 'basic trust' through its relationship with its mother, it is surely required that the mother herself should feel sufficient security in her own ability to provide for the child — whether on her own or jointly with the father. Those who have considered Basic Income recognise that an unconditional, individual grant is the most practical solution.

Development needs of very young children

On its own, 'basic trust' is not enough. During this century there has been increasing research into the personal and cognitive development of very young children. The contribution of Dr Maria Montessori to this research is well known. And there are many others. For example, in the sixties Professor J. McVicar of Illinois University agreed that very early cognitive encouragement by mothers was the only way out of the cycle of poverty. In the seventies, the Harvard Pre-School project reported that the most significant element in a child's development was the responsiveness of the carer — generally the mother — between the ages of 10 months and 18 months.

From an especially pleasing project organised by Barbara Tizard (Professor of Education at the University of London), we see unselected, very modestly educated mothers showing a high degree of spontaneous competence. Tizard's project taped and compared long periods of conversation between four-year-old girls at home and in nursery school:

> We realised how much they revealed the young child as a persistent and logical thinker. These were not the illogical and whimsical characters suggested by, for example, the theories of Jean Piaget; they were powerful and determined thinkers in their own right. Their limitations seemed to

be due far more to lack of knowledge and faulty assumptions than to any childish illogicality.

When we came to analyse the conversations between these same children and their nursery teachers, we could not avoid being disappointed. The children were certainly happy at school, for much of their time absorbed in play.... The richness, depth and variety which characterised the home conversations were sadly missing. So was the sense of intellectual struggle, and of the real attempts to communicate being made on both sides.

(Introduction to: *Young Children Learning, Talking and Thinking, at Home and at School*, Barbara Tizard and Martin Hughes, Fontana Paperback, 1984.)

A more famous name is that of Dr Benjamin Spock, author of *Baby and Child Care*, now aged 87. Interviewed last July, he said that if mothers understood the importance of a child's first few years, they would maybe postpone going to work until the child was a bit older.

The effects of advertising

I have laid the blame for increasing separation of mothers from young children on the market, as we know it. Living costs combine to require two incomes for what, by current standards, is quite a modest family life style. Current standards, of course, are not unrelated to advertising, nor is advertising something quite distinct from the market.

Passing through Paris last April I bought a magazine called *Enfants*. Splashed across the cover was the headline: *Crèches. Les bébés en colère*. Reading it I found no mention of how the babies were feeling — it was the mothers who were angry, because of the lack of state-provided child-care. So I counted the pages in that magazine, of which there were 178 in all, with 106 devoted to glossy advertisements, and most of the rest encouraging readers to buy something.

No life for a baby

Until the advent of modern contraceptive techniques, the hidden hand of the Market discarded babies as externalities whenever 'hands' were not urgently required — a fact correctly recognised by Malthus. Take Florence as an example. At the time of Lorenzo de Medici, when the Market would seem to have been functioning especially well, the famous foundling hospital of Santa Maria degli Innocenti was accepting 900 babies each year. It had been built in 1445. At about that time, in another foundling hospital (Santa Maria de San Gallo), only 32% of babies survived until the age of five. Move on to the early nineteenth century, and we still find that 43% of all baptised babies in Florence were abandoned.

Florence was no exception. In a recently published book, *The Kindness of Strangers*, James Boswell recounts how children were abandoned from late antiquity to the Renaissance.[4] Foundling hospitals were not set up to solve the problem of babies born to unmarried mothers. It seems that the custom of exposing unaffordable children continued from classical times for several centuries: the babies were left in public places, where there was a reasonable possibility that they would be taken to be brought up as slaves, or even adopted. Later the monasteries and convents became available as repositories, until gradually these found themselves with too high a proportion of monks and nuns who had not chosen to enter — having been simply left on the doorstep — a problem that did not arise in foundling hospitals.

Now all has changed. Infertile couples search in vain for babies to adopt. Despite unemployment, there are forecasts of future labour shortages, especially of skilled labour. With all the knowledge that has been accumulated about early development, one would suppose that the community would make every effort to provide existing babies with what they need. Instead of gathering them into crèches and nurseries, they would concentrate on the welfare of the parent-child unit.

But not a bit of it! It is enough to be out and about at seven in the morning and meet mothers wheeling their babies to be minded while mother works at something else to be convinced that our system is disastrously wrong. Baby has had to be roused from sleep, be changed and dressed and fed in a hurry — to be collected at some time or other by a tired mother who then has to organise everything for the following morning's rush, as well as look after her husband.

This is no life for a baby.

Babies are enjoyable

A Basic Income paid unconditionally to every member of a society would banish the need for such excursions. It would also, as Keith Roberts has explained[5], make possible a genuine market economy. One reason that it is not available is that politicians, bankers, philosophers, economists fail to recognise babies as people — with a natural right to their mother's company.

I also suspect that lurking somewhere there is a fear of allowing women to become too independent. Unfortunately, as in that French magazine, women who claim to be campaigning on behalf of women are the very ones who frequently demand more (subsidised) child-care. They, too, are forgetting that babies are people — people who prefer their own mothers.

Galbraith has well said that, since the supply of servants dried up, middle-class wives have been enlisted as surrogate servants. The women who campaign for crèches want servants; they want minders to take on the work of child-care. But who will liberate the minders? In the US they are paid less than car park attendants. The mothers claim that an hour or so of 'quality time' is an adequate maternal contribution, but some of the best quality time is that spent learning by watching or sharing in adult work, while the right moments for instruction are unpredictable.

To me it seems clear that with BI young people would feel a new confidence in themselves as independent citizens, without the need to rush into parenthood, to capture a partner, or to prove that they are grown up. Within marriage a woman with her own income need never feel the shock of dependence. Cooperation in child-care, between parents and between families, would be made very much easier than it is now.

This might be welcomed even by the mothers who demand crèches. Many work because they need money and do not know of an alternative. A paper from Finland, presented at the BIEN conference in Florence, mentioned a desperate shortage of recruits for the 'caring professions'. When mothers were given the option of an allowance instead of free child-care, 60% chose that option. Babies are, after all, enjoyable.

References
1   Locke, John, *Of Civil Government* (1690), Cassel, London, 1905
2   Morgan, Elaine, *The Descent of Woman,* Souvenir, London, 1972
3   Eibl-Eibesfeldt, I., *Love and Hate,* Methuen, 1971
4   Boswell, James, *The Kindness of Strangers: The Abandonment of Children in Western Europe from Late Antiquity to the Renaissance,* Pantheon, New York, 1989
5   Roberts, Keith, *Automation, Unemployment and the Distribution of Income,* European Centre for Work and Society, Maastricht, Netherlands, 1983